FRESH TAKES ON TEACHING

Literary Elements

How to Teach What Really Matters About Character, Setting, Point of View, and Theme

Michael W. Smith & Jeffrey D. Wilhelm
FOREWORD BY DEBORAH APPLEMAN

SCHOLASTIC

NCTE National Council of Teachers of English

New York • Toronto • London • Auckland • Sydney
Mexico City • New Delhi • Hong Kong • Buenos Aires

Dedication:

To our students

Acknowledgments:

This book is the culmination of years of thinking about literature and the teaching of literature. And through those years we've been pushed in our thinking by more people than we can name, from our own teachers to our students to our fellow book-club members to our colleagues, especially those with whom we've shared ideas in the National Writing Project and in our inservice work. The specific people we mention in the book are just the tip of the iceberg. Thanks to all.

We'd also like to thank the institutions that have supported our work. Jeff thanks Boise State University for valuing his work with teachers, and Michael sends similar thanks to Temple University, especially for the 2009 Summer Research Award that enabled him to devote the time he needed to complete the manuscript.

And a special thanks to the people at Scholastic, especially our wonderful editor, Gloria Pipkin, who was always smart and gracious even during trying personal times. We couldn't have done it without you.

Editor: Gloria Pipkin
Cover design: Brian LaRossa
Interior design: LDL Designs
Copy editor: Eileen Judge
Proofreader: Carol Ghiglieri
Cover photos: girl, heart: © Dustin Steller/Design Pics/Corbis; house, woman: © Photodisc

ISBN-13: 978-0-545-05256-6 • ISBN-10: 0-545-05256-4

National Council of Teachers of English

1111 W. Kenyon Road
Urbana, IL 61801-1096
www.ncte.org

NCTE Stock #: 17953

Contents

Foreword

I f you thought that teaching literary elements was old-fashioned, stuffy, or even irrelevant, think again. In their latest collaboration, two of the most savvy scholars in literacy education, Michael Smith and Jeff Wilhelm, invite us to see that teaching literary elements can be lively and engaging, providing an essential component to reading and comprehending literary texts. In fact, when presented in the active and compelling ways that Smith and Wilhelm suggest, literary elements can become a central dimension of literary understanding for even the most reluctant student.

For far too long, the teaching of literary elements has either been the province of college-bound classrooms designed to prepare students for the Advanced Placement exam, turning adolescents into novice structuralists, or it has reduced the reading and interpretation of literature in mainstream secondary classrooms to meaningless symbol hunts. Flannery O'Connor, upon hearing that students were being required to read her work wrote: "If teachers are in the habit of approaching a story as if it were a research problem, for which any answer is believable so long as it is not obvious, then I think students will never learn to enjoy fiction." All too often the perfunctory and mechanical teaching of literary elements has ruined students' enjoyment of literature. Like reluctant acolytes, adolescent readers have been forced to memorize the catechism of literary elements: character, setting, point of view, and theme.

Through their refreshing and innovative approach, Smith and Wilhelm turn these seemingly tired literary elements into a vital and dynamic dimension of any literature curriculum. In many ways this book draws on their impressive previous work (*Getting It Right*, 2007, New York: Scholastic; *Going With the flow: How to Engage Boys (and Girls) in Their Literacy Learning*, 2006, Portsmouth, NH: Heinemann; *"Reading don't fix no Chevys": Literacy in the Lives of Young Men* 2002, Portsmouth, NH: Heinemann). As they did in those field-changing books, Smith and Wilhelm focus on ways to make the literature classroom become more active, contemporary, intertextual, developmentally relevant, and interactive. Not only do they provide a theoretically well-grounded approach to the teaching of literary elements, but they also offer classroom teachers a wide range of specific and engaging activities. In their hands literary elements are not the mere province of formal classroom study; they are active and lively ways of making meaning with texts. For example, teaching character makes creative use of personality tests and Mac/PC ads and teaching setting becomes an artistic and aesthetic adventure into Van Gogh's bedroom.

In his provocative book, *The Crafty Reader*, Robert Scholes writes: "What is the craft of reading? As with any craft, reading depends on the use of certain tools, handled with skill. But the tools of reading are not simply there, like a hammer or chisel; they must be acquired through practice." (2001, xiv). Scholes also makes the point that it is not just literary texts that deserve our crafty reading; it is cultural texts as well. Adolescents in particular need to become crafty readers of the relentless media that surrounds them. By learning how these texts work, it is less likely that they can be helplessly manipulated by them.

Mark Twain famously declared that if all you have is a hammer, everything looks like a nail. In some ways you can think of literary elements as a full tool kit, where students have a variety of interpretive tools to make meaning of texts. By providing such useful and animated explanations of literary elements, Smith and Wilhelm provide adolescent readers and their teachers the tools to craftily and productively read the complex textual words of literature and of life.

In their inimitable style, Michael Smith and Jeff Wilhelm have indeed provided a fresh take on literary elements, one that will help literature become the meaningful site of exploration, as the authors put it, of "what is and what could be."

Deborah Appleman
Hollis L. Caswell Professor of Educational Studies
Carleton College
author of *Critical Encounters in High School English: Teaching Literary Theory to Adolescents*, Second Edition (2009, Teachers College Press and NCTE)

CHAPTER ONE

The Principles of Our Instructional Approach

This book stems from a deep conviction and an equally deep concern. The conviction: Literature provides a unique and powerful way of knowing—and therefore offers us new ways of becoming and being. Reading literature allows us to explore both what is and what could be. Teaching literature, therefore, can open doors that nothing else can open, at least not in the same way. The concern: The way the elements of literature are typically taught does not open these doors, at least not for most kids, and may in fact serve to close them for many.

The purpose of this book is to share our ideas about how we can teach the literary elements in such a way to achieve two crucially important goals: 1) fostering a deep appreciation for and understanding of literature and 2) helping students read as writers, thus providing them with tools for their own creative activity.

More specifically, our plan is to explore new and expanded ways to help students understand characterization, setting, point of view, and theme in literature, and also to consider how these elements can help students understand and navigate their daily lives. We'll have a separate set of chapters on each of these elements, but our work with each one is undergirded by the same set of instructional principles, which we'll outline here. In the chapters that follow, we'll share our thinking about each element along with lots of ideas for classroom practice. We'll also provide many lessons that we hope you can use "as is" and as models for other activities you can develop with your particular students in mind.

PRINCIPLE 1:
The Importance of the *Why*

It's astonishing to us, in reflecting both on our own teaching and on other teaching that we've seen or read about, how often teaching totally misses or fails to address the true significance of what is being taught. Many studies in cognition highlight the reason it's so important for students to realize why we ask them to do what we ask them to do. Understanding the purpose of an activity drives our motivation and engagement in that activity (see, e.g., Brown, Collins, & DuGuid, 1989). Classic studies like those of Bransford and Johnson (1972) have established that what's true for activities in general is also true for reading: Our purpose for reading drives what we attend to, comprehend, and actually use. Without a clear and articulated purpose, there is no traction for reading, for remembering, or for anything close to what we might call learning or understanding. (And as Jeff likes to say: "If you aren't teaching for understanding and use, then what the heck are you teaching for?") It's hard even to get started in an activity without clearly understanding why an activity is important. On the other hand, as Neil Postman (1996) once proclaimed: "For a student with an adequate *why*, almost any *how* or *what* will do!"

In our own studies into the literate lives of boys (Smith & Wilhelm, 2002, 2006), we found that our informants could not tell us the genuine purpose of any assignment in any subject over the course of a semester. Instead, when we asked them about why they undertook schoolwork, they said things like: "You have to do your homework or you can't pass and play ball." Or "My mom will ground me if I don't do my work." In fact, the young men seemed almost to get angry at us when we pushed them to articulate a *real intrinsic* purpose for their work in English. In his frustration, Rev, for example, proclaimed that "English is about nothing! It doesn't help you DO anything!"

We try to proceed in our own teaching from the premise that we have to begin by asking: Why does what I am teaching right now matter right now? What work can it possibly do? How does it count for readers, writers, problem solvers, workers, and citizens in a democracy? What is, in fact, significant and functional about it?

We've been helped in our thinking about what counts by a very elegant notion from cognitive science called the *correspondence concept* (Bereiter, 2004). In cognitive science, inquiry is a process of accessing, building, extending, and using knowledge in ways consistent with how expert practitioners think, know, and perform. If we adopt that perspective, student understanding can only be measured by student progress toward how experts know and use concepts and strategies. As Nickerson (1985) explains: "One understands a concept, principle, process or whatever to the extent that what is in one's head regarding that concept corresponds to what is in the head of an expert in the relevant field" (p. 222).

Therefore, students need to do what expert readers and writers do, and come to understand and use concepts and strategies as experts do. All of what is in our curriculum actually could be meaningful and usable because it was in fact constructed to solve real-world problems and compelling disciplinary questions. This is the heart of the matter! But much of what we do in school actually undermines true understanding and leads to student misconceptions about knowledge, the discipline, and basic acts like reading or problem solving (Dykstra, 2006; Wieman, 2005).

And as a consequence, our students resist our teaching. Listen to Buda, one of the participants in our study of boys: "I'm not going to do this crap. . . . The teacher wouldn't do this crap!" This has become a mantra for us: Would we do the crap we are assigning? If not, why not? And how can we reframe it so the task achieves obvious and meaningful personal and social work in the here and now?

The most powerful way we have found to demonstrate the why of what we're teaching is to embed our instruction in inquiry units that focus on essential questions. Essential questions are the big and enduring questions that organize disciplinary conversations. We know that we love literature because it helps us think about critical questions: "What makes me me?" "To what extent are people responsible for what happens to them?" "To what do we owe our primary allegiance?" "What makes a good relationship, or parent, or family, or leader?" We could go on and on, but we won't, as we've written about this idea at length elsewhere (Smith & Wilhelm, 2006; Wilhelm, 2007).

A look at Jeff's teaching journal when he first began using inquiry units provides some insight into the power of the approach:

Somehow I've lost sight of teaching purposefully. I've just been assigning stuff and letting the curriculum or anthology be my guide. Asking the essential question moves me from teaching a bunch of texts to using a variety of materials to consider and really explore an exciting and important issue!

And later:

Asking a big question [about survival, like "who and what will survive?"] immediately makes the unit a social project of exploration. I mean, it makes it clear we are doing something important together. It shows the kids how they can contribute and invites them to bring in stories and material of their own about hunting and fishing limits, and letting fields lie fallow, and all kinds of other things.

In the chapters that follow, we'll be providing lots and lots of suggestions for classroom activities. But we wanted to stress right from the start that we don't want you to regard these activities as a bag of tricks. Rather we hope you see them as tools that you can use to engage your students in grappling with the kinds of issues that brought us and, we suspect, you to the profession of teaching in the first place.

PRINCIPLE 2:
The Importance of the *How*

The first recommendation made in the Reading Next report on adolescent literacy is that teachers provide "direct, explicit comprehension instruction" (Biancarosa & Snow, 2006, p. 4). Classic research by Durkin (1979) establishes that even at the younger grades, teachers overwhelmingly tend to provide comprehension evaluation rather than comprehension instruction. Teachers tend to identify their evaluations of reading—and even telling students what a story means—as actual instruction in how to read. Teachers confuse the *what* with the *how*. It seems so obvious that we should teach students how to do what we want them to do, but sadly, many reviews of what and how we teach in our English language arts classes show that it is rarely done. In our experience, however, rather than focus on teaching students how to read literature, teachers often substitute teaching two other foci: technical vocabulary and the details of a particular interpretation of a text. We understand both impulses but think that both must be energetically resisted.

Literature, like any specialized field, has a technical vocabulary. In fact, terms abound—from the ordinary (e.g., the elements we'll be focusing on in this book) to the arcane (e.g., synecdoche, doppelganger, zeugma). As in any field, the technical terms gained their status because they provided practitioners with tools that allowed them to do something important in the field. Unfortunately, it seems that the terms have become ends in themselves rather than aids to understanding. Think, for example, of the common exercise of asking students to underline the simile in a poem. Such an exercise sheds light on whether students know a definition but does not indicate whether they can use their knowledge. Educational psychologists would call the focus on literary terms and definitions an emphasis on *declarative knowledge*, that is, knowledge of *what*, a kind of knowledge that can be spoken.

Another kind of declarative knowledge that's often at the forefront of language arts classes is the specific interpretations of the texts we read with our students. Once again, we understand the impulse. Both of us regularly taught texts that we loved and had read many times. When we did, we sometimes fell into the trap of working to help our students to come away with the same understandings of those texts that we had. We're not alone. Marshall's research (Marshall, Smagorinsky, & Smith, 1995) establishes that many teachers want their students to come to a shared understanding of a text and that as a consequence they tend to dominate classroom discussions, speaking on average three times as much as their students. They also tend to end up telling students what to think instead of helping them use particular tools and conventions to learn how to create their own interpretations or engage in their own writing.

George Hillocks has helped us understand why this emphasis on declarative knowledge is so worrisome. Throughout his writing (1986, 1995, 1999, 2007), he draws a distinction between declarative knowledge and *procedural knowledge*—that is, knowledge of *how*, a kind of knowledge that has to be performed. That distinction is crucially important, for, as Hillocks demonstrates again and again, declarative knowledge doesn't result in procedural knowledge. Knowing the names of the tools that a writer employs or the terms a literary analyst uses doesn't mean that students can use them on their own. Recalling the details of one interpretation doesn't help students create a new one themselves.

Let's do a thought experiment to make the point. Think of all of the technical vocabulary associated with cooking. Our kitchens are full of tools, each of which has its own name. We own whisks and colanders, Dutch ovens and graters. We own lots of knives, each with its own name: paring knife, slicing knife, oyster knife, cleaver, and so on. And each of the knives has multiple parts: the blade, the handle, the tang, the shoulder, the fuller (or blood groove). And those are just the nouns! Our cookbooks are also full of different verbs: bake, blanch, poach, roast, simmer—we could go on. Our point is simply this: Knowing all of this vocabulary is perhaps useful, though not absolutely necessary, but knowing it doesn't mean we can cook. And this vocabulary isn't really *ever* useful unless it is used to talk about, think about, or actually perform real cooking—attached to and in service of the procedural. The *what* is best learned and is most useful when learned in the context of the *how*.

When we talk about "fresh takes" on teaching literary elements, we're talking about two things: a deeper understanding of the complexity of the elements themselves and an emphasis on helping students apply this deeper understanding to their reading, and to their writing as well. In this book, then, we share our ideas about what we can do to teach the procedural knowledge students need to become more accomplished readers and writers.

PRINCIPLE 3:
The Importance and Difficulty of Transfer

Focusing on procedural knowledge is key, but it will not help students become more accomplished readers *unless* they transfer what they learn to new reading situations. That's why, as we've argued elsewhere (Smith & Wilhelm, 2006), we believe the issue of transfer is perhaps the single most important issue we need to address as teachers. That is, we need always to think about how what we do today prepares students for what they'll do later—today, tomorrow, next week, and next year. We want them to transfer the knowledge they have gained about people and stories to their understanding of the literature they read, and to their writing. We want them to transfer what they learn from reading one text to their reading of other texts. And we want them to transfer the understanding they've gained from reading to the way they think through problems and live their lives.

Although teachers often count on the fact that transfer occurs, the evidence suggests that it typically doesn't. As Haskell (2000) points out, research on transfer paints a pretty bleak picture. He puts it this way: "Despite the importance of transfer of learning, research findings over the past nine decades clearly show that as individuals, and as educational institutions, we have failed to achieve transfer of learning on any significant level" (p. xiii).

But Haskell does offer some hope. According to Haskell, transfer *can occur* under these conditions:

1. If students have command of the knowledge that is to be transferred;

2. If students have a theoretical understanding of the principles to be transferred;

3. If a classroom culture cultivates a spirit of transfer that encourages students to bring knowledge forward to new situations and shows them the benefits of doing so; and

4. If students get plenty of practice in applying meaning-making and problem-solving principles to new situations.

Haskell's analysis is consistent with one offered by Perkins and Salomon (1988) in an article that has long influenced our thinking. They argue that teachers are too sanguine about the likelihood of transfer, relying on what Perkins and Salomon call the Little Bo Peep view of transfer; that is, if we "leave them alone" they'll come to a new task and automatically transfer relevant knowledge and skills. However, they note that "a great deal of the knowledge students acquire is 'inert'" (p. 23), something that shows up on a multiple choice test but not in "new problem-solving contexts where they have to think about new situations" (p. 23).

As a consequence, Perkins and Salomon argue that teachers must work hard and quite consciously to cultivate transfer, and they suggest two mechanisms for doing so: *low-road transfer* and *high-road transfer*. Low-road transfer occurs when two tasks so closely resemble each other that you automatically use the same strategies that you used in the first task as you approach the second one. For example, if you get a rental car, you transfer what you do to drive your own car to driving the rental. High-road transfer, on the other hand, requires "mindful abstraction of skill or knowledge from one context to another" (p. 25). For example, if you suddenly had to drive a forklift or a truck, you'd probably have to ask yourself, "Okay, what do I do first?" The mindful abstraction they talk about resembles Haskell's (2000) theoretical understanding; that is, to transfer knowledge from one context to a dissimilar context requires you to know just what it is you do, why you do it, how you do it and how you know it works, and how to self-correct and think through problems if things don't work. This book, then, shares our ideas about how to help students transfer what they've learned from one reading experience to the next and, we hope, from their reading to their lives.

PRINCIPLE 4:
The Importance of Sequence

One of the most important insights of cognitive science over the last 50 years is that from a field called *schema theory*—namely, that all learning is metaphoric, that learning occurs by connecting the known to the new. If new knowledge is consistent with previous knowledge, it is added to existing schema—an organized set of knowledge pertaining to seminal ideas or processes—in an act called assimilation. If what was previously known is inconsistent, it must be accommodated to the new learning. Otherwise, people will not only fail to understand the new data, but they will also quickly revert to prior misconceptions (Science Media Group, 1989, see also Dykstra, 2006; Wieman, 2005). In fact, the only resource a learner has for learning the new is what she already knows and can do. This prior knowledge must be activated, even if such knowledge is impoverished or incorrect, in order for new learning to proceed.

Schema theory (Bransford & Johnson, 1972) has shown that a prerequisite for comprehension is the activation and use of prior knowledge. What does this mean for teachers? It means that we must begin instruction by activating students' existing knowledge (and related interest) about what we want them to learn.

As important as it is to sequence instruction by moving from the known to the new, it is also crucially important to think about how we can develop progressively richer understandings as we move from day to day. Thinking hard about sequencing instruction is something that math and science teachers do as a matter of course. They understand that chapter 1 prepares students for chapter 2, which prepares them for chapter 3, and so on. However, we don't see this kind of thinking in most of the language arts classes we've seen.

We're not alone in making this observation. When Applebee, Burroughs, and Stevens (2000) examined the curricular structure of the classes of a group of experienced and highly regarded literature teachers, they found that in the vast majority of them, teachers and students made very few connections across texts. In fact, as we've argued elsewhere (Smith & Wilhelm, 2002, 2006), some common practices (for example, the chronological organization of American and British literature classes) actually work against attempts at sensible sequencing in that students start by reading the texts that are hardest and furthest from their experiences. The notion of preparation and consolidation of strategies necessary for success is sadly absent from such a sequencing plan. Yet leaving this out is akin to a coach's never practicing basic skills or plays before putting his or her team on the field for an actual game, or not learning from one game what needs to be practiced and improved upon before the next game.

Unless curricula are structured so that the understandings students gain in one text or activity can be brought forward to the next one, students won't develop a sense of competence. Instead, as we found in our study of the literate lives of boys, both in and out of school, students are likely to feel overmatched and resistant. But if students can bring their learning from one text to the next, they can feel equipped to encounter their new reading. Because developing competence is highly motivating, they are also more likely to be engaged and feel up to the challenge (Smith & Wilhelm, 2002).

Throughout this book, we'll explore more fully the issue of sequencing assignments so that students develop strategic knowledge in one activity or assignment that they can bring forward and build on in the next. In so doing, we're making the learning that students do in their English classes much more like the kind of learning they do outside of school. We also make the learning in school applicable to their lives and futures outside of school.

Consider the learning context that so many of our students are so devoted to: the learning of video games. When you play a video game, you develop strategies and understandings in the game's lowest levels that you then apply in increasingly complex ways in harder levels of the game. That's one reason video games are so addictive: They're built to provide a sense of developing competence. The levels, scores, strength points, names, and ranks you earn in such games provide visible signs of your accomplishment. The instruction that we share in the chapters that follow is designed to provide this sense of emerging and growing competence.

PRINCIPLE 5:
The Importance of Providing Opportunities for Choice, Co-Production, and Discussion

Our greatest-hits list of instructional insights includes the pedagogical power of providing students with meaningful choices. Eric Erikson (1963) has demonstrated that the primary task of adolescence is to develop and demonstrate one's identity through evolving interest and competence. But without choice, students lack the opportunity to stake their identity in their pursuit of individual interests and in their developing competence. As one of the boys in our study informed us, "All you do in school is play 'guess what the teacher already knows'" about texts that the teacher has selected. This cannot lead to staking one's own interest, competence, or identity—the primary task of adolescence.

Jeff's older daughter, Fiona, experienced precisely this problem when she moved from her long-time school (where she was well known) to a new junior high. She complained vociferously that no one knew her. When asked why not, she replied that "all you do in school is sit in rows and listen to the teacher go 'yadda yadda yadda.' No one gets to see what you care about or what you can do. No one gets to know you."

When we provide meaningful choices in different activities and in culminating projects, and when we help students enact the how in service of finding, expressing, and enacting their own meanings, we get to know them and they get to know each other. They learn interpretive processes and concepts as they interact, connect personally, and create personal meanings. We engage them in co-producing the curriculum. They no longer play the game of merely guessing what the teacher already knows, but rather put what they are learning in service of their greatest developmental needs of building competence and staking identity.

Let's return to our video-game analogy for a moment. While the game of school isn't very engaging for many students, video games are. Students' engagement in those games is a consequence of a profoundly important educational insight made by video game designers: Gamers must be put in the position of co producing a game (see, e.g., Gee, 2003). Certainly gamers navigate the existing game and play by its conventions and rules (just as students must navigate curriculum), but they do so by assuming a very strong role and exercising decision-making power in that role, by consulting and working with other gamers, and by developing and deploying a strategic repertoire. Everything they decide to do or not do will have an impact on the gaming experience that unfolds. Helping students navigate curriculum in individual ways could provide a similar unfolding personal experience, as all students engage in different ways and make different meaning around a common project. This does not necessarily require new curricula, but a new way of framing and participating in existing curricula.

Both of us have argued in separate books that one such common project is engaging in a discussion with an intelligence behind the text. In Jeff's work in *You Gotta BE the Book* (Wilhelm, 2008), he describes reading as a transaction that involves ten dimensions of readerly response, including two that will loom large in this book: the recognition of a text's construction and the conventions used to construct it, and the recognition of interaction with the author who constructed that text. Several of Jeff's informants in this study regarded a new book by a favorite author as a chance to "talk" with the author and to get to know that author better.

Likewise, Michael's work in *Authorizing Readers* (Rabinowitz & Smith, 1998) foregrounds the notion of an author whose ideas are respected, discussed, comprehended, and perhaps then resisted through the medium of text. Authorial reading requires readers to apply the cues and conventions the author has coded into the text and then to evaluate their experience in making that application. Considering reading as a transaction with an author brings many benefits—reading is now seen as a dialogue with another intelligence from whom we might hear or experience something outside our normal way of thinking—i.e., we might learn something! This learning follows not only from experiencing another perspective and from living through an experience shaped by that perspective, but also from how we respond and react to that perspective, which helps us explore, question, justify, revise, or adapt our own self-knowledge and belief system. As readers we are brought to the point of asking: What if things were otherwise?

Discussion is an invaluable tool for fostering the kind of reading we're hoping for and for casting students in the role of co-producers of knowledge. Studies of textual understanding and discussion show that discussion contributes greatly to articulating tentative interpretive understandings, testing and honing those interpretations, and learning new meanings and ways of making meaning. A review of the literature around the use of classroom discussions in middle and high school English and language arts reveals that although discussion is much lauded, students seldom experience it. Nystrand and his colleagues (Nystrand, Gamoran, Kachur, & Prendergast, 1997), for example, note that

> by discussion we mean turn-taking among students and teachers, which departs from the normal IRE (teacher initiates–student responds–teacher evaluates) structure of classroom discourse and does not obligate students to wait for the teacher's evaluation before responding themselves to another student's response, and where their teacher, rather than evaluating a student's response, joins in and becomes a conversant. (p. 16)

Describing high-quality discussion as more like conversation, as dialogic and exploratory versus monologic, information driven, and preordained, these researchers note that such discussion involves "more probing and substantive interactions. . . . The talk is more like conversation than recitation" (p. 18). Students' questions and responses, and not just the teacher's questions and itinerary, shape the course of the discussion. In other words, all participants in the conversation, the students and the teacher, listen and respond to each other, and the course of the discussion is determined and shaped by what both the teacher and the students bring to the encounter.

This kind of discussion is co-constructivist, meaning that the teacher's contributions may help students use new tools and consider new perspectives. In such discussions teachers assist students in developing interpretations rather than imposing their own. This type of discussion foregrounds students as negotiators and creators of meaning, who are engaged in explaining both what they know and how they came to know it. Unfortunately, discussions like these are very rare. In an examination of 451 class periods in 58 eighth-grade language arts classes and 54 ninth-grade English classes, Nystrand et al. (1997) found that discussion averaged 50 seconds per class in eighth grade and less than 15 seconds per class in grade 9.

In the chapters that follow, we hope that you see myriad opportunities for students to create meanings through choice, individual expression, discussion, and other forms of creative activity.

PRINCIPLE 6:
The Importance of Connecting Reading and Writing

Though our focus here is primarily on reading, another central insight for us is the interconnectedness of reading and writing. What a reader must decode from a text—everything from words to complex conventional codes like symbolism or irony—must have been encoded into the text by an author. Likewise, what a writer encodes into a text, she expects a reader to notice and interpret.

In our work with George Hillocks's (1986) inquiry square (see, for example, Wilhelm, Baker, & Dube-Hackett, 2001; Wilhelm, 2001), we have shown that readers and writers go through similar processes and have similar needs. Both need to have articulated purposes for what they do. Writers need to know how to get the material about which they write; readers need to access and apply appropriate background knowledge and be able to mine texts for what they want to learn from them (Hillocks calls this *procedural knowledge of substance*). Writers need to be able to create the formal features of the texts they are trying to produce; readers need to know and be able to enact the reading conventions those texts invite (Hillocks refers to this as *procedural knowledge of form*). Though we will concentrate on promoting more wide-awake and strategic reading throughout this book, we will frequently use writing in service of this focus by pointing out how we can use students' writing as a resource for their reading, and vice versa. We'll also show how what students learn about reading and interpreting literary elements can be applied to their own composing.

Let's get started.

CHAPTER TWO

Thinking About What It Means to Understand Characters

When Michael was a kid, he and his friends used to play strikeout when they didn't have enough guys for a proper game of baseball. They'd draw a box with chalk on the windowless wall of the local elementary school that would act as a strike zone. If you hit the ball past the pitcher in the air, you'd get a single, and extra base hits were indicated by other landmarks: a tree, the jungle gym, and so on. If you didn't swing, the pitcher would call a strike or ball, depending on whether the pitch hit within the chalk strike zone.

Michael remembers one game in particular he played with his buddy Ernie. It was just the two of them. Michael was pitching to Ernie, and all of a sudden Ernie started doing a play-by-play of his at-bat, just as he would if he were an announcer. But instead of pretending to be real players, he was pretending to be the characters of the book he was reading, a novel titled *Relief Pitcher* by Dick Friendlich. To this day, Michael remembers Ernie's saying as he stepped up to the plate, "Batting fourth, Dixie Fleming, the Actor." "Why the Actor?" Michael wondered. "What kind of guy is this Fleming anyway?" The next month when Michael got his flyer from the Scholastic book club, you can be sure he bought *Relief Pitcher*. The next time they played, Michael knew just what pitcher to pretend to be in order to get a strikeout.

When Jeff was in fourth and fifth grade, he ripped through all of the Hardy Boys books. He would trade books with his friends Bobby Fisher and Bret Bartolovich, and when they got together, they would often pretend to be Frank, Joe, and Chet solving mysteries. There was one occasion when Jeff planted clues around the neighborhood and the three friends took Bobby's beagle for a walk and used him as a bloodhound to go sleuthing. Jeff's prize possession was a complete collection of the original leather-bound Hardy Boys books. He read them over and over, imagining what it would be like to be Joe. In role as Joe, he made a dictionary of underworld terms used in the books, such as "he took a bath in the canal" for "they drowned him for being an informer." Sadly, his mother sold his collection in a garage sale when he was in college. He doubts whether he has ever really completely forgiven her.

The Importance of Understanding Literary Characters

Our interest in literary characters hasn't waned over the years. When Michael makes reservations at a restaurant, he doesn't leave his real name. Instead he leaves Fred Trumper, the main character of John Irving's *The Water-Method Man*, a character who was very important to him during a very trying time of his life. When Jeff takes a kayak trip down a canyon stretch that's new to him, he often pretends that he is John Wesley Powell, the one-armed Civil War hero who explored the Colorado River. Jeff first got to know Powell through reading his journals; now Jeff imagines what it would be like to have been Powell and make a first descent down a river about which he's heard only vague rumors.

Our relationships with literary characters and with the authors who created them are what brought us to reading. Our love of reading is what brought us to teaching the English language arts. In some way, then, literary characters have made us what we are today.

Literary characters have affected more than our choice of occupation; they've affected who we are and how we act. When Michael started teaching, he used to worry so much about students' cheating or taking advantage that it sometimes prevented him from building an environment of trust in the classroom. Then he read Henry Fielding's *Joseph Andrews*. Andrews's sidekick in the novel is Parson Adams. Parson Adams is a comic figure, and throughout the novel he's taken advantage of by scoundrels he attempts to help. But he's also a good man. When Michael read the book, he never said "Shame on you" to Parson Adams for trying to help. He did say "Shame on you" to the scoundrels who deceived him. Since reading the book, Michael has resolved to apply what he's come to think of as the Parson Adams test to his work with students: He asks, "Have I acted in a way such that I can honestly say if students take advantage of me, it's not my bad, but theirs?" If the answer is "yes," he's content. Michael's resolution has made a world of difference in his work with students.

Likewise, Jeff's thinking and his parenting is consciously informed by the negative example of the father in Alan Paton's *Too Late the Phalarope*. The scene in which the father blots his son's name out of the family Bible seared itself into Jeff's mind, and he resolved—before he had children of his own—

that he would love his children no matter what, that he would tell them every day that he loved them, and that he would never let the ways they disappointed him come between them. During the most trying times in his life as a parent, he often thought of this literary father and how he could avoid becoming like him.

We're not alone in recognizing the impact that literary characters can have on our lives. In Wayne Booth's wonderful book *The Company We Keep* (1988), he talks about how literary characters can affect a reader's character. He notes that stories typically center on the characters' efforts to face moral choices and argues that "In tracing those efforts, we readers stretch our own capacities for thinking about how life should be lived" (p. 187). In *The Call of Stories* (1989), Robert Coles relates one of our favorite quotes. It's from one of his students, who is talking about the importance of literature in his life:

> When I have some big moral issue, some question to tackle, I think I try to remember what my folks have said, or I imagine them in my situation—or even more these days I think of [characters in books I've read]. Those folks, they're people for me . . . they really speak to me—there's a lot of me in them, or vice versa. I don't know how to put it, but they're voices, and they help me make choices. I hope when I decide "the big ones" they'll be in there pitching. (p. 203)

We realize that we're probably preaching to the choir, but we think it's a point worth making: Getting to know—*really* getting to know—literary characters enriches our reading and our lives. Think of all of the essential questions that motivate our reading that depend on our understanding literary characters: What does it mean to be a good parent (or teacher or friend)? What makes a real hero? To what extent do we discover (as opposed to create) our true selves? We could go on. Indeed we will go on throughout our work on character to provide other examples of essential questions into which instruction on understanding character can be embedded.

Getting to Know Literary Characters

What does it mean to get to know literary characters? Well, if characters are to play the significant role in our students' lives that they have played in ours, getting to know a literary character would mean much the same thing as getting to know the flesh-and-blood folks who populate our lives.

HOW DO WE UNDERSTAND PEOPLE IN OUR DAY-TO-DAY LIVES? CREATING A GENERAL IMPRESSION ON THE BASIS OF A PERSON'S TRAITS

Research in social psychology sheds light on a process we engage in so often that we pay it little attention. A classic article by Asch (1946) begins this way:

We look at a person and immediately a certain impression of his character forms itself in us. A glance, a few spoken words are sufficient to tell us a story about a highly complex matter. We know that such impressions form with remarkable rapidity and with great ease. Subsequent observation may enrich or upset our first view, but we can no more prevent its rapid growth than we can avoid perceiving a given visual object or hearing a melody. (p. 258)

The first sentence seems to us to be the most telling. The premise with which Asch begins, one that is corroborated by his research, is that we get an impression of a person's entire character, not just his or her characteristics.

Asch established this premise through a set of studies that have a similar design. He gave participants in his research a list of traits and asked them to form an impression of the kind of person the traits describe. Here's one list of terms that he used: "energetic, assured, talkative, cold, ironical, inquisitive, persuasive" (p. 260). And here are a couple of the sketches of the impressions his participants created on the basis of those terms:

He seems to be the kind of person who would make a great impression upon others at a first meeting. However, as time went by, his acquaintances would easily come to see through the mask. Underneath would be revealed his arrogance and selfishness.

* * * * *

He is the type of person you meet all too often: sure of himself, talks too much, always trying to bring you around to his way of thinking, and with not much feeling for the other fellow. (p. 261)

Two things seem especially striking about this study. In the first place, Asch's adult participants were adept at creating a unified general impression of the person described. None of the more than 1,000 people who participated in the research project responded to the request with anything that approximated a list of traits. Second, the general impression people developed went beyond the list of traits that they were provided. That is, in the words of Grabes (2004), they turned "words on a page into 'real' people" through the process of "figuring forth."

HOW DO WE UNDERSTAND PEOPLE IN OUR DAY-TO-DAY LIVES? RECOGNIZING THAT SOME CHARACTERISTICS MATTER MORE THAN OTHERS

Asch's work has other interesting findings as well. One is that not all traits carry equal weight in creating a general impression. Asch gave the following list of traits to another set of participants: "intelligent, skillful, industrious, warm, determined, practical, cautious." He substituted *cold* for *warm* with yet another set of participants. He found that participants regarded the designation of the person as warm or cold was more important than any of the other traits and that the way they understood the other traits was colored by whether the person was warm or cold. For example, intelligence in a warm person was perceived as a trait that allowed the person to do good works for others, while intelligence in the cold person was perceived as being calculating.

Given Asch's discussion of the immediacy of the impressions we make, it's not surprising that he found the traits that were encountered first tended to be more influential than those encountered later. His research corroborates the exhortations of our moms: "You only get once chance to make a good first impression." Here's the general impression of one participant when presented with the words "intelligent—industrious—impulsive—critical—stubborn—envious" (p. 270): "The person is intelligent and fortunately he puts his intelligence to work. That he is stubborn and impulsive may be due to the fact that he knows what he is saying and what he means and will not therefore give in easily to someone else's idea which he disagrees with" (p. 270).

Here's the general impression of another participant who was presented with the same list of words but in the reverse order: "This person's good qualities such as industry and intelligence are bound to be restricted by jealousy and stubbornness. The person is emotional. He is unsuccessful because he is weak and allows his bad points to cover up his good ones (p. 270)."

In short, Asch's research establishes that we create coherent general impressions on the basis of a person's traits, although the impact of different traits varies. And, of course, when we read literature, we may get an explicit statement of a character's traits through direct characterization, but, as in life, "the discovery of the traits in a person is a vital part of the process of establishing an impression" (p. 280).

HOW DO WE UNDERSTAND PEOPLE IN OUR DAY-TO-DAY LIVES? CREATING EXPECTATIONS ON THE BASIS OF GROUP MEMBERSHIP

But those individual traits are not the only thing upon which we base our judgments. Let's do a thought experiment: Imagine that you have a job in a new school. You've just received your class list. All you know about your class is your students' names. Will you be getting an impression of that class before meeting your students? The answer for many teachers is "yes." As part of our study of the literate lives of young men both in and out of school (Smith & Wilhelm, 2002), we've had lots of informal conversations with teachers who have admitted checking their class lists to see how many boys they have. The more boys they have, the more trouble they anticipate. That doesn't mean that these teachers aren't alert for individual differences once they meet the class. But it does establish that at least some of the time we base our initial impression of a person on that person's membership in some group.

In fact, lots of curricular choices are made because of students' membership in groups. A school might assign Gary Paulsen's *Hatchet* as summer reading because the school believes that boys will like it. Or Walter Dean Myers's *Monster* because they think it will appeal to kids of color. What's true of us as teachers is true of people in general as well. West and Zimmerman (1991), for example, argue that gender is a superordinate grouping; that is, they argue that we understand ourselves and others first in terms of gender. Omi and Winant (1994) make a similar argument about race (at least in the U.S.): "One of the first things we notice about people when we meet them (along with their sex) is their race. We utilize race to provide clues to *who* a person is" (p. 59, italics in original).

It is not just race, nationality, ethnicity, religion, and gender—what Fishman (1995) calls the "A List" of cultural markers—that we draw on. We also draw on age, geography, education, occupation, family status, and sexual orientation (Fishman's "B List"). We know that because we're college professors we have to fight the impression that we're theory-heads who are unconnected to and unconcerned about what really happens in schools.

In an often-cited article, Kunda and Thagard (1996) build on Asch's approach, making a persuasive argument that top-down impressions formed on the basis of membership in a group interact with the bottom-up impression formed by particular information one gets about an individual. They argue that when we encounter someone new, we notice individual details about that person as well as make inferences about groups to which the individual belongs. The inferences we make about the individual are affected by both kinds of information. According to Kunda and Thagard, we try to integrate those inferences into a general impression, making additional inferences or modifying existing ones as we get additional information. The more individuating information we get, the more the inferences we make on the basis of group membership are put to the test. Ultimately, we'll form a final impression (final, at least, until we learn something that forces us to reconsider). We understand character by making a series of inferences that we must keep categorically tentative as we get new information, so we have to connect more dots that give us a fuller and more complex picture. Of course, the processes we use for evaluating people in real life can also apply to characters in stories. (Our thanks to Julian Krisak for helping us think through this issue.)

Whew! We know we've taken a long detour over what is probably unfamiliar terrain, but we hope the detour has been warranted. Let's think about the instructional implications of the work we've done so far:

1. To understand characters, our students must recognize not only a character's particular traits but also how those traits interact to form an overall impression of the character.
2. Because first impressions are so powerful, we have to help students recognize when they ought to modify them.
3. Students will make inferences about characters based on stereotypes of the groups to which they belong. We have to make sure students test those stereotypes against the individuating information that they glean from their reading.

(Consider how important all of this is not only in literature, but also in life.)

HOW EXPERIENCED READERS UNDERSTAND LITERARY CHARACTERS

We began this chapter by arguing that the moral *and functional* force of literature resides in the fact that it provides, in George Santayana's words, "imaginative rehearsals for living" (cited in Booth, 1983b, p. 212). That is, literature allows us to try on perspectives other than our own and to test what comes from adopting those perspectives. Literature also allows us to try out new ways of being or acting—to rehearse what we might say or do in new situations. Michael, as we noted above, tested Parson Adams's perspective, and because it passed, has tried to make it his own. Jeff tested the father's perspective in *Too Late the Phalarope* and found that it failed, and so he has worked to avoid it.

Once again, although the importance of trying on alternate perspectives sounds obvious, it's not. Consider, for example, the rule that Lee offers Samuel in Steinbeck's *East of Eden*:

> [P]eople are interested only in themselves. If a story is not about the hearer, he will not listen. And here I make a rule—a great and lasting story is about everyone or it will not last. The strange and the foreign is not interesting—only the deeply personal and familiar. (1992, p. 276)

We fear that many teachers believe this rule and apply it to their teaching. Bleich (1975), an influential reader response theorist, for example, bases his pedagogical ideas on the beliefs that "the role of personality in response is the most fundamental fact of criticism" and that "all people, young and old, think about themselves most of the time and think about the world in terms of themselves" (p. 4). Probst (1992), an influential advocate of Louise Rosenblatt's theories, says this: "If we could learn enough about adolescent psychology, we might be able to develop a literature curriculum that would promote reflection upon one's own experiences" (p. 76). Reisman (1994) goes so far as to argue for eliminating references to cultural markers at the beginning of texts so that students can see themselves in those texts. (For example, Arna Bontemps's story "A Summer Tragedy" begins this way: "Old Jeff Patton, the black share farmer, fumbled with his bow tie. His fingers trembled and the high stiff collar pinched his throat." In Reisman's view, it could be edited to eliminate the appositive in the first sentence.)

Developing self-knowledge is certainly an important goal. But we think that learning about others is equally important and may, in fact, be more important if we want to foster personal growth. The unique power of literature allows us to pay a respectful attention to people and perspectives that are distant from us in time, place, and experience.

Let's take a brief sojourn to another discipline once again to articulate what it means to pay respectful attention to others. Our thinking on what this means has been informed by the philosophical work of Downie and Tefler (1970). They argue that respect has two dimensions. First, "we respect [others] by showing active sympathy with them; in Kant's terms we make their ends our own" (p. 28).

Second, "we respect them by taking seriously the fact that the rules by which they guide their conduct constitute reasons which may apply both to them and to ourselves" (pp. 28–29).

In other writing, Michael has developed what this means for readers (Rabinowitz & Smith, 1998; Smith & Strickland, 2001), but we think the point is important enough to make it again here. One of the most surprisingly educative encounters Michael has had with a story is one he had some years ago in a multiracial literature discussion group he initiated in a GED class at a local adult education center. The group was discussing Alice Walker's "Everyday Use," a story that turns, at least in part, on the tension between two sisters, Dee and Maggie. The story is set in the rural South. Dee, the older sister, always pushed to leave home, both physically, by attending a school in the city, and metaphysically, by forging an African identity, exemplified by her taking on Wangero as her new name. Shy and frightened, Maggie provides a stark contrast in the way she clings to home and all that it means. The story chronicles a visit home by Dee. During her visit she seems taken by the artifacts of everyday life. She especially admires quilts her grandmother made, and asks that she be allowed to take them. She plans on displaying them on her walls. But her mother, the narrator of the story, says no, for she had promised the quilts to Maggie. Dee is furious. She argues that "Maggie can't appreciate these quilts! She'd probably be backward enough to put them to everyday use." Her mother offers what Michael had always considered a telling retort. She says that it doesn't matter if Maggie wears the quilts out, for "She can always make some more . . . Maggie knows how to quilt." The argument causes Dee to leave after criticizing her mother and sister for not understanding their heritage and for being content to live as they always have. The story closes with the mother and Maggie's sitting next to each other on a bench, "just enjoying, until it was time to go in the house and go to bed."

After Michael read the story aloud, the group discussed it. And then came the surprise. Michael had read the story many times prior to the meeting of the group. He had always read the story as illustrating the primacy of the family. But in the discussion several African American participants in the group offered a different understanding. They argued that in their experience progress toward racial equity was only made by those who thought first about the race and that Dee's desire to display the quilts as objects of pride was very much in line with those who worked to foster African American pride.

As he listened, Michael came to realize that he did not pay Dee an ethical respect. Instead of trying on her perspective, he dismissed her. The literature discussion group required him to make a new assessment. Paying Dee an ethical respect forced Michael to consider whether his tendency to think first about interpersonal and familial relations as opposed to larger political issues was justified or whether it was a luxury that being White and being male afforded him. And as a consequence, he left with a new appreciation both of the story and of his discussion group colleagues.

Trying on a character's perspective doesn't mean adopting it. Ultimately one might decide that Dee is wrong. But if that decision is to be useful, it requires that it be informed by a respectful attention. Providing that respectful attention not only teaches us about others, but also about ourselves. Part of the way we learn about ourselves is by examining those with whom we align and those we reject.

But taking seriously the rules by which characters guide their conduct is no easy matter. In the first place, it means trying on perspectives far different from our own. It also means noticing the kind of people who are often invisible to us in our day-to-day lives, people like Maggie, who do not demand our attention. Finally, it means recognizing the limitations of our own experience as an aid to understanding others. When we try on the perspective of a literary character, we must, of course, use our life experiences as aids. But we also have to be aware that our experience may not be enough and may, in fact, mislead us. Michael's daughter Catherine brought this point home to us when she said, "Dad, I'm a Black, adopted girl. Three strikes and you're out. I know that you love me, but you can't really understand me." Hard words to hear, but, we think, true ones. Catherine's words don't suggest that Michael shouldn't try to understand her; they suggest that he needs to be alert for when he is applying his perspective rather than hers to the situations she faces.

Our consideration of the ethics of reading brings us to our fourth instructional implication (see 1–3, page 24):

4. If students are to experience the greatest possible benefit from reading, then they need to try on, at least provisionally, the various perspectives of the characters about whom they are reading.

THE PROBLEMS WITH TRADITIONAL INSTRUCTION

Before we present a variety of activities designed to address these four implications, let's take a quick look at one popular anthology to see how traditional instruction fares in achieving them. The ninth-grade book of McDougal Littell's The Language of Literature series (Applebee, et al., 2002), the anthology series used at Michael's daughters' high school, has character development as the literary focus for its second unit. The instruction introducing that focus provides students with definitions and examples of a variety of terms associated with characters: major and minor characters, protagonist and antagonist, round and flat characters, and dynamic and static characters. After these definitions, it moves on to discuss strategies for making inferences about a character's background, feelings, and behavior. The book urges students to question why specific details are included and to assess the significance of those details by applying what they know from reading or from their own personal experience. In the story that follows, "The Beginning of Something" by Sue Ellen Bridgers, a few questions are inserted to help students make inferences about the characters. Here's the first one: "Why is Roseanne surprised at her mother's reaction to the death of cousin Jesse?" (p. 327).

We think that the McDougal Littell series has much to recommend it, especially the variety of opportunities it provides for extended interpretations, and we like and admire its senior consultants. Moreover, the instructional approach it takes resembles the approach of many other anthology series and is consistent with what we've seen many teachers do over our years of observation. Despite its ubiquity, though, we worry about this approach for three important reasons:

1. It emphasizes declarative rather than procedural knowledge.
2. It doesn't lend itself to transfer.
3. It doesn't reflect the way we understand people in our lives.

Let's examine each of these in turn.

Declarative Versus Procedural Knowledge

We talked about the importance of procedural knowledge at some length in the last chapter, so we won't belabor the point here. But we think it's worth noting that the technical vocabulary associated with characterization doesn't help readers *do* anything, although it may highlight some of the things they need to pay attention to as they read. Take, for example, the difference between dynamic and static characters. The key issue isn't knowing the definitional distinction, but is rather being alert for details that signal that a character is changing and being willing to modify initial impressions. Modifying initial impressions isn't easy, as classic research in schema theory (Anderson, Reynolds, Schallert, & Goetz, 1977) makes clear. That research establishes that readers often resist new information if it requires them to give up or modify schemata they have already developed. Knowing a definition cannot change this tendency toward resistance. Repeated practice assessing the extent to which new information supports or challenges existing schemata is what's needed. And using a technical term to label what students have been rewarded for doing makes it far more likely that they'll learn the term, if it's important that they do so.

The Question of Transfer

In our introductory chapter we also discussed the importance and difficulty of transfer. Once again, we won't belabor the points we made there. But it's important to note that the primary instructional move the anthology makes beyond providing a definition of terms is asking questions. Although asking discussion questions is an important element of literature teachers' stock in trade, we have real worries about over-reliance on that practice. Why? Think about what students need in order to transfer their knowledge to a new situation. Answering questions that a teacher asks cannot help students do the kind of mindful abstraction they need to do to transfer what we teach them to new situations. This is true for two reasons. First, questions like the one from the McDougal Littell anthology mentioned above are story specific. The only story for which you can ask "Why is Roseanne surprised at her mother's reaction to the death of cousin Jesse?" is "The Beginning of Something." Second, in asking the question, the teacher or book has done most of the interpretive work by calling readers' attention to the passage. A crucially important interpretive skill is *noticing* (Rabinowitz, 1987; Rabinowitz & Smith, 1998) a detail as one that carries significant meaning. If we are interested in our students' applying what they learn from reading one story to their reading of the next, *they* have to be the ones to do the noticing. To do this, they need to understand the kind of cues authors provide for them to notice and depend on them to use to interpret character. If we ask questions about a text, it must be in the service of helping students to notice similar cues and ask the same kinds of interpretive questions for themselves.

Reading in Literature and Reading in Life

Our final concern is that what some instruction tells students about how to understand characters doesn't jibe with how we understand actual people in our lives. In the first place, traditional instruction suggests that we build our understanding of characters solely from the bottom up, that is, by noticing details. As we have argued previously, although building from the bottom up is crucially important, so too is developing a general impression and then checking it against the details. If instruction is to match what we do in our day-to-day lives, it has to do both. Moreover, it has to result in a general sense of the character rather than in recognition of a discrete set of traits. That is, understanding why Roseanne (from the anthologized Bridgers story) is surprised tells us something both about Roseanne and her mother. But the key is how what we learn affects our general impression of the characters, the impression that we'll carry with us once we've finished the story.

In the next chapter we'll detail a set of lessons designed to help students understand literary characters. We hope that you'll evaluate our lessons using the same criteria we used to assess the instruction on the McDougal Littell anthology—that is, considering whether they help students develop procedural knowledge, whether they reflect what we do when we try to understand people in our lives, and whether they foster transfer, both to other works of literature and to life.

CHAPTER THREE

Putting Theory Into Practice:
Preparing Students to Understand Character

Have you ever been in a group of people when someone tells a joke and you're the only one who doesn't get it? When you greet the joke with a quizzical look instead of laughter, typically someone notices and then tries to explain it to you. After the explanation, the characteristic response runs something like this: "Ha, ha, ha. That's really funny." But of course, it's not. If you don't get a joke the first time through, it's impossible to rehabilitate it.

The same thing is true for literature. If our students don't have a good experience with a text as they are reading it, it's impossible to rehabilitate it, no matter how good our post-reading instruction. Given how critically important understanding characters is to understanding literature, it's crucial, therefore, to take some time to help students understand just what they ought to be up to when they are working to understand characters. This means both helping them understand the importance of the four instructional implications we discussed in the last chapter and avoiding a number of problematic interpretive moves that we have often witnessed students make.

Two problems seem especially noteworthy to us. In our experience, students often focus on surface features of characters rather than on their impression of the character's character. When we've asked students to talk about what they learned about a character, they've often responded with something like the following: "He's fourteen," or "She's blonde," or "Their favorite sport is basketball." Now all of those details may well be worth noticing and remembering, but as experienced readers, we know that physical attributes, age, and interests are noteworthy only when they tell us something deeper about a character. A second problem we have encountered is when our students focus on states (e.g., She was happy when she won the race) instead of traits (e.g., She's a happy person.) The activities that follow are designed to help your students avoid these problems and to enact the four instructional implications we discussed last chapter. Here goes.

Using Personality Tests

We recommend beginning instruction by helping students recognize what they should be doing as they read. One great way to do so is to tap a literacy practice that many students have already developed: responding to personality tests. Teen magazines are replete with such tests. Phillips (2006) has published a compendium of these tests, such as "Your Inner Fashionista: Which STYLE Is Really You." Students could also take more serious, empirically validated tests—for example, versions of the Myers-Briggs Type Indicator test. You can find a collection of tests that are available on the Internet at http://www.geocities.com/lifexplore/tests.htm.

The point of giving students such tests is to help them see the kind of information we want to know about ourselves and others, for that's just what they should try to learn about characters as they read. One enjoyable and interesting activity to see if students have really thought about character is to have them fill out one of these personality tests from the perspective of a character. (More on this later.) In fact, Pevsner speculates on the Myers-Briggs types of a wide range of movie and television characters at http://www.geocities.com/myersbriggstypology/.

The tests could also provide the opportunity to think about what characteristics matter most to our understanding of people. After students had taken a number of tests, they could rank them in order of their importance. If a single test had a number of dimensions, they could rank those dimensions in order of their importance. You could tally the responses and have large- or small-group discussions about them. The goal of these discussions would not be to come to a consensus but rather to establish the understanding that some characteristics matter more than others.

Another way to establish this consciousness would be to draw on the work of Asch, either by repeating his experiments with the class by having them write their impression of someone on the basis of a set of descriptors (you might remember the list—intelligent, skillful, industrious, warm, determined, practical, cautious—from our earlier discussion) and then asking students to compare what they wrote with what their classmates wrote. The class could then compare what they wrote with what Asch's participants wrote, allowing students to see what understandings are shared, and which ones are idiosyncratic. Students should be especially alert, then, for evidence of those traits that most people think are particularly important.

Yet another way to establish this consciousness is to ask students to create checklists of characteristics of a best friend, life partner, teammate, leader, and so on. Doing so demonstrates that discrete characteristics are important not so much in and of themselves but rather in terms of what they add up to. These checklists, indeed all the work with personality tests, would be especially useful in inquiry units in which students are examining a range of authors' ideas on questions about friends, leaders, heroes, and so on. (On the life level, think how these different activities would help students in considering how they are perceived by others, critiquing how they evaluate and judge people, mulling over what is most important in their own friends, leaders, etc.)

Using Simulated Texts

As you recall from our argument on teaching for transfer, if students are going to be able to transfer what they learn to novel situations, they have to have a deep understanding of what they've learned. It's important, therefore, to have them reflect on how they understand people and, consequently, how they ought to understand characters. One way to do so is to present them with targeted practice using texts designed to focus their attention on the particular interpretive skill you are trying to teach. Langer (2001) calls this providing *simulated* instruction because "the tasks themselves are especially developed for the purpose of practice" (p. 856). She argues that providing such instruction is one characteristic of teachers whose students beat the odds—that is, teachers whose students perform better on high-stakes assessments than their SES would predict. "Simulations," we would add, provide practice—in situations that are analogous to the actual activity being prepared for and that develop actual expertise that can be applied in real-life situations. Simulations, therefore, can and should meet the "correspondence concept" (see Wilhelm, 2004).

ADS AND PORTRAITS

One kind of text that provides the targeted practice that Langer calls for is ads, both for print and for TV. For example, the ubiquitous Mac/PC ads (available on Apple's Web site), call for viewers to make inferences about the computers based on the characters who represent them. The lesson could consist of showing an ad, asking students to list three to five of the most important traits they think each character has, and tallying students' responses. As a next step, ask students to explain the reasoning underlying the decisions they made. As they articulate the evidence, track it based on whether their inferences were derived from group membership (e.g., "I know he's old-fashioned because he's a nerd and nerds don't know what's up") or individuating information (e.g., "I know he's old-fashioned because of the way he dresses. Who wears a suit?"). They could also rank the traits in order of importance to the general impression. This kind of work would be particularly useful in an inquiry unit built around an essential question such as "To what extent do the media manipulate what we think?" (This question could also be a sub-question in an inquiry organized around a larger question of who or what determines what we think and believe.)

Iconic images such as these tend to rely on group membership rather than on individuating information (think of the Marlboro cowboy). But other images available on the Internet are more complex. We used "photographic portraits" as a search term and found a number of photos that could be shared with the class. If you include such an activity, we suggest that you lead the discussion of each photo (or each set of photos) in a similar way. Begin by asking students (or groups of students) to list the single most striking characteristic of the person in the image and then to explain the evidence they relied on to make the inference. (Evidence could be a connection to personal experience or the world that is implied by the photo as well as evidence in the text itself.) After sharing, you could consider together how students used group membership versus how they used individuating information as the basis of their judgments.

Michael has used the collection *The Family of Man* (Steichen, 1955), a book that includes more than 500 photographs from 68 countries. The fact that the photos are of many different kinds of people from many different times and places provides the opportunity for just the kind of discussion we're calling for. For example, comparing a photo of an impoverished older man with an impoverished younger woman allowed Michael and his class to consider the extent to which the general impression they perceived was a function of the age and gender of the subject and to what extent it was a function of the specific details of the particular photo.

Another alternative is to use fine arts portraits as the focus of discussion. Michael's favorite portraitist is Diego Velázquez. Images of his are readily available online. Michael's particular favorite is *A Dwarf Sitting on the Floor* (1645), a painting that challenges generalizations on the basis of group membership (just look at the eyes). Jeff's favorite is John Singer Sargent. Think of the work you and your students could do on *Madame X* (1884).

We can see the power of simulated instruction by thinking through just how many of these visual texts students could consider in a class period. Students could make more inferences about more characters in a day or two of interpreting photographs or fine art portraits than they would in a month's worth of classroom discussion of literature. And because they'd constantly have to explain how they made the inference, they'll begin to develop the kind of conscious control that fosters transfer. This work should transfer not only to their subsequent reading but also to their writing. Seeing the impact of descriptive details and group membership should help students understand what they need to do to make their own characters come to life when they write narratives.

PERSONALS

A more complex activity could follow. As you recall from Chapter 1, a foundational instructional principle of this book is that we build from students' existing literacies to help them develop new academic literacies. That means drawing on their understanding of nonacademic texts to help them develop strategies they can apply to reading literature. One kind of nonacademic text that puts a premium on making inferences about a character is the personal ad. What follows is an activity that uses texts that resemble personal ads to provide students the kind of targeted practice that characterized effective instruction in Langer's (2001) study.

Rating Roommates

Pretend that you are going away to summer camp and the camp has sent you the profiles of five potential roommates. Rank them from the person you'd most like to room with (1) to the person you'd least like to room with (5). If you're a boy, pretend that all of the profiles were written by boys. If you're a girl, pretend that all the profiles were written by girls.

_____ **Chris**

Favorite subject: Math   **Future occupation:** Fngineer   **Favorite TV show:** *Star Trek*

What I like to do out of school: I spend most of my time outside of school on the Internet.

Statement: I know I don't have a lot of friends, but I'm the kind of kid that when I'm your friend I'm really your friend. I enjoy getting to know new people. My friends tell me that I'm a good listener. Maybe I developed that ability because I don't talk much. But I hope that when I do, I have something worthwhile to say.

_____ **Alex**

Favorite subject: PE or English   **Future occupation:** Basketball player

Favorite TV show: *SportsCenter*   **What I like to do outside of school:** Play ball

Statement: I guess most people think of me just as a basketball jock. I really shouldn't complain because I love basketball. It's the most important thing in my life. But I really like other things too, like art and reading. It surprises people sometimes. I'm not exactly sure why that is.

_____ **Sam**

Favorite subject: NONE!   **Future occupation:** Something that makes lots of $

Favorite TV show: *American Idol*   **What I like to do outside school:** Hang with friends

Statement: I'm kinda bummed that my parents are making me do this summer camp, so I REALLY hope I get a cool roommate. Somebody funny who's willing to bend the rules a bit. I'm not wild, but I really like to have fun, and that's what summer's for anyway. I have to say that one thing that's okay about camp is that I like being outside. So my roommate should like that too.

_____ **Dana**

Favorite Subject: Art   **Future occupation:** Something involving music

Favorite TV show: Anything about the supernatural   **What I like to do outside of school:** Play my guitar

Statement: Music is my life. If I'm not playing it, I'm listening to it. I especially like head-banger stuff. But I'm open to enjoying almost anything. I'm a bit nervous about this camp thing, to tell the truth. My friends at school tell me it's weird that I want to go. But anything beats sitting at home. I like new experiences, so I'm sure I'll like it.

_____ **Pat**

Favorite Subject: Biology   **Future occupation**: Doctor

Favorite TV show: Anything having to do with science   **What I like to do outside of school:** Read

Statement: I'm looking forward to coming to camp. I think it'll be a great learning experience. It's not just all the activities we have a chance to participate in, it's also a chance to meet lots of new people. It's kind of like college in a way. You learn from classes but you might learn even more from the people you meet and from living away from home.

Whenever we do a ranking activity of this sort, we tend to follow the same procedure. First, we ask students to do the ranking independently. Then we assign them to small groups and ask them to try to convince each other to adopt their ranking. As we circulate during the group work, we keep an eye out for disagreements because they foster elaborated explanations of the reasoning involved. If we notice that a student's personal rating is at odds with something that was being said in a group, we encourage that student to respond by saying something like, "You disagree. Tell _____ why." We found that a little nudge like that works even with some of our most reticent students.

Once the group discussions start slowing down, we put a matrix on the board like this one:

	1	2	3	4	5
Chris					
Alex					
Sam					
Dana					
Pat					

After tallying individual responses, it's easy to facilitate a very active whole-class discussion. We suggest beginning with the profile about which there was the most disagreement. For the most part, we encourage you to stay out of the discussion except for asking probing questions such as "What makes you say so?" As students make their arguments, you should track the evidence they cite, writing it on the board. After the discussion is complete, you can reflect on the kind of evidence that students used. Some of the judgments that they made will have been because of the character's membership in a group—for example, "He likes *Star Trek*!" Other judgments will be based on individuating information, such as, "She sounds like a really thoughtful person because she wants to learn." To help students begin to develop conscious control over what they are doing, you can ask them to look

Tips for Using Ranking Activities

1. The items being ranked need to be problematic. If everyone gives an item the same ranking, it's not useful.

2. Have students do the ranking individually before small-group or whole-class discussions.

3. Tally responses so that the whole class can see them.

4. Begin discussion with the item that has the widest array of responses.

5. Make sure to ask students why they thought what they thought.

6. After the discussion is over, do some debriefing to highlight the strategies students used to come to their judgments and the criteria they applied in making them.

back at the clues they used to infer the individuating information. This discussion should result in students' generating at least three or four of the inference cues that authors typically draw on to flesh out their characters: their actions and interests (e.g., reading versus playing the guitar), their language (e.g., "I'm kinda bummed"), and their thoughts or strong beliefs (e.g., "Anything beats sitting at home"). The discussion should also help students understand what perspectives they're most open and resistant to.

A follow-up activity (see page 38) that asks students to rank a set of fathers from the one they most admire to the one they least admire will help them apply what they've been doing to a new situation. Once again, they have to use both group membership and individuating information to make overall judgments about characters.

We recommend proceeding in the same fashion with the good father activity as you did with the roommate activity. Once the final large-group discussion is complete, it's time to engage students in reflecting on what they did. This discussion can revolve around what is revealed about each character, how this was revealed, and what we learn about ourselves from our judgments and interpretations.

In both the roommate and good father activities, students have to develop a general impression of someone. In both activities they can draw on either group membership or individuating information to develop that impression. Their judgments will depend on making inferences based on combining data from the text with experiences from one's personal life and the world. After the discussion you can have them write about what they relied on and why they relied on it. And both activities would not only help students understand character but also prepare them for an extended examination of an essential question like "What makes a good friend (or parent)?"

What Makes a Good Father?

Each of the following scenes features a father. Read each scene carefully and then rank from the father who is the best (#1) to the father who is the worst (#5). Make sure you can support your decisions. You'll be talking about them in small groups and then we'll be sharing them as a class.

1. Julie is an eighth grader. Her parents got divorced when she was six years old. For seven years she spent about the same amount of time with each of them, but three years ago, her dad moved to California, all the way across the country from her. He had a great job opportunity and he said that the lifestyle there suited him. These days Julie spends every other Christmas vacation and three weeks each summer with him. He calls every week, but it's hard to talk. He has trouble keeping track of current friends and classes. A couple of times when Julie faced a really big decision she called, and her dad was really helpful. She knows he'll help her decide what college to go to. Somehow he senses what's best for her. But she wishes he were more interested in the day-to-day details of her life.

Ranking for Julie's father _____

2. Joseph is a high school junior. He has a lot of friends, but they sometimes wonder about him. He'll never do anything that might get him in trouble with his father, a police officer. Joseph won't even go to a party where beer might be available or a concert where somebody might bring drugs. He says, "Can't. I think that kind of stuff is stupid. But more than that, you guys just don't know my dad. He'd kill me." Joseph's father has never hit him, but he's really strict. He makes Joseph do 90 minutes of schoolwork every night, whether he has homework or not.

Ranking for Joseph's father _____

3. Terry is a high school sophomore. Her dad is a biker. He makes a good living repairing motorcycles, and he's very generous with Terry. Plus, he's promised to put her through whatever college she chooses. Terry loves the time they spend together at home. Her dad is a whiz at math and he's great at helping her with her homework. He also teaches her how to fix his bikes. Terry could probably get a job as a mechanic, but she doesn't want to. She feels it's kind of a weird scene.

⟶

In fact, she wishes that her dad weren't so into it. He has the earrings and tattoos like many of the other riders. It embarrasses Terry a bit, especially when he shows up to school in his leathers. She tried talking to him about it once, but he just laughed and said, "Don't tell me that you're ashamed of your old man."

Ranking for Terry's father _____

4. Rorie is a seventh grader. But lots of people don't realize she's so young because she's such a great golfer. She's already won the women's championship at her golf club. Rorie loves to compete. She just wishes that she had more time to spend with her friends. But her dad is always pushing her to practice, practice, practice. He's always wanted the best for her. In fact, he worked two jobs and took a second mortgage out on their house so they could afford the club's $150,000 initiation fee. He said that it was a worthwhile investment, both because it would help Rorie's golf game and because her dad says, "At clubs like ours you only meet the best kind of people. You know what I mean. It's not for everyone." When Rorie plays, her dad always caddies for her. He's really a big help. She doesn't much mind when she hears other players call her "Daddy's little girl."

Ranking for Rorie's father _____

5. Thomas is a ninth grader. His first year at the high school has been a bit rough, much more work than middle school was. As a result, his grades aren't what they should be. Thank goodness his dad understands. In fact, his dad blames Thomas's poor grades on the teachers. His dad barely graduated from high school because of a learning disability. He's glad Thomas finds school easier than he ever did, but he worries that it takes up too much of his time. He always tells Thomas that there's more to being a kid than doing well in school. Friends and activities are at least as important. If Thomas's dad thinks he has too much work, he calls Thomas's teachers and complains. Neither Thomas nor his dad want homework to interfere with the time they have together. They like to play catch or go to a movie on the weekends. Thomas enjoys his dad's company so much that he even includes his dad when he does something with his friends, like going to a concert.

Ranking for Thomas's father _____

TARGETED WORK ON SPECIFIC INFERENCE CUES

The discussions should highlight a set of inference cues that students relied on. Another set of simulated texts would help them gain conscious control of those cues. What follows is a set of activities, each focusing on a single inference cue. We used to do them all, but if you think that doing so would take too much time, you could modify the activity by taking one example from each set and compiling them.

Characters' Actions

Directions: We've talked about how a character's actions can tell us something about him or her. In each of the following four selections consider carefully the actions of the specified character. On the basis of those details, decide what we learn about the character in question. On your own paper write the major characteristic(s) of this character. Be prepared to defend your answers, citing specifics.

1. Joan

It was a cold rainy day. Joan heard a whimpering from behind the dented, empty garbage can. She walked over to the sound, unsuccessfully attempting to avoid the muddy puddles that were in her way. She saw a small dog, its hair filthy and matted. Quickly she scooped it up, hugging it against her newly dry-cleaned coat.

2. Peter

Peter was one of the most popular students in the school. He was captain of the football team and president of the student council. For a long time Katy had liked Peter, but from afar, for she was very shy. A week before the turn-about dance, Katy, after building up her courage for weeks, asked Peter to go with her. He looked at her, smiled, and explained that he already had a date. Katy's face fell. Peter noticed her look. He then asked her to a movie the next week.

3. Lisa

Lisa pressed her lips together after applying fresh lip gloss. She walked quickly down the hall, her purse swaying at her side. She knew that eyes were on her and she smiled. When she passed the glass showcase, she turned and smiled at her reflection. She smoothed out the one wrinkle in her skirt and walked on.

4. Paul (From *Slaughterhouse Five* by Kurt Vonnegut)

[The dog] bit me [Paul]. So I got me some steak, and I got me the spring, out of a clock. I cut that spring up in little pieces. I put points on the ends of the pieces. They were sharp as razor blades. I stuck 'em into the steak—way inside. And I went past where they had the dog tied up. He wanted to bite me again. I said to him, "Come on, doggie—let's be friends. Let's not be enemies any more. I'm not mad." He believed me.

Characters' Language

Directions: We've talked about how a character's language tells us something about him or her. In each of the following four selections consider carefully the language of the specified character. On the basis of those details decide what we learn about the character in question. On your own paper write the major characteristic(s) of this character. Be prepared to defend your answer by citing specifics.

1. Mr. Smith

Mr. Smith had been teaching school for 15 years. On the day of a scheduled spelling test, the class took five minutes to settle down. He said: "Shut up! Now! I'm sick to death of you talking. If you don't shut up, I'm tellin' you . . . I . . . I. . . I . . . Shut up!"

2. Julie

Julie was a new student in freshman composition. Ms. Jones, her teacher, asked her to introduce herself to the class. Julie said, "For the last several years I have been residing in Los Angeles, California. My primary sources of relaxation there were ballet dancing and attending art galleries. I hope to continue these pursuits in my new home. Thank you."

3. Freddy

"Oh, man, I'm tellin' you, man, it was the best, man. When they came out, the lights go down and then the lasers shootin' all over the place. Totally awesome. And then these awesome speakers, man, unbelievable. The best."

4. Huck (From *The Adventures of Huckleberry Finn* by Mark Twain)

You don't know about me without you have read a book by the name of *The Adventures of Tom Sawyer*; but that ain't no matter. That book was made by Mr. Mark Twain, and he told the truth, mainly. There was things which he stretched, but mainly he told the truth. That is nothing. I never seen anybody but lied one time or another, without it was Aunt Polly, or the widow, or maybe Mary. Aunt Polly—Tom's Aunt Polly, she is—and Mary, and the Widow Douglas is all told about in that book, which is mostly a true book, with some stretchers, as I said before.

Characters' Thoughts

Directions: We've talked about how a character's thoughts can tell us something about him or her. In each of the following four selections consider carefully the thoughts of the specified character. On the basis of those details, decide what we learn about the character in question. On your own paper write the major characteristic(s) of this character. Be prepared to defend your answer by citing specifics.

1. Tom

It seemed the class would never end. Tom's mind began wandering. He thought about that big problem in the cafeteria. At least Tom thought of it as a big problem. He just couldn't seem to decide what he wanted in the lunch line. The line must have been a mile long and they were all laughing. "I'll never go back," thought Tom.

2. Ed

Ed had been sitting next to Kris all semester. She was the most popular girl in the school. And the nicest, thought Ed. Ed himself was quiet and serious, a good student. He was friendly but had few real friends. The Homecoming Dance was coming up. It took all of Ed's courage to approach Kris. ''Kris, you know next Saturday, well the dance is coming up.''

''Umm, it is. But I'm, well, I'm, ahh, busy. And . . . I can't get out of it. . . . Sorry.''

"That's O.K. I know you must keep a busy schedule," Ed said. And then he thought, "Wow, she didn't say no. She must like me. Maybe the Winter Ball."

3. Lisa

As Lisa walked the aisle of the store, she thought back to her years when her career was just beginning, when food shopping was unnecessary because she went out to eat so often. She remembered going out every night, meeting new men. They were enthralled. Jake was enthralled. He was so romantic ten years ago, she thought. Things were great ten years ago.

4. Esperanza (From *The House on Mango Street* by Sandra Cisneros)

I [Esperanza] like to tell stories. I tell them inside my head. I tell them after the mailman says, Here's your mail. Here's your mail, he said.

I make a story for my life, for each step my brown shoe takes. I say, "And so she trudged up the wooden stairs, her sad brown shoes taking her to the house she never liked." I like to tell stories. I am going to tell you a story about a girl who didn't want to belong.

Characters' Body Language

Directions: Another clue that tells about characters is their body language. In each of the following four selections consider carefully the body language of the specified character. On the basis of those details, decide what we learn about the character in question. On your own paper write the major characteristic(s) of this character. Be prepared to defend your answer by citing specifics.

1. Sam

Everyone was there. Of course, it was the first dance of junior high. Sam watched from the corner. He held his hands behind him, occasionally bouncing them to the rhythm of the band. When laughing couples passed him, he dropped his eyes and held his breath.

2. Sharon

The whole table was laughing, except Sharon. Frank, an EMS student, had just stumbled by, spilling his milk all over his tray. The laughter continued as the girls watched him try to clean it up. Sharon's eyes flashed around the table. Her jaw was set tightly and a vein stood out in her neck. She clutched her books tightly to her chest.

3. Tom

The oak door of the dean's office was closed. Tom sat outside. He tapped his feet quickly, one after the other. His eyes darted about. His lips were dry, so he licked them constantly.

4. Margot's Classmates (From "All Summer in a Day" by Ray Bradbury)

''Margot!''
''What?''
"She's still in the closet where we locked her."
''Margot.''
They [the classmates] stood as if someone had driven them, like so many stakes, into the floor. They looked at each other and then looked away.
They glanced out at the world that was raining now and raining and raining steadily. They could not meet each other's glances. Their faces were solemn and pale. They looked at their hands and feet, their faces down.
"Margot."
One of the girls said, "Well. . . ?"
No one moved.
"Go on," whispered the girl.
They walked slowly down the hall in the sound of cold rain. They turned through the doorway to the room in the sound of the storm and thunder, lightning on their faces, blue and terrible. They walked over to the closet door slowly and stood by it.
Behind the closet door was only silence.
They unlocked the door, even more slowly, and let Margot out.

Physical Descriptions

Directions: A character's physical description can also tell us something about him or her. In each of the following four selections consider carefully the physical description of the specified character. On the basis of those details, decide what we learn about the character in question. On your own paper write the major characteristic(s) of this character. Be prepared to defend your answer by citing specifics.

1. Pete

When you looked at Pete, the first thing you noticed were those crazy glasses. He was a little guy but his glasses were huge. Really big and really black, and usually broken and stuck together with some kind of tape. It's because of those glasses that we called him "owl-eyes." But if you could look past them, you'd notice other things too, like the crooked teeth that were usually in a smile and those crazy freckles that dotted his face. And his eyes themselves, a really warm brown.

2. Joanne

She wore not the slightest bit of makeup. Her eyes, blue, round, and enormous, dominated her face. She seemed never to blink. She parted her hair down the middle. Its ends hung softly around her shoulders. Though she was nearly 40, she had no wrinkles. Her faded jeans and blue denim work shirt were clean, though they were worn.

3. Annie

These eyebrows weren't Annie's. Hers had been plucked and new ones drawn in at a more radical angle, an angle repeated by the line of her hair, which was pulled severely off to one side. Her lips were painted a deep red. Her brown eyes were highlighted by silver stars carefully affixed to her enormously high cheekbones.

4. Father (From "Marine Corps Issue" by David McLean)

I was six years old but I can still see [my father] clearly, playing [handball] alone as always. He wears olive green shorts, plain white canvas shoes and long white socks, a gray sweatshirt, the neck ripped loose down the front, and a fatigue-green headband wrapped tightly around his bony forehead. Black thinning hair dipped in gray rises up like tufts of crabgrass around the headband. He wears dirty white leather gloves.

How Others Relate to Characters

Directions: Another way to learn about characters is how they relate or compare to other characters. In each of the following four selections, pay attention to the other characters. On the basis of those details, decide what we learn about the character in question. On your own paper write the major characteristic(s) of the specified character. Be prepared to defend your answers by citing specifics.

1. V.J.

The cafeteria was packed. Ten to twelve people were crowded around tables designed to seat eight. The chatter of conversation and the clicking of glasses and silverware were a symphony in disarray. But when V.J. entered the cafeteria, conversation stopped. Four freshman boys stuffed half-finished lunches into paper bags and left. V.J. sat down, looked about, and smiled.

2. Jennifer

Every year the Women's Club offered one college scholarship. All of the brightest and most active girls at the high school applied for the award. The day of the scholarship presentation was a tense one for all of the applicants. At 7:30 that evening, one girl would receive a scholarship that might be the beginning of a successful life. Finally, the announcement came.

"We are proud to announce the winner of this year's scholarship: Ms. Jennifer Randall." The crowd burst into applause. Girls who lost looked at each other, nodded, and smiled. As Jennifer received her check, she also received a standing ovation.

3. Jesse

They had been losing close games all season, so when they fell behind by a run, the crowd groaned. Looking out into the field, the coach saw players with their heads down. The team was quiet except for one voice that carried in from right field. "All right, all right. We'll get these guys. Get 'em out now, and I'll get things started."

"Jesse," the coach thought. "She's leading off next inning. She'll probably get things going."

4. Willy (From *Death of a Salesman* by Arthur Miller)

Howard: Say, aren't you supposed to be in Boston?
Willy: That's what I want to talk to you about, Howard. You got a minute? (He draws a chair in from the wing.)
Howard: What happened? What're you doing here?
Willy: Well . . .
Howard: You didn't crack up again, did you?

⟶

> Willy: Oh, no. No . . .
>
> Howard: Geez, you had me worried there for a minute. What's the trouble?
>
> Willy: Well, tell you the truth, Howard. I've come to the decision that I'd rather not travel any more.
>
> Howard: Not travel! Well, what'll you do?
>
> Willy: Remember, Christmas time, when you had the party here? You said you'd try to think of some spot for me here in town.
>
> Howard: With us?
>
> Willy: Well, sure.
>
> Howard: Oh, yeah, yeah. I remember. Well, I couldn't think of anything for you, Willy.

As students grapple with the texts on each of the character activities, they'll be developing a heuristic, or thinking tool, for the understanding of character. They'll know that they have to pay attention to the groups to which a character belongs and relate the inferences they make on the basis of that group membership to what they learn from a character's actions, thoughts, words, body language, and looks, as well as from how others relate and compare to the character. (Our thanks to Damir Mujcavíc for his help in thinking through this last inference cue.) They'll also be practicing the kind of thinking they have to do when they write character analyses.

USING MEDIA

Students are now ready to apply what they learned in the simulations to actual texts. But before they get started on stories, it might be a good idea for them to practice with media texts. We have two suggestions in this regard. One is to use movie trailers, a kind of text readily available on the Internet. After showing students a trailer, you can ask them what impression they get of a character and what they base that impression on. You could do a similar activity by looking at the Facebook page of a public figure, an activity that has the additional benefit of helping students consider how they portray themselves online and how they might be interpreted and constructed by others.

We also recommend that you engage students (or groups of students) in an ongoing media study that focuses on how TV shows use group and individuating information. Students or groups could choose (or be assigned) a popular TV show and then track when the show seems to rely primarily on membership in a group to create an impression of a character and when the show moves beyond group membership to draw upon individuating information.

If you think about a show like *Fresh Prince of Bel-Air*, you can see the kind of work you could do. In that show a number of characters seem defined entirely by their group. Carlton is a preppie, Hilary a rich kid. Sometimes it seems that Will (urban hip-hopper) and his uncle (upper-class achiever) are defined by their groups, but sometimes those definitions are complicated by the details of a particular episode. Discussing a variety of shows would help students see how characters are created and also help them begin to make judgments about the effectiveness and ethics of using or privileging one source of implication over another. It would also provide the occasion for teaching terms such as *round/flat* and *dynamic/static* in a meaningful context.

USING STUDENTS' WRITING

Another way to make sure students have conscious control over the ways authors create characters is to have them create their own characters. For example, they could take one of the impressions they wrote from a list of characteristics and then answer a series of questions about that person: What would the person carry in his/her purse or pockets, what kind of clothes would the person wear, what would the person's favorite movie/song/sport/TV show be, what would the person's occupation be, and so on. The list of possible questions is endless.

They could also write additional entries for the roommate and/or good father activities, to be shared with and ranked by other students. One fun way to assess the extent to which they can control the impressions they are creating is to ask them to predict what ranking their additions will receive and compare their prediction to what actually occurred.

Another way to have students apply what they've learned to their writing is to provide a group of students with a basic situation—a middle school student's asking a parent to go to a concert, for example—and have them decide what kind of parent and what kind of child they want to create. They'd have to act out and then write out the interaction between the characters. Students could read each other's dialogues and talk about the general impressions they formed of each character. The student writers could then discuss how those impressions jibed with the impressions they were trying to create.

WHY IT'S WORTH IT

We realize the preparation we're advocating is much more elaborate and time-consuming than what you probably do now, but we think it's worth it. If you did all of the activities we suggest above, it would likely take five to seven days of a 45- to 50-minute period. And that's a lot. But because understanding characters is so crucially important, we think that time is well spent. We also think that teaching deeply ultimately saves time, for it makes reteaching less necessary. If we work to meet the conditions for transfer that Haskell (2000) describes, students should be able to apply what they learned as they encounter characters in their subsequent reading and writing. Moreover, through your use of the kind of prereading activities we present here, you can also promote deep understanding around an inquiry topic that relates to character, such as one of those we proposed throughout the chapter. In this way, students accrue deep and applicable conceptual and procedural understandings at several different levels (e.g., in general, in terms of the inquiry, in the context of specific texts).

Of course, the precise way one would teach a unit or text with a focus on interpreting character would vary from unit to unit or text to text. Nevertheless, we do employ a repertoire of general instructional strategies for the different kinds of specific texts we teach. We'll share those strategies in our next chapter.

CHAPTER FOUR

Putting Theory Into Practice:
Teaching Character With Particular Units and Texts

One way to support the prereading instruction we discussed in the last chapter is to create a context that directs and rewards students' attention to characters.

Creating a Context That Fosters Attention to Characters: Inquiry Units

As we have argued elsewhere (Smith & Wilhelm, 2006; Wilhelm, 2007), we think that inquiry units provide powerful motivation and support for deep understanding. Inquiry units are centered around essential questions, the kind of timeless and debatable issues that draw us to literature.

For example, imagine that you are teaching a unit on the question "What makes a good parent?" and that you've begun that unit with the "good father" activity that we presented in Chapter 3 (pages 38–39). If you and your class read a group of stories that take up that issue in different ways, students can focus on the qualities of the parents they're reading about and assess whether those qualities in fact make the parent good or not. In order to compare the characters, they have to understand them. In inquiry units such as these, students get the conceptual (*what*) and the procedural (*how*) together, and the procedural is immediately functional and in service of the conceptual inquiry.

The culmination of such a unit would likely be a written argument of judgment that assesses whether one or more of the characters is a good parent or which of the characters is the best parent. Another option might be an argument providing an extended definition of good parenting, using examples and non-examples from all the unit readings and the students' personal experiences. This kind of character analysis depends on articulating the primary criteria that make someone a good parent, criteria that the prereading activity sought to develop, and using those criteria as a lens to evaluate characters. Creating a context in which argument is essential forces students to provide evidence, to explain how the evidence links to the construct, and to consider alternative points of view. In short, the unit context would not only foster students' careful attention as they read but would also help them develop an understanding of fundamental characteristics of effective argumentative writing. (See Smith & Wilhelm [2006, chapter 5] for a more complete discussion of the essentials of argumentation.) It also provides the reflective (as opposed to didactic) character education that Smagorinsky (2000) calls for.

As we have already noted, a variety of essential questions would work well to keep the focus on character. Any question similar to "What makes a good parent?" requires students to articulate their general impressions: *What makes a good friend? A good teacher? A good leader? A hero?* The list goes on.

Another option is to pose an essential question that calls on students to develop an extended definition of one or more important or governing qualities of characters. (See pages 22–23 for our previous discussion of Asch's warm-cold experiment.) Possible essential questions might include *What makes a person mature? What is loyalty? What is courage?* Again, the list could go on.

Finally, some questions really require kids to grapple with the relative influence of group membership and individuating information. If you pose the question "What makes me me?" students will have to think about the relative impact of their membership in groups (race, ethnicity, gender, class, generation, etc.) compared to such things as family, personal interests, and so on.

Using Autobiographical Writing Before Reading

Another way to create a context that fosters attention to characters is to use autobiographical writing before reading. When we talked about transfer in Chapter 1, we noted that instruction needs to cultivate a spirit of transfer, assisting students in bringing knowledge forward to new situations and proving to students that transfer will be rewarded. And as we noted in Chapter 2, we want students to transfer what they know about understanding people in their own lives to understanding characters in the story that they are reading (and vice versa).

One way to foster this kind of transfer is to have students write about relevant autobiographical experiences before they read. Prompts for autobiographical writing before reading ask students to take up issues that are relevant to stories without cueing particular readings of those stories. Here's a slightly revised prompt that our good friend Brian White (1995) used in his study of the impact of autobiographical writing before reading:

> Most parents hope to teach their children what life is all about. They want to prepare their kids for life's possibilities, for life's pitfalls, for life's activities, for important decisions. Describe a parent you think is a "good teacher." What does a parent need to be like in order to be a good teacher? Be as specific as possible and remember to write about parents you know, you've read about, or you've seen on television or in the movies.

As you can see, this prompt could be used with almost any story that included both young people and their parents.

Brian analyzed the impact of autobiographical writing before reading by examining students' performance in class discussion. He found that the students who had done the writing were less apt to make off-task responses. But more important, he also found that the students who did the writing were significantly more likely to make abstracting as opposed to describing responses. *Describing* comments are those that focus on surface details. *Abstracting* comments are inferences about a character's traits. It seems that setting up a context that asked students to draw on their life experience (but not substitute that life experience for the experience of a character) was very effective in helping students understand the characters about whom they were reading. Doing autobiographical writing before reading activates students' prior knowledge and teaches them that it's powerful and necessary to apply that prior knowledge.

Using Character Response Sheets

In Chapter 2 we argued that story-specific questions are unlikely to prepare students to understand more than the particular story they're reading. In contrast, a set of questions that can be applied across stories is likely to be much more useful. The following character response sheet isn't very complex, but it does capture the heuristic for understanding character that you and your students have been working with. You could use it to guide individual work, perhaps in lieu of a reading check quiz for assigned reading, or to guide group work. You could have students work on the same character, or have different students or groups of students work on different characters. The number of check points you have will vary with the length of the reading. You may have only one for really short stories, or one per chapter of a novel.

Character Response Sheet

Character's name:

First impression of the character (Remember, you should explain as much as you can about the kind of person the character is):

This impression is based on. . .

   The groups to which the character belongs (be specific):

   The character's actions (be specific):

   The character's language (be specific):

   The character's thoughts (be specific):

   The character's body language (be specific):

   The character's looks (be specific):

   How others relate/compare to the character (be specific):

Check point #1: Explain how your impression of the character has changed or been confirmed. The change or confirmation is based on. . .

   The groups to which the character belongs (be specific):

   The character's actions (be specific):

   The character's language (be specific):

   The character's thoughts (be specific):

   The character's body language (be specific):

   The character's looks (be specific):

   How others relate/compare to the character (be specific):

Before we move on, we think it's worth noting that as simple as this response sheet is, it does depart from traditional instruction in important ways. Because it explicitly reinforces the activities that preceded its use and because it can be used across stories, it fosters transfer. To use it, students must be alert for inference cues rather than waiting for teachers to highlight those cues through their questions. Finally, it assists students in internalizing the kinds of questions necessary to a sophisticated interpretation of character in literature or in life.

Using Drama

Another instructional strategy that helps students develop and explore their understanding of character is drama. By drama we mean any activity that requires students to play a role other than themselves. Classroom dramas are often thought of as a formal presentation by a set of students on some part of a text (usually a play). Because of our belief in the importance of activity and in the ethical imperative to at least provisionally try on characters' perspectives, we're much more interested in short, scriptless, and simultaneous dramas that allow all students to participate as actors rather than as an audience. Jeff (2002, 2008; Wilhelm & Edmiston, 1998) has written extensively on using drama as a support for literary reading, but we'd like to highlight four types of dramas that we think work especially well in support of students' understanding of character.

IN-ROLE WRITING

In-role writing asks students to put themselves in the shoes of a character to comment on the events of a story. We typically ask students to write a diary entry as though they were a character. Think back to our short summary of "Everyday Use" (page 26). Remembering that Michael, at least, too easily dismissed Dee, you could ask students to write a diary entry as Dee on what she anticipates will come of her visit, or as Maggie after she receives the quilts. The possibilities are endless. In writing the entries, students are making the characters come alive through two of the inference cues you've taught them: the characters' thoughts and language.

In this and all drama activities it's important to articulate the dramatic frame carefully. That is, you have to make sure students know who they are, what their situation is, what they will create, and how they will share what they create. A frame for the in-role writing we discuss above could go as follows:

> You are Dee. You are traveling to visit your family just prior to the events in the story that you have just read. You take out your diary to record your anticipation regarding your visit. You decide to discuss your feelings about the impending visit and the experience you think is causing these feelings.

Be sure to write legibly because we will share these and use them as the basis of a choral montage conversation between Dee and her sister.

After students have done the in-role writing, they can share what they've written in pairs or groups or even in a whole-class read-around. The discussion that follows the sharing should focus on why the students wrote what they wrote. If you identify different approaches that students take, you can use those differences as a probe; for example, "Pat, you seemed to think Dee would be optimistic about the visit, but Tracy saw her dreading it. Can you explain what you learned about Dee by reading the story that encouraged you to take the approach you did?"

PRESS CONFERENCES

In a press conference drama (this and the following two techniques are variations on hotseating [Wilhelm, 2002]), students play the roles of characters who are then asked questions by other students who are playing the role of reporters. Once again, the dramatic frame is key. Here's one that you could use for "Everyday Use":

> You are all going to be reporters for CNN working on a story about historical buildings, sites, and artifacts—which ones need to be saved, which are not that important, and why. You have heard the story of "Everyday Use," and a press conference has been arranged with the characters. Your job is to solicit the characters' feelings and thoughts about the importance of objects, such as the quilts.

So, for example, if Mama were part of the press conference, some students would be sure to ask: "Why didn't you give the quilts to Dee?" Once again, these dramas can be arranged in different ways. The whole class can ask questions of a single student or of several students in role, or different groups of students can have the same press conference simultaneously in small roundtables. We often do a large-group model and then have small groups interview one character at a time.

Once again, after the dramas have been completed, you'll want to do some debriefing, focusing especially on what students learned about the characters that made them respond the way they did and on how they learned what they learned. You might also explore how the drama work deepened or complicated their understanding of the story.

ALTER EGO/INNER VOICE

Of course, some characters may be deceiving themselves or may be purposefully deceitful when they respond to the kind of questions that a reporter might ask. In those instances, a second student could play the role of the character's alter ego or inner voice and after every response provide a translation of what the character was really thinking or feeling (at least as the student sees it.) For example, although

Maggie says that Dee can have the quilts in "Everyday Use," her alter ego might say, "Dee gets everything. And now she wants the quilts Mama promised me."

GOOD ANGEL/BAD ANGEL

Remember those cartoons in which a character faced a decision and a good angel stood on one shoulder trying to persuade the character to make the moral choice and a bad angel stood on the other, encouraging a less moral choice? Students can enact those dramas, either simultaneously in groups of three or with a series of good angels alternating with a series of bad angels while a single character sits in front of the class. After the appeals, the character could announce who was most persuasive and why. The good angels and bad angels could discuss what it is about the character that led them to make the appeals they did.

As an aside, this activity is also a great chance to develop transfer from students' reading to their living by listing the rhetorical devices used by good angels (who usually argue with ethical appeals, long-term consequences, concerns for all involved, logic, etc.) and bad angels (who use unbridled persuasion to prey on vulnerability, talk about immediate gratification, say things like, "This is your one last chance," and so on).

Dramas, by their very nature, require students to pay characters an ethical respect. They also allow students to use their tacit understandings of human behavior as a way to understand the characters about whom they read. That is, students don't have to have an articulated understanding of a character in order to portray him or her. But having performed the character, they can reflect on their performance to articulate why they did what they did. Drama provides them with a concrete experience to think with and abstract from.

Activities to Take Stock of Characters Once the Reading Is Complete

As we noted earlier in the chapter, the essence of understanding character is creating a general impression of the kind of person a character is. That means much more than knowing how the character is feeling at one particular point or what one trait of a character might be. Consequently, it's crucially important to engage students in post-reading activities that require them to display their general impression of characters. One type of activity that engages students in making their general impressions public is what we think of as "stock-taking" exercises like those that follow.

RETURNING TO THE PERSONALITY TESTS

One great way to encourage students to display their general impression of a character is to have them fill out the same personality tests they took earlier as a front-loading activity, but this time from the perspective of one or more of the characters about whom they have been reading. Students could work alone and then compare with others, or work in groups that negotiate and justify their answers. Various small groups could do the same character, or different groups could each address a different character. After groups complete their discussions, they then report back to the class on how they responded and why they responded as they did.

RETURNING TO THE SIMULATED TEXTS

Students can do similar work by returning to the ranking activities we presented in the last chapter and do the rankings from the perspectives of different characters. The work could proceed much as the work on the personality tests. Once again, the key is not the answers the students come up with but what they use to come up with those rankings and how well they seem to be internalizing the heuristic for understanding character.

CREATING REPRESENTATIONS OF THE CHARACTERS

Students can also work to develop a variety of different kinds of representations of the characters. Here are some ideas to do just that. We suggest using each activity on more than one occasion so that your students get increasingly comfortable using the activity.

When Michael was at Rutgers, he worked with a high school teacher named Georgia Pelios, who devised a wonderful tool that her students used. Georgia is a gardener, and she made good use of that interest. Early in every semester, she distributed to her classes a list of the symbolic significance of different flowers. For example, Wikipedia (http://en.wikipedia.org/wiki/Language_of_flowers#Symbolic_meaning_of_flowers, accessed September 11, 2009) provides an extensive list of flowers that represent such important traits as dignity (dahlia), ambition (hollyhock), and faithfulness (blue violet).

After students read a text (and sometimes as they were reading), Georgia would simply say, for example, "Okay, develop a three-flower bouquet to represent [name of the character]." Students could work individually, in pairs, or in groups to do so.

The number of flowers in the bouquet changes the kind of thinking students have to do. A bouquet of a single type of flower would call upon students to determine what they see as the character's governing characteristic. Asking them to choose several different types of flowers would help them reveal how they think the characteristics add up.

Because Georgia regularly used this activity, her students were comfortable examining characters as they read in a way that would allow them to create a bouquet. Her regular use of the activity also meant that she was able to use it very efficiently. Students knew just what to do. Not only did the activity have the benefit of helping students display their understanding of character in an effective way, it also had the side benefit of providing meaningful instruction in symbolism.

Another way to help students display their understanding of characters involves tapping existing literacies. One great method is to ask students to create a Facebook or MySpace page. Remember the quote from Robert Coles's student about how he hopes literary characters are "in there pitching" when he considers big decisions? That can only happen if he is able to take the characters out of the context of the story or novel and understand how they would behave in new contexts. Asking students to develop a Facebook or MySpace page for a character requires them to do the same thing.

Of course, there are myriad other similar possibilities. Students could develop a coat-of-arms for a character, or a body biography. (See http://homepage.mac.com/mseffie/handouts/bodybiography. html for how one teacher adapted this activity from a presentation by Cindy O'Donnell-Allen. See also O'Donnell-Allen & Smagorinsky, 1999; Smagorinsky & O'Donnell-Allen, 1998a, 1998b, for a full discussion of the pitfalls and potential of using body biographies.) The list of possible activities could go on and on. To get inspiration for different activities, ask yourself how you display your character or reveal your understanding of other characters outside school and then ask students to do likewise with the characters they've read about. Quilts, scrapbooks, eulogies—the possibilities are limited only by your imagination.

LIST OF VALUES

Our friends Betsy Kahn, Carolyn Calhoun Walter, and Larry Johannessen (2009) developed another activity that requires students to think hard about characters in the works they're reading. They call it "Literary Characters' Value Profile," and it is simply a list of 22 values alphabetically arranged from "acceptance" to "wealth." They ask students to rank these values in their order of importance as though they were a character.

A variety of permutations of this activity is possible. You could provide this list of values to your students, or you could develop a list with them. You could have them do a complete ranking or identify the top (or bottom) three values. Students or groups of students could work on the same characters or different ones, always attempting to justify their rankings with evidence. Likewise, students could compare dominant values at the beginning and the end of a story and how this relationship contributes to theme. Like the list of flowers, the list of values could be used over and over with different stories. It's an efficient tool for fostering discussions and for highlighting the kinds of things students should be thinking about as they read. The discussions and debates students undertake in this activity can provide data and reasoning that can be used in the arguments they might write at the end of the unit.

SEMANTIC DIFFERENTIAL SCALES

One of the reasons that the "Literary Characters' Value Profile" works so well is that it provides students with an easy in to discussion. That is, it's not very hard to write a number down (especially if you ask students to identify only the top few values). And once they have, it's easy to involve them in discussion with probes like "You have a different top value. Why?" and so on. This requires students to draw on textual evidence, as well as their prior experiences and life knowledge. Another activity that provides students an easy in is the use of semantic differential scales.

Semantic differential scales are simply pairs of words that are opposites. A six-point semantic differential scale would look like this:

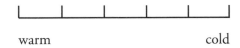

warm   cold

Students simply have to mark the scale where they think the character should be placed.

Once again, there are many ways to use the scales. You could develop a set of scales with the class and use them throughout the unit. If you do so, we recommend that you focus on identifying sets of governing qualities—that is, those qualities that are so important that we understand other qualities in relation to them.

Once students have filled out a single scale or a set of scales, you can display their assessments easily by drawing a scale on the board or by taping a scale onto the classroom floor and having students vote by standing where they feel the character should be placed.

One great feature of both the scales and the "Literary Characters' Value Profile" is that interesting discussions can ensue, no matter how the class distributes itself. If there is a variety of opinions, you simply ask students "What makes you say so?" If there is a consensus, the question becomes, "What did the author do to make us all come to the same conclusion?" Students can discuss these probes in pairs or small groups and then report out and compare in whole-class discussions. The small-group work will ensure that everyone has something to say. Journal writing can follow, and what has been learned can be used in more formal writing.

You can use these tools to provide snapshots of characters at any given point in the story. Then you might use the tools again as a way to engender discussion about how, if at all, the characters have changed and what meaning or themes can be ascribed to these changes.

TAKING CHARACTERS OUT OF CONTEXT

Kahn, Walter, and Johannessen (2009) also developed an activity that requires students to do the same kind of "figuring forth" that the Facebook/MySpace activity does. They developed a set of multiple choice questions, asking students to consider what a character's favorite subject would be, where he or she would choose to live, who his or her hero would be, and so on. You could write the questions yourself or ask your students to develop items that they think would be especially telling. Students could then be asked to justify their conclusions in a short journal entry.

Conclusion

We hope you see what we mean when we say that this book is about fresh takes on teaching the literary elements. We firmly believe that understanding character is at the very heart of what readers must do when they read fiction. And if that's so, it's well worth the time it takes to help students develop robust interpretive strategies that they can employ whenever they read fiction or nonfiction. If that's our goal, we have to engage students in thinking hard about what we do when we understand people in our daily lives and how we must do similar things when we read. We have to go beyond definitions of character and kinds of character to helping students know how to create and evaluate characters in their reading and in their writing.

The ultimate purpose of reading literature is to explore what kind of person we want to be as well as how to become that kind of person and avoid becoming something else. That's why we love literature and find it such a powerful pursuit to undertake with students. We think that the lessons on understanding character that we've described here have a chance to help students experience something of the feelings about literature that we have. That's an important goal—one that's well worth the effort to achieve.

CHAPTER FIVE

Setting Up the Story:
The Importance and Power of Context

Jeff is drafting this chapter while sitting on his screened porch on Meddybemps Lake in Washington County, Maine, very near the ocean and the Canadian border. The house is a green design, both because Jeff wants to keep costs down and because he wants to be a good steward of the earth. It is cloudy, cool, and threatening to rain. Mosquitoes cluster on the screens. It is the early afternoon during the first week of August (summer VACATION!), and Jeff is a bit tired from his morning bike ride. On that ride he passed the houses of many locals, all of them modest and some falling into disrepair. Jeff's family is playing cards on the porch, and his daughter Jasmine is laughing loudly and periodically complaining about her "crummy" cribbage hands.

Why Setting Matters

Think for a minute about all of the issues embedded in that very brief description. If Jeff were to write a story set in that place and time, his decision about what elements of the setting to stress would be an important indicator of just what he was trying to accomplish. An emphasis on the proximity to the ocean could mean that Jeff was taking up the causes of global warming and pollution. Long descriptions about the houses that have fallen into disrepair might indicate that the story would, at least in part, be about how social class plays out in America. If he kept his attention on the porch itself, he'd be suggesting a narrower focus, maybe something about family dynamics. Setting, then, is crucially important in helping readers understand what a story is about and in helping writers see what events are probable and what events and consequences would be possible but surprising. In this chapter we'll take up the questions of what readers really need to know about setting to make meaning and what writers have to do with the setting to make their stories meaningful, enjoyable, and understood. We'll also consider the issue of transfer: How does an understanding of setting and context enhance our understanding and navigation of our own personal lives?

A LITTLE BIT OF THEORY: ACTIVITY THEORY AND SITUATED COGNITION

Before we proceed with thinking about setting as a literary convention and tool, let's situate our work in a wider way. The foundation of many disciplines outside of education is a consideration of situation and context. Anthropology, history, and sociology are prime examples. In recent decades, education has also increasingly recognized the importance of context. One clear manifestation of this tendency is the growing importance of cultural-historical activity theory—otherwise known as CHAT—in the field of education. By looking at CHAT and a school of thought called "situated cognition," we can see how our discipline understands the importance of context for human action—inside and outside of stories.

As Roth and Lee (2007) explain, CHAT is a psychological framework that derives from Vygotsky's sociocultural work in psychology. His followers Leont'ev and Rubinshtein founded this theoretical framework to explore human activities as complex, *socially situated* phenomena in ways that went further than the then-current behavioristic (stimulus-response) notions of human behavior. (Interestingly, many current educational practices such as grading, information-transmission instructional practices, and standardized testing hark back to behavioristic notions of teaching and learning that are considered outmoded in their psychological conceptions of teaching, learning, and understanding.)

For our purposes, activity theory is useful to a consideration of setting because it highlights that any human activity—whether internal or external—is in fact allowed, encouraged, shaped, and constrained by the particular social situation in which it occurs. Activity theorists argue that human behavior can be highly creative and non-predictable, but it is always situated and must be understood in situations. Engeström (1993), who builds on the work of Leont'ev in many interesting ways, argues that all human activity is goal-oriented and rule-governed. Rules are designed by humans in particular settings for the purpose of achieving certain goals. Over time these rules become the unquestioned way of doing things in those settings, whether it's using statistical analyses in fantasy baseball, playing bridge at your club, conducting science in a lab, or interacting socially at a formal dinner party.

Likewise, disciplines are rule-governed, and so are particular kinds of reading and writing, so learning math or how to read lyric poetry means learning how to follow the rules for those activities. For our purposes, it is important to note that every setting will imply certain rules for behavior. How people follow, adapt, or violate these rules says a lot about their character and their relationships to the social settings in which they are operating.

Research on what's known as situated cognition (see, e.g., Brown, Collins, & DuGuid, 1989) proceeds from similar assumptions. The theory of situated cognition holds that situations always co-produce thinking, learning, and understanding. Researchers who study situated cognition argue that the setting in which cognition occurs shapes and, in fact, co-produces all the thinking and problem-solving that is done there.

In exactly this regard, the Nobel Prize–winning psychologist Herbert Simon (1996) has compared the human mind to a pair of scissors: one blade is the mind and the other blade is the specific environment and situation in which the mind is currently operating. Simon emphasizes that thinking and learning and understanding cannot occur in a vacuum—they occur only in specific contexts that shape and make them possible. The two work together like scissors. Only the two aspects working together will be effective.

One way to test the tenets of activity theory and situated cognition is to see how they help explain what we observe about what does and could happen in schools. We think they hold up pretty well. One particular application that we often see is how the preservice teachers with whom we work tend to take on the ethos and practices of the classroom and teacher with whom they're placed. This in turn reflects the culture of the school and community. Instead of doing what they planned and were excited about doing or what they learned in their methods classes, these teachers often succumb to the influence and conventions of the particular setting in which they are placed. Likewise, as teachers of writing, we notice that writers from different disciplinary backgrounds write in dramatically different ways, with different styles and different understandings of genre and what counts as evidence, for instance. What they write, how they write, and what counts as good writing are all profoundly influenced by their discipline, occupation, or particular workplace—that is to say, by the setting in which they do their writing. A journalist at *The New York Times* behaves in much different ways than does a journalist at the *National Enquirer*. Their professional setting dictates what acceptable behavior is.

The takeaway: Research in psychology, education, and numerous other fields shows very clearly that context dramatically affects what people think and do.

AN INSTRUCTIONAL ASIDE

Before we move on to think some more about what setting means and why it is important, we wanted to look back at activity theory and situated cognition to see what they mean for our teaching. Activity theory argues that when individuals meaningfully engage and interact with their environment, including other people in that environment, the production of "tools" is the result. These tools—which can be conceptual or procedural (that is, *usable ideas* for doing work in the situation, or *strategies for application* in the situation) or actual physical tools (something like a lever, a bridge, or a tool such as a spreadsheet that you can use to perform a function in the situation)—are "exteriorized" forms of mental processes.

Here's a simple example. Jeff is a passionate marathon cross-country skier. He knows that he must put his weight squarely on each ski to get the best glide. He has a mnemonic that acts as a conceptual tool to help him do so: "knees, nose, toes." The mnemonic reminds him how his head, knees, and toes should line up, which in turn ensures that he has the proper bend in his ankle and knee to place his weight where it should go. If he can actually line up his body in this way, he has a procedural tool that he can put to use. And if he does so, his skis become physical tools that allow him to ski really fast! (Faster than he otherwise would have, anyway.) Obviously, these tools can only be developed and are only useful in a particular context: that of skiing on a cross-country ski trail.

The same process holds true for using literary conventions. Our students need to have understandings that can become both conceptual tools for noticing and thinking and procedural tools for interpretation and subsequent action. If all they know is a definition, they possess only inert pieces of information, not *tools* for knowing and doing work in flexible and transferable ways. As is always the case, the only way to develop such tools is to pursue meaningful work in a purposeful context. No one is going to be truly motivated to understand a literary convention as a reader and writer, nor have the support to really do so, unless developing this understanding is in immediate service of something personally and socially meaningful in a larger context. No student was ever motivated to read by the strategy of prediction or making text-to-text connections, but learning such strategies might be exciting if they can immediately be used to achieve something important. In fact, the arguments that we have been making throughout the book about embedding instruction in inquiry contexts is based on what we have learned about situated cognition. That's why throughout the book we're calling for teachers to make their classroom settings similar to the ones in which real experts operate—for example, by engaging students in the discussion of essential questions and by using dramas and simulations (Heathcote & Bolton, 1995; Wilhelm, 2004), labs, or other kinds of hands-on learning about real problems.

One of our mantras is that we want to make what we teach our students "toolish" and not "schoolish." It seems to us that it is often the case in schooling generally, and in English and literary studies in particular, that we concern ourselves with details that are often off-point and insignificant, that don't do too much work for students as evolving readers and writers. (And when there *is* work to be done, as we pointed out in the introduction, it is too often the teacher doing the talking and the work for the students, instead of modeling it, then working with them to apprentice them, and finally setting up the situations in which students can master the learning by using the tools to do the work of real readers and writers by themselves.) Within a meaningful situation and with focused instruction that hands over performance capacity to students, inert informational nuggets can be alchemized into a conceptual or procedural tool with great power to inform how students interpret stories (in literature, film, photography, etc.) and create stories, whether they tell them, write them, draw or film them.

What Experienced Readers Do to Understand Setting: A Heuristic

Certainly one of the most important principles of our own instructional planning and reflections over the years has been to get at *the heart of the matter*, that is, to focus on what's truly important about what we teach. We try to keep this principle in mind whenever we consider curriculum, frame units, plan individual lesson activities, or reflect on our teaching and how to improve it. Too often we have found that students do not understand the purpose and function of what they are learning, why it is important, and what work it can help them get done. As activity theory points out and classic research in schema theory has made clear (Bransford and Johnson, 1972), purpose drives motivation, attention, memory, and transfer, and little of import can be achieved if we do not highlight the purpose, application and the heart of the matter at hand. So, what is the heart of the matter of setting? What does the reader need to know, what does the writer need to do, what should the teacher be thinking when it comes to this literary element?

A tool we both use to help us think through what is at the heart of the matter for any genre or convention is the inquiry square, which we learned from our mentor George Hillocks. We've written about it extensively (Smith & Wilhelm, 2006; Wilhelm, 2001; Wilhelm, Baker, & Dube, 2001) and introduced it in Chapter 1 of this book. This tool reminds us to consider 1) the procedural (strategic) knowledge a writer or reader needs in order to get what's necessary to construct meaning in this genre or with this convention (*procedural knowledge of substance*); 2) the procedural/strategic knowledge necessary to shaping the material one has collected into a powerful iteration of this genre or convention (*procedural knowledge of form*); 3) the declarative (nameable) conceptual tools about the form the genre or convention takes (*declarative knowledge of form*); and 4) the declarative conceptual tools that practitioners use to think about the subject of the reading and writing (*declarative knowledge of substance*).

So what do students need to know and be able to do with regard to setting? CHAT and situated cognition establish that our thinking and teaching about setting have to be much deeper and more nuanced than it generally is. In many literature textbooks and in much instruction, setting is taught simply as a definition along the lines of "the time and place where a story occurs." This is a classic case of missing the point. As we have already argued, by itself this kind of declarative knowledge or definitional statement is inert; it doesn't do much work, promote much understanding, or create tools that can be used by students as readers or composers of meaning, particularly not in creative, transferable, or transformative ways.

LEVELS OF SETTING

To be an effective reader or composer or interpreter of settings, in story and life, we need to know what it is that is salient in a setting—what must be noticed, attended to, and interpreted. But even the notions of time and place aren't such easy terms as they may first appear. All contexts are nested in other contexts. In different texts different levels of context might be differentially important. And various levels of context might interact in ways that need to be considered.

This idea is nicely expressed by what are known as systems or cybernetics views of development, behavior, and learning. These views reflect a transactional approach to educational and developmental psychology (Gordon, 1975; Schiamberg & Smith, 1982; Thompson, 1971) that is consistent with our own views of learning and of reading literature as transactional, as occurring in "a relationship in which each element, instead of being fixed and predefined, conditions and is conditioned by the other" (Rosenblatt, 1993, p. 380; Rosenblatt, 1978; Wilhelm, 2008).

An aspect of various models in systems theory and cybernetics is that human beings do not develop in isolation; they develop in a variety of contexts—different environments that surround the individual human being and with which she is in constant interaction play a major role in development (Bridge, Judd, & Moock, 1979; Bronfenbrenner, 1977, 1979, 1989). The first level of the ecology or the context of human development is called the microsystem. This level has the most immediate and earliest influences and includes the family, along with local friendship and peer groups, and neighborhood or community institutions such as a particular school or church.

Figure 5.1: LEVELS OF SETTING

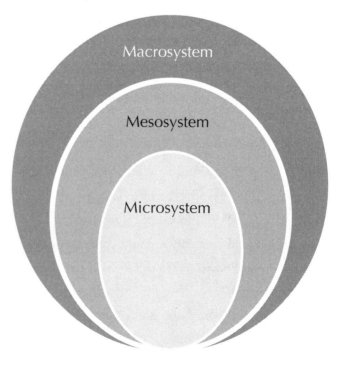

FRESH TAKES ON TEACHING LITERARY ELEMENTS

Interestingly, Jungians and other depth psychologists see the self as "embedded"—meaning that anyone must be understood as operating inside of various levels—or nestings—of different contexts. Depth psychologists also see "interactive spaces" as contexts; for example, how two or more people relate in a setting creates a unique nested context within that setting (Gerson, 1996).

The next level of nested context is the mesosystem. This possesses intermediate levels of influence such as larger and less personal social institutions like government, transportation, entertainment, news organizations, and the like, or geographic regions larger than the neighborhood. The influence of these systems and institutions interacts with, and is filtered through, the microsystem institutions. This is society at large with embedded community and cultural aspects. The local community and culture is embedded or nested within society and the culture at large; the microsystem is part of the mesosystem.

The most global level of contextual surrounding is the macrosystem. This is the most distant from individuals and their influence and includes aspects such as international relations or global changes or even more abstract aspects of culture. For example, the movement from agricultural and industrial economies to an information-age, global economy is having widespread influence on the ways societies, communities, and families are operating. Global climate change provides another example.

As readers and writers of stories, we need to remember that there are multiple contextual influences on characters and situations, and we need to consider deeply which ones are important to describe as a writer and to notice and interpret as a reader. We also need to consider how to understand the interplay of various elements. Which are important? Which are not? Which can be assumed? Which must be described and considered? How do macro-levels, perhaps unmentioned, affect the micro-level? (Interestingly, Polyani [1979], points out that what is important in the context is construed differently in different cultures. These differences can lead those with inappropriate cultural or macro-level expectations to find stories from a different culture difficult to understand or even pointless.)

The question under consideration then is this: What counts as the relevant context? So is the setting of the story Mr. Wilhelm's classroom, or West Junior High School, or Boise, or Idaho, or the United States? Or something even larger? In the terms of socio-cultural psychology, the issue would be termed as one of being able to assume the "culture" (e.g., the universe, United States and Boise, Idaho) but needing to describe the microsystem or "idioculture" (e.g., the specific cultural issues and idiosyncrasies that make Mr. Wilhelm's classroom interesting and unique). Now, if Mr. Wilhelm's class were getting ready to fight wildfires that were threatening Boise, or mudslides coming down the foothills, then the meso-level of Boise and the fact that it is in the high desert surrounded by foothills must be mentioned as part of the relevant setting. Or if tensions sprang up or were defused among Mr. Wilhelm's Christian, Jewish, and Muslim students because of the rescue work, the larger global macroculture might be what's most important.

It is usually very important to be specific about the microsystem (both as a writer who describes the microsystem, and as a reader who decodes or infers specific elements of that system). However, it is sometimes important to pay less attention to the microsystem and more to the meso- or macrosystems, as in the case of an allegory in which bigger context is what counts.

Expert readers attend to the level(s) of contextual nests that are salient and important to the story. Take, for example, a story about a family that has a different set of norms from the community where they live. In Jeff's hometown, an Amish family bought a nearby farm. A story about them would have to include that family's microsystem and how it clashed with the surrounding mesosystem.

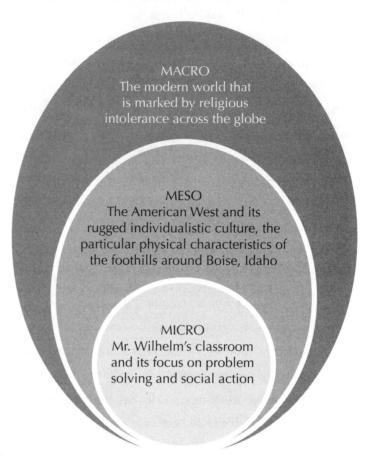

Figure 5.2: LEVELS OF SETTING: AN EXAMPLE

MACRO
The modern world that is marked by religious intolerance across the globe

MESO
The American West and its rugged individualistic culture, the particular physical characteristics of the foothills around Boise, Idaho

MICRO
Mr. Wilhelm's classroom and its focus on problem solving and social action

Likewise, a story might feature a family trying to downshift and resist pervasive consumerism. This would be a story where you would have to pay attention to the family's microsystem, and how it interacts with various levels of the mesosystem and macrosystem.

Suffice it to say, we must avoid oversimplifying the notion of setting. If we do oversimplify it, then we can hardly understand real people, human development, education, or literature and how it works. Settings—and levels of setting—are vitally important to understanding human activity, character, perspective, and how these unfold.

Using the inquiry square as an organizing device, let's proceed backwards, beginning with the declarative knowledge about setting students would need to truly understand and be able to use setting as a tool in their own reading and writing. To review where we have come so far, and to look ahead to where we are going next, let's again take up the example of Jeff in Maine. Remember that all activity is situated and must be understood in that context. There are different levels of context/situation. We must attend to the level that is important to the story and can assume other levels, unless levels are interacting as part of the story.

So we must ask: What is unique in the microsystem? What are the unique aspects of physical setting that might interact with the other aspects of setting? In terms of Jeff's real life, what opportunities and possibilities are there for him in Maine? Well, he can visit his friends in Maine. He enjoys sea kayaking, and Maine is one of the best places for doing this. It is also good for whitewater kayaking. He could also backpack, if he is willing to brave insects and rain. As we previously expressed, there are other things that are not possible or probable to do in Maine, like taking a beach vacation and expecting to get a tan—at least in northern Maine where Jeff is.

If he is writing a story, it might be important to mention that the story takes place in Maine, since Maine can be considered a microsystem, particularly if the story will involve town meetings or robbing lobster traps or something unique to Maine. But if the story will involve being stranded on Jeff's island in Meddybemps Lake, then the island is the microsystem. Maine (now a meso-level) might figure somewhat if it is important to the story that the characters become stranded on the island when a sudden freeze ices the lake, but not thickly enough to walk across. Being Maine, of course a town meeting is called to plan out a search and rescue mission. Emotions are running high. People disagree about what to do, but being Maine, no one is afraid to voice his or her opinion.

Certain stories Jeff might tell about his camp would involve more of the meso- or macro-levels. For example, if the story is about flying in his octogenarian pilot friend's plane (Flying Ed Lardo), then the meso-level of flying near the Canadian border could be important, like the time they were asked by the FAA if they had seen a suspected drug-running float plane cross the border. Or if Jeff wrote about how he moved his family to an eco-cottage in Maine because of global climate change and to escape materialistic, consumeristic culture, then the macrosystem would play out in relationship to the microsystem.

DIMENSIONS OF SETTING

But it's not just determining the relative importance of the macrosystem, mesosystem, and microsystem. Each of these levels also has a variety of dimensions, each of which could be more or less important. To derive these dimensions of setting, we first considered what elements of setting are typically taught. We then thought about how setting is important in our real lives and did some informal ethnographic research about how settings seem to shape our own activity and the activities of others. (This is something that we will propose that students could do in the next chapter on instruction in setting.) We then tested these ideas against work about setting in screenwriting, work that we found immensely helpful (McKee, 1997; Norton & Gretton, 1972). Finally, we used the inquiry square to think about using these dimensions of setting in our instruction with students.

The inquiry square helped us consider how students need to be able to name and talk about these aspects of setting and how they are shaped (declarative knowledge of substance and form).

More important, we found that students need to be able to strategically create and interpret settings along these dimensions (procedural knowledge of substance and form). And undergirding all of this, students need—as activity theory and situated cognition assert—to have a profound understanding of the purpose and possible applications in immediate settings (e.g., as inquirers, readers, and writers in the context of an inquiry unit, and as navigators of everyday life) of what they are learning (knowledge of purpose).

Setting as Physical

One dimension of setting is physical location. This is the story's specific geography as far as the particular location, climate, and physical features; its address as far as country, city, neighborhood, and street; its features as far as natural artifacts, style, architecture, floor plan, rooms, and furniture. The physical setting is how a story is located in a specific space or spaces (McKee, 1997; Norton & Gretton, 1972).

Think of your own life. You are invited to a party. Is it the address that counts? The street itself? The neighborhood? The traffic? Which side of the tracks the address is on? What properties abut the property? Is it in an area of industry, business, or homes? Depending on what topic, conflict, or point will be explored or expressed in a story, writers and readers will need to attend to different physical details.

Setting as Temporal

Setting is temporal in two respects: 1) the period or era in which a story is set, and 2) the duration of time in which the story takes place. The period or era is the point and place in historical time. Is the story set right now in the present contemporary time, or in the past, or in the future, or in a fantastical/hypothetical future or past? Almost all stories are set in one of these eras, and this significantly impacts the story and its meaning. (However, there are fantasies, quite uncommon, that are not set in a specific time and seem to float at any time we want to imagine, such as *Alice in Wonderland*, *Animal Farm*, or *Watership Down*.) The second level of time is duration or time span, which is the length of time that the story contains. Some stories occur in a very short time frame of an hour ("The Story of an Hour" by Kate Chopin) or a day (*One Day in the Life of Ivan Denisovich*, by Alexander Solzhenitsyn). Other stories span generations. In most cases, stories that occur in a short time frame emphasize the micro-level of context, while epics that extend over years or decades or generations focus on larger, more macro concerns.

Setting as Social and Psychological

Settings also typically contain a social/psychological dimension, what we might call a human dimension. The social/psychological dimensions of setting are a function of the systems of relationships among the characters there. So Jeff's Maine porch would be a different setting if his kids were intensely competitive as opposed to friendly and fun-loving, or if Jeff joined them in a game that he takes seriously, like cribbage, or if Jeff's family had gathered to witness the death of a close friend or the birth of a neighbor's child. An important aspect of the human/psychological dimension is what might be considered the "interactive space" of a setting—the kinds of interactions that occur there and their psychological aspects. This is something we will take up in some detail in the next chapter.

Setting always provides a situation that is going to deeply influence what can happen in a story and how the characters feel about what happens. This is another way of saying that conflict is a function of setting—just as the level and intensity and results of conflict are—on the story's ultimate meaning. Conflicts and the resulting possible consequences derive from settings and situations, and these are what contain and drive story action.

Putting It All Together: Setting as Rule Setting

With this knowledge of the levels and dimensions of setting, we now hope that you can see how a very important concept about setting is that *setting is really about "rule setting."* In other words, setting "sets" or determines rules, constraints, and possibilities, potential conflicts and possible consequences. In essence, the discussed levels and dimensions of setting work together to *define and confine* all of the possibilities that might follow. You can see how this is an insight of activity theory: that particular groups make rules that apply to particular settings/situations in order to achieve certain goals. It is also an insight of discourse theorists (e.g., Gee, 1999) who argue that entry into a discourse community (or community of practice) means learning the rules of that community and being able to play by those rules. Knowing and playing by the rules makes one a valued insider who can participate with that group in their setting. Testing, questioning, and violating the rules will inevitably lead to conflict, as the activities of Abigail and the girls, Abigail and John Proctor, and John Proctor himself all lead to various conflicts in Arthur Miller's *The Crucible*.

It might sound as if setting is a kind of straitjacket and, in fact, it is. But you might also see it as a kind of river channel in a canyon. There are only certain directions things can go, but slightly different routes can be taken and different events can happen. Trying to navigate a new channel is possible and can bring conflict and problems. Going outside the river is not possible.

Even when writing a fictional story, not any old thing can happen. Writers are constrained by the rules of the world they have invented, and only very particular things can happen there. Where do these rules come from? First, from what we know of the world. (We are arguing in this book that this is a powerful point for teachers: it allows you to use what students already know from the world, and it means that what you learn about literary conventions has application to reading of all kinds, including reading of the world. This makes the study of these tropes triply meaningful.) In different actual settings in the world, only certain things are possible and even fewer things are probable. Stray from the probable, and a reader is going to feel misled and maybe even betrayed; if something impossible happens for that setting, then the rules of setting have been violated and the story loses its capacity to mean something.

Let's consider Jeff back in Maine one more time. Maine is a fairly poor state, especially outside its southernmost confines. If Jeff sets his story near Meddybemps in the year 2009, it is improbable, and maybe impossible, to have a gathering of the rich and famous, or a political fundraising event. However, it is very possible that someone could get lost in a blueberry barren or even in a cove of the labyrinthine Meddybemps Lake. There could be a mysterious case of food poisoning from red tide or a sea kayaking accident. There could be a bear attack. Those things are possible and do not test the limits of the probable.

There are also *genre-specific rules of setting*. Fantasy, for instance, grants the writer one giant fantastical leap away from reality and then the reader demands the strictest adherence to the rules of that invented world. This adherence to probability is as strict as a Gradgrindian schoolmaster, and there can be no more fudging with the rules of the world after the initial leap, and no free association and no coincidence. When we interview passionate readers of fantasy books, they can tell us in the most articulate terms what is allowed and not allowed in the worlds of *Redwall* or *The Wizard of Oz* or Harry Potter or Earthsea. These readers know what is likely to happen, what could happen, and what will definitely not happen. (In our study of boys' literacy, we found that passionate fantasy readers saw fantasy as a comment on reality and their real lives, using the one fantastic leap to provide unique angles for examining reality (Smith & Wilhelm, 2002).

In pure science fiction, the rules include that nothing can happen that is not scientifically plausible at the time of the writing. In historical fiction, what we know from history cannot be violated, and nothing can happen in the book that violates what we know of historical events and the constraints of living in certain situations at that time.

This all serves to underscore the point that even fictional worlds and settings don't come from a vacuum, or from inspiration like Athena, fully formed, emerging from Zeus's head. They grow and evolve from the compost of all that we know from the world, from history, from our own experience and that of humanity, and from our experience with other books and movies from the genre we are reading. We pick up the implicit rules of particular situations and specific genres from our experience. Like a game, the satisfaction and meaning come from being governed by rules. For example, tennis would lose all its excitement and challenge if there were no rules, lines, or net.

Jeff remembers writing a story for his high school English teacher, Bill Strohm. Bill wanted to know the setting for the story, and Jeff said something vague like "the United States." When asked the time period, Jeff indicated it was the "future." In fact, Jeff had only a vague idea that he wanted to write about a social upheaval that occurred in the future, and (*surprise!*) he was having trouble getting started.

Bill pointed out that Jeff's writer's block was due to the lack of a specific setting that would give direction to the story and would confine the possibilities so Jeff could start writing. Bill asked Jeff whether his story would be realistic or fantasy, and Jeff said it would be realistic. Bill then pushed Jeff to limit the setting to a specific place. Jeff finally settled upon Los Angeles. Bill asked if Jeff had ever been to Los Angeles. In fact, he had never been west of the Mississippi River. Bill indicated to Jeff that he had to intimately know a setting, and its rules, its possibilities and probabilities, to be able to write about it. Now, this doesn't mean it would be impossible to write about a place you have never been, but you do need some kind of knowledge to proceed from, and having been in a place would be a big help.

Jeff then settled on his hometown, and the effect that a major earthquake might have on life there. Bill was pushing Jeff to create a very small and specific and known or knowable world as a way to get him over his writer's block and as a way to help him write an interesting and readable story. As Jeff began to write about the activities on the street outside Karl Smith's market across from the sandstone town hall building just prior to an earthquake splitting Main Street and bringing the High-Line railroad bridge crashing down on the Corner Liquor Store and Tommy's Rec and Pool Hall, his creative juices were flowing.

Jeff had experienced the freedom and creativity that comes from respecting the *rules of specificity and limitation* (McKee, 1997). Far from constraining creativity, being specific and limited in one's setting can free the writer, and makes a story more comprehensible to a reader. A setting should be specific and it should be deeply known by the writer and deeply knowable by the reader. Here's another essential point: The few salient details that the writer provides must imply much, much more, so that even through the use of just a few details a whole world and its laws are implied.

Bill pushed Jeff to know everything about his setting that would be germane to how life would change in the instant of a natural disaster. He communicated to Jeff that the more knowledgeable he was about the world, the greater the creative choices he would have as a writer, and the more engaged in the possibilities his readers would be. Bill emphasized that to be a good writer, you really have to *know* the world that you are writing about. But you only have to share those details that are necessary for implying the rest of the details.

Jeff had felt that writing about what he already knew and writing about his own small town would be limiting. But in fact, writing about something known helps the writer and the reader to know it even more deeply. And writing about a focused setting makes it more knowable and therefore more powerful, useful, and significant. Small does not mean trivial, and it can mean focus and power. A powerful story is at home in its own setting. The more powerful and honest the story, the more its setting seems to be the one true place for that story to happen. But to understand and create powerful settings, whether as a writer or in the mind as a reader, we must know what is salient and infer or create entire secondary worlds based on these few striking details.

Conclusion

It should be clear from our discussion that setting is a complex business. Traditional instruction, with its focus on terms and simple identifications of basic categories, just won't help students learn what is important about settings in their own lives, nor what is important to know and be able to do as readers and composers of setting. It just doesn't get the job done.

Using the inquiry square is a powerful heuristic for thinking through the kinds of knowledge involved in understanding the various levels and dimensions of setting To conclude, what is it that highly effective readers (and writers) do when they adequately account for the setting?

1. They identify the salient levels and dimensions of the setting and what is striking about each level and dimension.
2. They look for or invoke from their previous life and reading experiences the rules of these levels and dimensions and how they operate and interrelate.

CHAPTER SIX

Putting Theory Into Practice:
Preparing Students to Interpret and Create Setting

Four challenges seem especially important to us in regards to the targeted teaching of setting:

- Helping students attend to the appropriate levels and dimensions
- Helping students attend to the salient features of these aspects of setting
- Helping students use their prior experience to figure out the rules of how these levels and dimensions work with texts
- Helping students attend to the interplay of the dimensions—especially to assess the effect of this interplay on character and actions, and to make predictions and interpretations

The activities that follow are designed to address these challenges and to enact the instructional implications we discussed in the last chapter.

Using a Case to Introduce the Levels and Dimensions

We suggest beginning with an activity that will raise students' awareness to all of the complexity we introduced in the last chapter without overwhelming them. The following case study is short, but when Michael wrote it, he tried to include all of the dimensions and levels in one way or another.

New Friends

Every four years around the time of the Olympics, the Department of Education would put on a Middle School Olympics in which kids from around the world would come together to showcase their talents. The event lasted three weeks.

Every participating school could send five students. But each student had to have a different talent or interest. Joe felt fortunate to be selected to represent the athletes from his school. The other students who were going were Marcy, who played the cello; Zack, who was really into manga; Sharon, who starred in all the school plays; and Ed, who was a complete brainiac.

Once the kids were selected, they had to get together for lots and lots of orientation. Joe never would have hung out with any of the other kids who were going. Not that he had anything against them. At his school, though, athletes stuck with athletes pretty much. Well, really basketball players stuck with basketball players. That was the big sport. He knew some of the other kids resented basketball, and he could see why. Some of his teachers even seemed to favor him because he was the star. His mom, though, always kept his head from getting too big. She seemed to get along with everyone. Sometimes she took him to the African American neighborhood where some of the guys on his AAU team played pick-up games. Joe and his mom were the only White people there, but his mom seemed comfortable. More comfortable even than he was. Joe wasn't used to being in the minority. His school was all White. That didn't mean everybody was the same, though. Some of the kids, like Marcy and Ed, came from families who had lots of money. Some, like Joe, were from families who had a hard time making it, especially now with the unemployment rate so high. Joe didn't want to go to the pick-up games at first, but his mom convinced him that it was good to get out of his comfort zone and try something new.

The Olympics orientation activities were kind of boring, but Joe had to admit it was kind of cool to talk with people that he didn't usually hang out with. In fact, Joe was a bit surprised at how much he enjoyed the conversations with the other students from his school who were going to the Olympics. Sure, it was a little hard to get the conversation started the first few times they got together. Some of the basketball players had bullied Ed during the year, and he seemed especially edgy when Joe went up to him, but by the time they took the school van on the three-hour trip to Washington, D.C., they talked easily together. Ed really cracked Joe up. He knew more than the teachers who were chaperoning, and he wasn't afraid to let them know it. And Marcy, even though she played classical music, loved to listen to Lupe Fiasco, Joe's favorite rapper. Joe even started to appreciate manga a bit, and he promised himself that he'd go to the plays next year.

Once Joe arrived at the Olympics, he had to say good-bye to his new school friends. Each kid went off to a different dorm at the college where they were staying. Joe and all the athletes were in a dorm set off from everyone else behind a small woods. Some of the

➔

other kids were in apartment style rooms that held eight people. But Joe's dorm only had doubles.

The athletes were an amazing collection of people. His roommate, Aban, was a soccer player from Iraq. Joe thought that maybe they put an Iraqi kid and an American kid in the same room on purpose, just to show that sports was a way to bring people together. It was pretty interesting to room with Aban. Aban was Muslim. He prayed five times every day. And he had lots of amazing stories to tell about the war. Sometimes American soldiers were the heroes. But sometimes they were the villains. Aban didn't seem to hold that against Joe, though Aban tended to hang out with the other Muslim kids. But after a few days, they were comfortable with each other, and they started to share their hopes and dreams in quiet whispers after lights out in the dorm. It didn't seem so odd to be talking with someone so different. Everyone at the camp was doing it.

But Joe did have a chance to hang out with basketball players, too. He and this Nigerian kid, Chinedu, had great one-on-one games. They both played small forward. Both were already 6'2" and were still growing. Both liked to drive to the basket but could use more practice on their outside shots. After their games, they'd talk. Joe found out that Chinedu's family was really rich because his dad was in the oil business. His life was so different from Joe's on that end. Joe never even went to the movies because his mom couldn't afford it. Sometimes at dinner he and Sharon would talk about how unfair it seemed that some of the kids they were meeting had so much when the two of them had single moms who had to struggle to make ends meet.

And then there was the dorm counselor, Enrique, a 45-year-old teacher from Venezuela. Joe had never met anyone like him. And he didn't know much about Venezuela except something that his social studies teacher had said about the fact that Venezuela had a president who hated the United States. Enrique didn't know a thing about sports, at least not about basketball. But he sure was willing to learn. Joe had never met an adult who listened so hard to kids. Enrique mostly listened, but when he talked it was really worth paying attention to. He seemed so wise about so much: friends, girls, school, you name it. Most nights everyone would gather around Enrique, talking about anything and everything, from what happened on the courts or fields to what was happening at home.

Joe was really sorry when the three weeks were over. The whole experience was a life-changing one. The last days there everyone exchanged e-mails and promised to add each other as MySpace friends.

After reading the story to the class, give each student the following ranking sheet.

Making Predictions

Think about Joe and all the people he has met. Rank them from the person Joe is most likely to stay friends with (1) to the person Joe is least likely to stay friends with (7). Be prepared to defend your answers.

_____ Marcy, the cellist

_____ Sharon, the actress

_____ Ed, the brainiac

_____ Zack, the manga artist

_____ Aban, the roommate

_____ Chinedu, the basketball player

_____ Enrique, the dorm counselor

Which of the following had the greatest influence of your rankings? Please give a 1 to the factor that was most influential down to a 6 for the one that was least influential.

_____ The way things were at Joe's school and how they tend to be at middle schools in general

_____ Differences in nationality, race, and class

_____ The kind of person Joe's mom was at home

_____ The kind of place the camp was

_____ How other countries thought of the United States

_____ Other (Be specific.)

As we explained in Chapter Three, we suggest asking students to do both sets of ranking individually and then putting them into groups of four or five to discuss their rankings. Then we'd put a matrix on the board and tally the ranking so students can see areas of agreement and disagreement, and lead a discussion, beginning with the most contentious ranking. As the discussion goes on, we suggest tracking on the board the justifications that students use. Someone might say, "I think it'd be Chinedu because of the basketball and, after all, his mom made him get used to being with different kinds of people." Someone else might agree, saying, "And at his school he was used to hanging out with basketball players." A third student might add, "No way. Their lives are just too different."

After the discussion, we recommend looking back at what the class talked about and highlighting the different levels of setting that the class talked about. If you want, you could introduce the terms *micro* (e.g., How Joe and his mom related and what values they promoted), *meso*, or middle, (e.g., how cliques worked at Joe's school), or *macro* (e.g., the cultural and political differences between countries). But the vocabulary isn't really important. What is important is that students begin to see how smaller contexts are nested in larger ones.

After that discussion, give students the ranking sheet below and repeat the process. This time, the discussion will focus on the dimensions of setting. The first item changes the physical setting, the second changes the social/psychological dimension, and the third and fourth change the temporal dimension. Once again, the terms aren't important. What is important is that students begin to see the possible impact of each of the dimensions.

Evaluating Changes in Setting

Which of the following changes to the situation would most affect your rankings? Please give a 1 to the change that would have the biggest influence.

_____ If Joe's dorm were an apartment-style dorm near all of the other dorms

_____ If Joe's dorm counselor had been really strict and didn't seem to like kids all that much

_____ If the Middle School Olympics lasted one week instead of three

_____ If the story took place before kids had access to personal computers

---

A great follow-up to this introductory activity is to have students search for short summaries of movies to put on the bulletin board with a brief explanation of the levels and dimensions of setting that are most important. Here's the plot summary for *Arranged*, a movie Michael just watched:

ARRANGED centers on the friendship between an Orthodox Jewish woman and a Muslim woman who meet as first-year teachers at a public school in Brooklyn. Over the course of the year, they learn they share much in common—not least of which is that they are both going through the process of arranged marriages. (http://www.imdb.com/title/tt0848542/plotsummary)

The macro-setting involves the relationship between Jews and Muslims. The meso-level of setting is Brooklyn, a very diverse borough of New York City. The micro-level is the particular details of their friendship, and the school setting, which also creates the social/psychological background of the movie. Time is important because arranged marriages are rare these days in America. The actual physical spaces are of less importance.

Examining the Physical Dimension of Setting

In cognitive science, the principle of sequencing shows that when teaching something new, it is useful to start with concrete, highly visual experiences. As the famous anthropologist Jacob Bronowski once said on the PBS series *The Ascent of Man*, "There is nothing in the head that was not first in the hand." We need concrete experiences to abstract from. That's why we suggest organizing your work on setting around the three dimensions of setting (physical, social/psychological, temporal) and embedding discussion of the three different levels (micro, meso, macro) of systems into that organization.

USING PAINTINGS AND PHOTOGRAPHS

For this reason, we start the following setting sequence with the physical setting (the most concrete dimension) and look at the physical setting through concrete artifacts like visual art and photographs. Another advantage of using such artifacts is exposing students to interesting and important artwork; additional benefits result when using artwork that relates conceptually to an inquiry theme and essential question.

For a general pass at setting you can start with the famous van Gogh painting *Bedroom at Arles*. You can find it on a variety of Web sites, including http://www.usc.edu/programs/cst/deadfiles/

lacasis/ansc100/library/images/646.jpg. This picture has the advantage of portraying one small space without human figures. The painting is not an exact representation—it certainly doesn't include all the objects that were really in the bedroom, only those that were salient to van Gogh, and the colors are not direct representations. The painting directs us to notice some aspects and objects of the physical setting.

Guide the students through the following questions, which provide a framework for focusing first on the physical setting and then on how the physical interacts with the temporal and social/psychological dimensions. This will give students an overview of the physical dimension and how it relates to the other dimensions.

The questions walk students through the steps of noticing and interpreting these aspects. Of course the questions can be tweaked for your particular purposes, particular works of art, and the needs of your students at any given time. These are general questions that will work to help students internalize the kinds of questions to ask about any setting.

1. What would you name as the setting? (someone's bedroom)
2. What do you notice? (Students tell what they notice and why, which could be put on an anchor chart and added to throughout the unit.)
3. How do you know the artist wanted you to notice these aspects and objects?
4. What effect does what you notice have on you? Why is that?
5. How do the objects and aspects you notice form a pattern or patterns? What is the effect of that pattern?
6. What can you tell about where this setting is, as far as country, city, neighborhood, address, etc.? Is it, for instance, important to know that this is a room in a boarding house (micro-level) or that it is in Arles in southern France (meso-level)—indicated by the title? Or that the painting is set in the nineteenth century (macro-level)?
7. What kinds of things do you think typically happen/can happen in this space? What is probable and improbable? How do you know? (setting as rule setting, using prior knowledge and experience)
8. What era is expressed? What time of day? How do you know? Is the time important? (temporal aspect)
9. What kind of feeling or mood is created? How does the painting make you "feel"? How do you think it goes about doing that? (social/psychological dimension)
10. What kind of person sleeps or lives here? What details reveal that? What kind of interactions (both internal and external) might occur here? (setting as interactive space; assessing character, predicting character action)

11. What else might we infer about the character/s who might occupy this space? About the artist? Why might the artist have painted this picture and in this way? On what do we base these inferences? (assessing character through setting; considering the intelligence behind the text)

12. Write a description of the painting, but limit yourself to 25 words. You will have to determine your overall impression and reaction and choose only those details from the levels and dimensions that are significant in creating this central impression.

13. How do the details you chose create that flavor and convey what is essential in the setting? (salient details)

Another principle of sequencing is to move from socially supported work to work that is done in smaller groups and then more independently. Therefore, we typically go through a painting—or perhaps a few—with the whole class, first modeling how we use the levels and dimensions for understanding setting, and then having students help us with subsequent paintings. When we do the modeling, we name the levels and the dimensions as we address them, using the same language each time. Then we have students form small groups and ask students to work together on answers to the questions. We can wander the classroom and help any students who may be struggling. This follows the model of Gradual Release of Responsibility (Teacher Does-Students Watch ⇢ Teacher Does-Students Help ⇢ Students Do Together-Teacher Helps ⇢ Students Do Alone-Teacher Monitors), also known as Modeling-Mentoring-Monitoring (Wilhelm, Baker, Dube-Hackett, 2001).

Other great paintings that we have used include Munch's *The Scream* (great for looking at the physical—the pier; the temporal—the sunset; and how these are related to the social/psychological dimension; who are the people in the background? Why are they there?); Renoir's *La Loge* (excellent for physical space as related to social/psychological space—who is the man looking at? What does the loge (the opera house) say about the couple? Is the larger context of the opera house in Paris important? What kind of relationship can they have here? What kind of relationship do they have elsewhere?); Edward Hopper's *Lighthouse Hill* and *The Long Leg* are great for exploring natural setting and what might happen there. His *Office at Night* and *Nighthawks* are great for exploring physical urban spaces and the effect of setting on human interaction.

Just flipping through art books or online resources will give you hundreds of ideas for paintings or photographs to use—Grant Wood's *American Gothic*, Thomas Hart Benton's panoramas and murals, Bierstadt's landscapes, and much more. *National Geographic*, Smithsonian, and WPA photograph collections (among many others) are also excellent resources for exploring setting, particularly how the physical interacts with the temporal and the human dimensions.

A slight variation is one we call the "Matching Game," in which we ask students to look at paintings or photos without human figures and ask students to think who might fit in that setting and what they might do there. You can also do the same by matching character to setting. Here you show a portrait or photo of a person and ask students to describe that person's home, natural or urban setting, and what he or she would do there. Choose settings that are intense and psychological, or portraits that reveal idiosyncrasies of character for the best results.

Another idea we've used in our classrooms is to display canonical photographs, as well as photos that students find, bring in, or take themselves, and then have students write reviews, descriptions, or poetry based on the photographs. A great book to use with such an activity is Cynthia Rylant's *Something Permanent,* a beautiful book of poems she wrote in response to WPA photographs by Walker Evans.

Here's one high school student's response to Rylant's book, writing to the prompt, *What did you like about the book, what did you get out of it, and how could we use the book in class as part of our inquiry about how the Depression affected people?*

Something Permanent Journal Writing

Something Permanent contains the pairing of Walker Evans's photographs and Cynthia Rylant's poetry to demonstrate how settings can convey so much information, and how emotions can be rooted in objects, and how, through the use of strong, sturdy words, you can convey what a setting means to the people there and what possibilities exist for them there. Evans's photos resist all attempts at pigeonholing. The settings and objects he captures— slightly sagging bed, birdhouses in a backyard, the façade of a gas station, a rocking chair on a porch—all possess physical presence that communicates and controls so much more and allows you to guess what has happened there or might happen there.

The photos also suggest the scope of the human lives lived there in that place and that time. This is where Rylant enters the picture, no pun intended, flushing [sic] out the intimations offered by the pictures themselves with her poetry, never reducing the image to a single meaning but always widening the angle of vision to include more, to see farther. Moreover, best of all, the angles Rylant chooses to widen are rarely the ones we expect. Her poem about the sagging bed, begins, "Of course it was hard to make love/with the children in the room." What follows is a tenderly erotic lyric about a couple who "ease their weary minds/with sex, which makes them poorer/and richer/all at the same time!"

I think that these photos and poems will help us in our inquiry and discussion of the Great Depression and our inquiry into how hard times affect people. I think we can use these photos and maybe other ones by Dorothea Lange as prompts for writing our own poetry. Maybe we could write stories set in the photos, or tell what happened here before or what might happen next. — Bea Futch

Following is student Josh Hale's poem to his own "found" photograph, inspired by Rylant's examples. The challenge posed to the students was to describe what the setting suggested might have happened or could happen here.

Nothing Permanent, by Josh Hale

V-E Day
Last night we celebrated the end
of this damn war
this morning
back in the quonset hut
where we've lived together
and shared so much hope and agony
and no privacy whatsoever
my urine was the color of champagne
But I wasn't unique
or so was the story
from my peek in the other bowls

After each activity, it's important to have students reflect on what they are learning so that they can transfer it to new situations. In this case, here's what we asked:

1. What did you notice in the setting? Why did you notice this? (rules of notice about dimensions)
2. What level of the setting is most important? What about the other levels can be inferred? (levels/nestedness of setting)
3. By connecting the setting to your own life experience, what "rules" do you think are in place in this setting? (connecting and rule setting)
4. How did you play out these rules in your poem? (application—assessing and predicting human activity in a particular setting)

Any type of questions or prompts that get after these general and transferable aspects of setting will work. The reflection is essential for consolidating the strategies of interpreting and using the levels and dimensions of setting independently. As always, new insights can be added to an anchor chart about what to notice in setting.

We like to have our students go on "search and find" missions, asking them to bring in paintings or photographs they have found, or sometimes that they have created—then we can treat their artwork with the same seriousness we accord the masters. The different talents and interests of our students never cease to amaze us.

USING QUICK INFORMAL STUDENT WRITING

It's also useful to embed instruction in students' own personal experiences with setting. This is particularly true as you begin to explore how the physical setting interplays with the human dimensions of setting. Students could be asked to photograph, draw, or paint familiar or personally important settings and then to go through the questions on page 84, or they might present these "special settings" in small groups, explaining the important features and their significance. The next step is to ask students to write about a familiar or special setting and to share their writing.

We remind them that we are focusing here first on the physical/geographical dimension of setting (though other dimensions will be implicated) and to be *specific and limited*—choosing only those details that are most salient and get the most work done. We remind them to write about what they know and what is knowable! Keep in mind that other activities that pay similar types of attention to the aspects of setting will work just as well.

If students are going to collect pieces into a portfolio of places important to them or write a travel brochure or guide to another culture or place, or a story, then so much the better. Students can be reminded that this work will help them not only with their immediate reading, the pursuit of their inquiry, but also with a near-term writing experience.

The following is one way of proceeding with quick, informal kinds of exploratory journal writing. The point here is to work fairly quickly to get at underlying principles of setting, and to create a compost heap of ideas for future writing, not to create anything polished.

Ask students to consider their own bedroom and how to describe it. To model, you might describe your classroom and how this setting expresses your personality, your theories of teaching and learning (Is there a lectern? Do all chairs face the front or are students in groups? What kind of artwork or student work is displayed?), and what you are trying to encourage and discourage from happening here. You might also discuss the limitations of the space and how you are creative in trying to make it fit your purposes.

You may want to encourage students to write in their room, or to take a photograph or photographs of their room to use as a reference. Ask them to compose a list of important features and what each means or expresses about the room, what happens there, and how the room captures their personality. Then ask them to rank the details in order of importance to the significance of the room, its mood, and its human and interactive possibilities. Then ask them to use the ranking to write a description of the room in 35 words or less, concentrating on communicating what is most significant to someone else. Students could also describe their "dream" room. Have them share and discuss.

In another quick-write activity, have students brainstorm significant places in the school and grounds, or even the community. Have them think about what tends to happen in those spaces, both obvious and hidden; for example, the vice principal's office is usually a place to avoid, but sometimes might be the site of a friendly chat. What about these places makes these actions and/or feelings probable and possible? What kinds of things can probably not happen in these places? What can happen but might be surprising and, therefore, have special power in a story? What are the sensory details of this place?

Students could also brainstorm a list of favorite places and share with a small group. Have them talk about the features and aspects that make one place special, enjoyable, and functional for them. What would someone have to know about this place to understand it and appreciate its specialness? In our experience, students are intensely self-interested (all right, just like the rest of us) and are eager to share what is important to them and expresses their identity—this makes a good springboard for learning about settings that are farther from home and more distant from their time, place, and experience.

Students could be asked to think of places where they spend a lot of time—but these places don't have to be places they like; they might be places students dislike or feel ambivalent about. Have them quickly describe the physical characteristics of these places.

Ask: "What features make you like or dislike this setting? Think about the time you spend there, the other people who are there, what happens there, the psychological aspects, and so on." Remember to keep adding to the anchor chart about setting as new clues come up. (The point here is to build students' understanding of setting—what to notice and how to use what they know from their lives to think about the "rule-setting" dimension of setting.)

Students could write a thorough description, highlight what is salient, and then cross out what is unimportant. To explore what's implied by specific and perhaps seemingly small details, you could focus on a single detail from a description, a photograph, or a painting and ask what it means. After students have done this in small groups a few times, you could ask them to produce such a detail (like the ones below) for the rest of the class to think about.

> *A single dirty sock on the floor under the dining room table*
> *A handgun on the kitchen table*
> *A polished walnut desk with perfectly organized file folders of tax receipts*
> *A wood stove with a roaring fire in the corner of the room*

After you provide a few examples, students could do the same, always focusing on what is salient and what is less so, what level and dimension of context they are attending to, how this might relate to other levels (the tax receipts to the government and IRS), what they can infer from the few details offered, how they are using their life experiences to understand the rules of the setting and to make assessments and predictions about character.

This informal writing should lead to a formal writing assignment that is part of the unit design, as we will discuss next.

USING FORMAL STUDENT WRITING

The final assignment in this sequence could be to compose a "sensorium," a New Journalistic sensory place description, see page 88. (New Journalists apply many fiction devices to their writing to make it more alive for their readers, and students have fun with this). See Smith and Wilhelm (2007) for a complete discussion of this assignment and student examples.

Other writing assignments that students could complete at the end of a unit on setting could be arguments about the influence of setting (in a literary work, on particular characters or events), an extended definition of a particular setting, or a comparison/contrast of the influence of different settings on a character, on the action in different scenes, and so on.

USING DRAMA AND ROLE-PLAY

We've talked about using dramas and role-plays to teach character. They are also very effective in teaching setting. You can set up a role play around an issue, then change the setting and see how the role-playing changes.

For example, imagine a doting and overprotective single mother whose son is beginning to chafe a bit and seek independence, although he's still a little uncertain of himself. Because of a stupid mistake and losing his temper, he is now in serious trouble with the law. Because of where he lives, the son and his mother do not believe he will be treated fairly by the court system.

Role-play their conversation in these settings:

- at the police station in front of the detective who arrested him
- in the taxi on the ride home
- alone once they get home
- at home when his uncle, his mother's brother, a former Marine sergeant, arrives

Other such prompts can be composed to fit particular units, settings, and characters. Students love improvisational challenges where a setting is drawn out of a hat. Then they think of a character who might live in that setting and improvise a typical action or meeting in that place. Students can also be given a random line or verbal task to perform that they have to deliver in different contexts,

Sensorium Peer Editing Sheet

Considerations for first and second draft peer editing:

1. Is there a title that invites the reader immediately into the lived experience of the described place?

2. Does the opening have movement or dialogue that immediately draws the reader into the setting and its story?

3. Does the writing concentrate on the described place and the people there?

4. Is there one place described over a limited time?

5. Are all five senses specifically used? Are nouns, verbs, adjectives, adverbs, and modifying phrases as specific as possible, appropriate, and deliciously different?*

6. Does the reader experience the place in a totally stimulating way, just as the writer originally did?

7. How does the writer show the social status of the people described? Are symbolic possessions, gestures, actions, styles, and so forth used that truly reveal status and character?

8. Is the psychological feeling—how the space shapes interactions and activity—obvious?

9. Does the description stir up memories of similar places for the reader?

10. Is a sound device used so we can hear a sound that occurs in the setting?

*Note to peer editor: If there are places that need elaboration with specific details so that the reader can see, taste, hear, feel, and smell what the writer sensed, then highlight these sections with a mark in the margin of the paper. All details must do "work" in creating associations and experiences for the reader!

such as at school with a teacher, in the park with friends, or at church with a priest.

Another technique is that of *tableau drama* with its associated technique called *slide show* (Wilhelm, 2004; Scruggs & McKnight, 2008). In tableau, a group of students create a visual depiction or statue version of a scene with their bodies—they can play people, objects, trees, or animals to depict the scene. A variation is to have a second group narrating what they see, or advising the tableau group how to depict the scene more creatively. Scenes can come from a text being studied, or they may be brainstormed by the group.

In a *slide show*, the tableau group creates several scenes, one after another. Again, a second group can be advisors or narrators of the slide show. The advisors can coach the tableau group by reminding them to show the physical setting and the psychological aspects of that setting ("Show us how you feel!" "How would people be interacting here?"). The temporal dimension can be enacted as slides "unfreeze" and can become mini video clips with action (a technique called *tableau vivant*).

A good starting point for this activity would be to have students depict slides from a real or imagined vacation or highlights from the year at school. What happened in what places?

A nice follow-up is to use curricular material by having students visually or dramatically depict scenes from their inquiry unit: important places in the galaxy and what happens there, the ten most important scenes from the Civil War, the most important settings and scenes from *To Kill a Mockingbird*, and so on.

The possibilities are endless. Remember to have students reflect, either together or individually, on how the activity used ideas about levels of context and dimensions of setting, and about the rules of what happens where, so that they will be able to transfer their understanding of setting to new situations.

COMPOSING STAGE DIRECTIONS

After students have role-played a scene, they can write stage directions for that scene so that it could be recreated by others. Or, students could write a scene with stage directions so that another group could perform it the way they envision.

Since the audience of a dramatic scene or role-play does not see or read the stage directions, all directions must be for ideas that can be displayed visually (such as furniture and backdrop) or verbally (through words, tone of voice, etc.).

If you and your students have the interest in being technical, then you can tell them that directions are always written from the point of view of the actors facing the audience and use terms like *upstage left, center stage, downstage right*. We often have students who like to make iMovies of scripts, and this is a possibility for your classroom, too.

In setting the scene, the audience needs to see the physical setting: what is the general location? What are the objects in that setting? They need to know the time and whether the year, season, day, or hour is important. The passing of time can be depicted through dimming or blacking out a scene, or through music. The audience will need to know about the psychological and interactive dimensions of the space. Emotional tones can be set by music and lighting of different intensity and colors. Emotional and social features can be described through tone of voice, facial expressions, body position, and gestures.

Students could look at stage directions from a play they have read or are currently reading before trying to write some of their own, or they can download movie scripts of favorite scenes from the Internet. When another group tries to enact their scene, they will get immediate feedback about what they have communicated well or not so well.

USING A PLACE AND IDENTITY ACTIVITY

Place is a fundamental component of everyday life, the "where" that locates each event and experience in our lives. Place also evokes identity and possibility. You meet people and you ask where they are from. "I'm from the rural South." "I'm from New York City." "I work on a ranch in North Dakota." "I live near Jackson Hole." These responses conjure up very different cultural assumptions and associations. Geographic setting has a deep influence.

The same thing is true of a suburb or area of a city or town. "I'm from Harlem." "I live in Midtown." "My apartment is on the Upper East Side." Each of these responses is not only an identifier of culture, but also of opportunity and constraints. There are things you can do in each place, and things you cannot do.

One fun exercise is to have students look through the housing and apartment advertisements in the newspaper, or online. Have them choose a few places where they might like to move with their family, or on their own if they were able to. Where would they choose to live? What features of the dwelling would they look for? What opportunities and constraints, possibilities and problems might each address or each dwelling and its features provide? Students could be asked to rank the features of one of their choices in order of importance to them: address; section of town; nearness to schools; quality of schools; proximity to shopping, work, parks, libraries, and the outdoors; as well as the features of the yard and house itself.

This exercise is also salutary in that it can introduce students to the cost of rent, the relative cost of different areas, what one would pay for certain features and amenities, and so forth. Again, the cues and rules of notice for this dimension of setting can be added to the class anchor chart as they come up in the activity.

Examining the Temporal Dimension

In our experience, helping students infer temporal dimensions can go pretty quickly. You've already seen how the temporal comes up when dealing with the physical dimensions of setting. One caveat is that students need to have some background knowledge to make inferences about eras distant from the current day, but here's the good news: providing them with activities that help them infer era and the associated place can also build the background they need to read and understand issues surrounding the inquiry topic. So it's important to choose materials for your introductory work that serve the inquiry and build background.

For example, let's say your inquiry is centered on the essential question *Can war ever be justified?* You are going to do an integrated unit with the social studies teacher on World War II, and read parts of Studs Terkel's *The Good War*, as well as Young Adult literature such as John Marsden's novel *Tomorrow, When the War Began*, Aidan Chambers's *Postcards From No Man's Land*, or Art Spiegelman's graphic novel *Maus: A Survivor's Tale*. You're also planning to watch the movie *Band of Brothers*. Your students may not know much about the WWII era, the duration of the war, and so on, so starting with images and film clips from that era can build background while the kids learn to infer the temporal dimensions of setting.

USING VISUAL MEDIA

One thing Jeff did during such a unit was to use Norman Rockwell paintings as a kind of front-loading. He showed his classes paintings of soldiers preparing for war, going off to war, returning from war, telling stories in the garage about the war, and showing pictures from the home front. He asked the students to infer the era and cite the clues, such as style of the painting, the dress of the characters, the make of cars, the objects in the garage, references to historical events, and so forth. He also asked students to infer what point in the war was being represented and how long the war must have lasted—to help develop a sense of duration.

Erika Boas, teacher extraordinaire from Tasmania and a visiting fellow at Jeff's Boise State Writing Project site, came up with this activity for using photographs to infer era and duration:

1. Teacher selects a series of photographs that represent a particular place (could be a specific building, place on a street, or something more general, like a country) over time. Students could likewise be sent on "search and find" missions to get a series of such photographs. They might even have family photographs that show their home or a favorite spot over time, or a series of holiday photos over time. Camilo José Vergara's photographs of 65 East 125th Street, Harlem, 1977–2002, serve as great examples of photos to use in this activity. They are included in *Seeing & Writing 3* (McQuade & McQuade, 2006).

2. Place sets of photographs in envelopes and distribute envelopes to students in small groups

3. Ask students to work with their group to sequence the photographs chronologically and to justify their choices. (This could also work with prints, paintings, sketches, etc.) Record the cues they used to figure out what was earlier in time, and what was later. Display the photos on a timeline of some kind.

4. Lead the whole class on a "gallery walk" to see each display, stopping at each set of photographs to discuss the various problem-solving strategies students used to order the photos through time and the approaches they have taken in displaying this time order.

5. Have the students select one photograph and brainstorm a story based on the information it contains. They should be using story-building techniques with particular attention to setting and the ways in which setting will provide the impetus and the constraints for the story.

6. Organize a student visit to a memorable local place. Have students complete a series of reflective writing tasks, asking them to focus on the following:
   - the physical setting
   - sensory experiences
   - change through time (What was this place like in the past? What will it be like in the future?)
   - levels of micro-, meso-, and macrosystem that can be seen or inferred
   - atmosphere
   - mood
   - overall sense of place

7. Invite students to divide up the task of crafting a multi-genre piece that explores a particular place in one or more of the following ways:
   - across different times
   - from the perspective of different characters and peoples (or even animals, God, etc.)
   - through different literary genres
   - as a challenge to traditional narrative structure (e.g., using flashbacks, circularity, hypertext, and/or multi-voice text)

8. Have students publish and share their narratives along with a brief explanation of how they used the temporality of setting in their work.

9. Invite students to write in their journals about how their understanding of narrative, time, place, and continuity has developed during the learning sequence.

The images on the next page of dorm rooms from the 1890s to the present are another example of photographic texts you could use. For online images of more dorm rooms through the ages, see http://www.aavc.vassar.edu/vq/issues/Winter_2003.

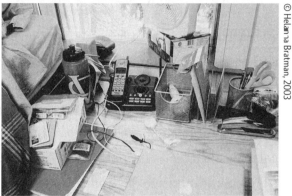

What is the era of each dorm room photo? What clues help you to know?

USING PICTURE BOOKS

Using picture books is also a great idea. Some useful picture books with artistic representations of time along with physical space are the following:

1. *Memorial* by Gary Crew and Shaun Tan. Have students explore the impact of time on place, and how the use of both time and place contributes to the success of this picture book.

2. Ask students to work in pairs to read and discuss other picture books such as *Window* or *Belonging* by Jeannie Baker or *My Place* by Nadia Wheatley, which also explore time, continuity, and change.

3. Check out the picture book *Zoom* by Istvan Banyai to explore notions of the macroculture, mesoculture, and microculture in a picture and the story that each picture tells.

Other picture books can be chosen that relate more directly to the inquiry theme at hand. All picture books make use of the dimensions of setting, particularly through the use of pictures. Typically, some pictures display mostly action, while others display mostly setting. Students can be asked to compare and contrast the kinds of work that various pictures do and that various segments of text achieve in combination with the pictures.

As a follow-up activity ask students to find an image with a temporal aspect. Each student's image could be placed into a PowerPoint slide, and other students could make inferences based on that image (likewise, a scene from a film could be shown, or a paragraph in a book read aloud). The class could also try to match the photo, clip, or paragraph to the person who chose it.

Another activity we've used is to show short film clips from a movie that explores the time period or concepts of the inquiry. One clip can be from early in the movie, and one from late in the movie. If the scenes are set in the same place, then students will have to use clues about era and the passage of time, and brainstorm how the change in time shapes the story.

The recent movie *The Curious Case of Benjamin Button* (based on an F. Scott Fitzgerald story) offers an interesting take on several issues, such as the power of time to shape experience, love and relationships (parental, familial, work groups, romantic), and dealing with loss. Showing clips of the boarding house from early in the movie and later on would use cues of era (e.g., style of American flag, furniture, dress) as well as cues of character (Benjamin gets younger over time, other characters get older). Again, throughout this work, students should name how they know the era and how they know time is passing and use these cues to help create a class anchor chart of cues/rules of notice.

As they go through this work, we ask students to think as a writer about reading or viewing. Based on what they are seeing and reading, ask these questions:

- How do artists and authors convey era through a single detail or combination of details, or the passage of time through a detail or combination of details? How could you do so in your art and writing?
- How do era and passage of time affect characters and shape action?
- How can you best have your readers experience the setting the way that your character does? How can you use specific details, such as those that appeal to the senses, to achieve this?

One of Jeff's recent seventh-grade classes came up with this list:

Cues for temporality
- Styles of dress, architecture in the image
- Makes of cars, transport, objects in the image
- Style of photograph or painting (e.g., black and white photos versus color, grainy, spotted black-and-white photos taken on gelatin)
- Language—like slang, other expressions

Graphic novels are another way to help students infer temporality. Graphic novels typically provide some large setting panels early in the text. (See Scott McCloud's 1994 book, *Understanding Comics,* for an explanation of how such panels work.) Find a few such panels from *Maus,* manga, and other texts kids are reading, such as Dennis O'Neil's *The Dark Knight* or *300*, a graphic novel by Frank Miller and Lynn Varley. We guarantee you have some passionate readers of such texts who'll be happy to help you. *Maus* is set in the thirties and in WWII-era Poland as well as in modern America, switching back and forth among the settings. How do we know when the time changes? How do we know how much time has passed? Lots of manga texts are set in the future. How do we know? What does this future look and feel like and how will that affect the story? *The Dark Knight* stories are set in a film noirish Depression era; what cues do we have that this is the case?

USING SIMULATED TEXTS AND EXCERPTS

Students can be given practice putting the dimensions and levels together through the use of simulated texts and excerpts. A chart such as the one on page 96 can help focus their attention on all dimensions and levels of setting.

Students could start by completing a chart for their own life with the microculture, mesoculture, and macroculture of American politics, economy, cultural values, etc. Next, they could individually complete a chart for a character in a short simulated text or a cartoon, and then compare their chart to others from their learning group to create a composite chart and infer the setting "rules" from that chart. Eventually students could do the same for a text such as a nonfiction piece or short story, before proceeding to a longer text.

Here's a simulated text based on the life of the famous tiger hunter Jim Corbett that Jeff created during a unit on "Who will survive?" Jeff's students responded to the text by filling out a setting chart. Note that this kind of text can be made up about any historical or fictional character, taking care to deal with different levels and dimensions of setting. Students, once they get the idea, can create and share texts.

> Jim Corbett is an Englishman but he lives in the highlands of India in the 1920s. He is single and works for the railroad as an administrator. It is a very time-consuming job, and he has many responsibilities. As an Englishman, he can sometimes have initial difficulties relating to native Indians as equals or communicating with them as a trusted confidante. Jim is also the greatest tiger hunter in India. When a man-eating tiger is on the loose anywhere in northern India, he is called upon to hunt and kill the tiger. He is then released from work at the railroad for the duration of the hunt. These tigers typically live in deep jungle and mountainous areas. Man-eating tigers are often injured, which is why they eat humans—who are easy prey. Once tigers develop a taste for humans they tend to stay in that area and continue attacking people. Tigers are very intelligent and can circle back, walk through water, hide in trees and rocky caves, cover their tracks, and use other strategies to evade being found. Jim needs the help of the locals and requires guides, although these people are often paralyzed by fear and are reluctant to help him.

Elements and Dimensions of Setting

ELEMENTS → LEVELS ↓	Physical	Temporal	Social	Psychological
Micro:				
Meso:				
Macro:				

Brainstorm:

1. Major character(s):
2. Character goal(s):
3. Obstacles to goal(s):
4. Actions taken or that could be taken to achieve goals/overcome obstacles
5. How setting is implicated in goals and obstacles
6. Rules in the setting that affect goals, obstacles, and the overcoming of obstacles/achievement of goals

To get deeper:

1. Circle elements that seem to be most important as far as their effects on the characters and their action.
2. With a line, connect elements that are related and identify, on the line, the nature of the relationship.
3. Consider the lines and come up with "rule setting" or rules that are implicit or explicit in the setting and that affect characters and their action on each level of setting.

The completed chart below provides an idea of how students responded.

Figure 6.1: ELEMENTS AND DIMENSIONS OF SETTING IN THE JIM CORBETT STORY

ELEMENTS → LEVELS ↓	Physical	Temporal	Social	Psychological
Micro: local area of a hunt	Jungle; rocky and difficult terrain	Some aspects of the hunt are socially very much like ancient times.	Relationship between local headmen and Corbett; between headmen and locals	Deep rules about male-female, superior and inferior relationships; intense fear
Meso: Northern India—culture of railroad employees	Mountainous; high expectations and high work load	Clash of more modern culture with more traditional; clash of English culture with Native Indian culture; clash of Indians' regard of tigers as mystical with English regard of tigers as animals	Caste system of Hindu culture—difficulty of communicating across castes; marginalization of women, who are often put to death when husbands die	Desire for independence on part of native Indians, in conflict with their need to rely on English and to work within the English system
Macro: English-Indian relationships/colonial power to occupied power	Passive resistance of some Indians to English colonials	1920s: No GPS No electronic communication No good maps	Difficulty relating across culture, from ruling class to ruled	Distrust/desire of native Indians for help in getting the tiger

Carefully chosen excerpts work in much the same way as do the simulated texts. We recommend selecting an excerpt from something you are reading or an excerpt from a book that students might want to read that is related to the unit and then examine setting and its dimensions.

Here's a slightly condensed excerpt from "Ann Story" by Dorothy Canfield Fisher (1956, p. 37), also from the "Who will survive?" unit:

Usually the first to come over the Indian trails was the father. He might bring a helper: a son, brother, or a friend who also planned to resettle. These men came by canoe or on foot or with a packhorse, carrying the minimum of tools and supplies—axes, wedges, a gun, powder, lead, salt, flints, seed for the first crop, a kettle or two (very precious), a frying pan, blankets, and a very small ration of food, generally Indian corn, to fall back on in the infrequent days when neither fish nor game was readily available.

Ask students the following questions:

1. When is the story taking place? (If students don't have the necessary background, then you

can assist by giving them choices—the 1700's, modern times, the future— and asking how they know.)

2. List four cues that locate the story in time.

3. In what country do you think the story is set?

4. Circle the cues that helped you determine place.

Doing a couple of these with students can be very helpful, particularly if the excerpts build conceptual as well as procedural knowledge that is related to the ongoing inquiry.

Using Two-Sided Stories/Recasting

Another idea we've had fun with is what we call "two-sided stories" or "recasting" stories, for example, from one time period to another.

Using the excerpt from "Ann Story" on the previous page, we could ask students to describe the site the father is looking for and then describe it again ten years later when the family is there—for example: "Laura hauled up a bucket of water from the deep well her father had dug. She scanned the horizon line for her father and brothers, who were hoeing the far field, where last year they had cleared logs from the forest to use for their new home. Wood smoke poured from the chimney where her mother was cooking a hearty lunch of venison and succotash."

Examining the Social/Psychological Dimension

How do different features of setting cause, shape, and intensify psychological effects and other human responses? One idea for exploring this is to present students with an extract from a story where a character is faced with a very direct challenge based on the setting—for example, Will Hobbs's *Downriver* or Gary Paulsen's *Hatchet*, or a nonfiction piece like an excerpt from *Into the Wild* or *Into Thin Air* by Jon Krakauer, or Suzanne Fisher Staples's books about girls growing up in Pakistan and India (*Shabanu: Daughter of the Wind*, *Haveli*, and *Shiva's Fire*)

Then you could ask questions like these: How would the story be different if the setting were a more supportive or peaceful place, in a different location, or in a different time period? What if there were just slightly different features of the setting? How might the character or characters behave differently in this changed setting? How might the results differ? Exploring these questions offers an opportunity for drama work or another kind of "two-sided story" or "recasting."

USING A "MOODY" WORDS ACTIVITY

One of Jeff's student teachers, Ruth Anna Spooner, came up with the following assignment to help students attend to the cues that create the psychological dimensions of setting:

"His Last Bow" by Sir Arthur Conan Doyle

It was nine o'clock at night upon the second of August—the most terrible August in the history of the world. One might have thought already that God's curse hung heavy over a degenerate world, for there was an awesome hush and a feeling of vague expectancy in the sultry and stagnant air. The sun had long set, but one blood-red gash like an open wound lay low in the distant west. Above, the stars were shining brightly, and below, the lights of the shipping glimmered in the bay.

1. Circle all of the sensory details you see in the paragraph.

2. Choose three or four details/phrases that you think are the most interesting or descriptive, and list them here.

Sensory Details/"Moody" Words →	Resulting Emotion/Mood

3. What is the mood you think the author wants you to feel as you read this? (Answer with THREE words or fewer.)

4. Based on the clues here about the mood and setting, what do you anticipate the rest of the story will be like? What might happen next? How might it end? (1–2 sentences)

After students fill out the chart they can then label the moody words for the level of setting they imply (e.g., "the sultry and stagnant air" cues the microculture while "the most terrible August in the history of the world" cues the macroculture with the threat of war between countries. After doing short exercises like this, students could be asked to perform a similar analysis on a description of setting from their own free reading, or they could go on a search-and-find mission, bringing results back to class for comparison and contrast.

CASTING STUDENTS AS ETHNOGRAPHERS

An important aspect of the social/psychological dimension is the kind of interactions that can occur in a given setting. This can be impacted by the culture and cultural constraints of the setting, the rituals and routines of the setting, the values and ways of doing things that are salient in that setting, competing values and perspectives that are at play in the setting, and so forth. In other words, the various levels of micro-, meso-, and macroculture can be at play in this regard in any setting.

Students can be asked to play the role of ethnographers, going through their day listing the different settings they find themselves in, the kinds of interactions that seem to occur in each setting, the possibilities and constraints put on action and interaction in each setting. They could then be asked to visit an unfamiliar setting like a religious service of another faith, or an ethnic grocery store, a pool hall or bowling alley, and to record the interactions and how they seem to be shaped by that setting. Here's an assignment (pages 101–102) inspired by the work of Hubbard and Power (1993) that you could use. Once students have completed such an assignment on a particular place, they could play ethnographers about a place they are reading about, such as 1930s Maycomb, Alabama, as they read *To Kill a Mockingbird*.

Why It's Worth It

We hope you are convinced that setting—in both human contexts and in literary texts—is very nuanced and powerful. Spending time understanding setting has many benefits to students as readers of literature and as writers and composers of various genres. Understanding setting deeply will enable students to be wide-awake researchers into the power of setting in reading and writing, in their own lives and those of others, helping them to be more democratic citizens and lead more cognizant and, possibly, fulfilling lives. These are goals well worth going after.

"Hanging Around"
Ethnography Assignment

YOUR JOB: Observe a place in the school or elsewhere that students frequent. (You can also observe a place in the community that is frequented by a group that you are unfamiliar with, such as a grocery store, church of a different faith, etc.) Your job is to try to understand the importance of the place to the students, to see how the place works to fulfill that importance, and to learn about students from their behavior in this place.

You should observe the place (cafeteria, ball field, mall, etc.) for an extended period of time (45 minutes or so), or for several shorter segments of time, as your schedule allows. You may do this with a partner if you wish.

Content: What is THE story?

1. You need to find a story, maybe even *the* story, about the place you are observing. Ask yourself the following question, as you consider your observations, read your notes, and plan your next visit:

   Where is the story?
   Now, a story involves a tension; this tension could be a dramatic conflict, a problem (overt, evolving, or hidden), or an unactualized possibility. This is where ethnographic studies always start to roll: when a tension is discovered.

      So, try to identify the major character or characters. What parts do they play? What struggles and purposes are involved? Where's the energy in this place? How is this shaped by the setting—the physical, temporal, and psychological dimensions—the possibilities for interaction. Is it with the customers? Between the customers and waitresses? Between different players' purposes? Move from the exterior tensions to the interior tensions that might occur in this particular environment.

Content: What needs to be included in the story?

2. Now you need to tell about the story of this setting in a way that should describe the scene, physical features, time, psychology, events and possibilities, actors, and interactions. How does the context affect the interactions and experiences? Do it in such a way that your audience will feel they understand both the experience of being in this place and the major underlying story of being there.

Is there anything more you need to know to tell your story? What is it? How can you find out?

····➔

Format: How do you want to tell your story?

3. You may tell your story as a straight narrative, but I encourage you to experiment. If you choose to write a narrative of the report, limit yourself to four single-spaced pages maximum, please, with a detailed map.

Go for It! Creative Formats:

If you choose a creative storytelling mode, please make sure you have met the content criteria and use your best judgments. Your classroom presentation should take 4–5 minutes if you do it on your own; 5–8 minutes if you do it with a partner.

You could mix a narrative with poetry, song, posters, pictures, drawings, graphics, or artifacts from the scene. Or you could do the report completely in poetry, pictures, or song. Other options are a museum exhibit, a video documentary, an exposé, a newspaper article. You could also perform skits or a tableau drama.

What is the best way for you to communicate your story to your audience? And by the way—have fun!

CHAPTER SEVEN

Putting Theory Into Practice:
Teaching Setting With Particular Units and Texts

To make the most of the kinds of instruction on understanding setting that we shared in the last chapter, this instruction should be embedded into units that make immediate and obvious use of the knowledge that students are in the process of developing. This meaningful context of instruction is the setting that lends purpose, promotes motivation, provides assistance, co-produces knowledge, *and* offers a place for applying what is learned and for receiving feedback about how deep the understanding is. As you can see, activity theory, situated cognition, and the whole tradition of socio-cultural psychology argue for the necessity of teaching in meaningful contexts such as inquiry units.

Creating a Context That Fosters Attention to Setting

As we explained in our chapters on character, in our own teaching and in our work with other teachers, we have found that framing instruction with essential questions is powerful for achieving goals like those outlined above and for changing the dynamic of the classroom from being teacher-centered and information-driven to being community-centered and problem-oriented. Organizing curriculum as inquiry around essential questions means that we can get many related and complementary things done around one central project. This makes the most of your time and reinforces the most important concepts and procedures since things that go together are now being taught together in synergistic ways. Inquiry makes the most of time and energy through its focus. Inquiry allows you to get many things done through an extended examination of one issue.

A good inquiry unit will fit very nicely to meet many various standards and curricular goals (Wilhelm, 2007). Here are some that foreground and reward an understanding of setting and context as they meet many other standards and goals:

- How does culture shape who we are? (Jeff has done this one in language arts and in combined language arts-social studies classes.)
- What do we need to know if we are going to live in a German/Spanish/Middle Eastern/ Native American culture? (great in foreign language classes, social studies classes, etc.)

One of the ways we have proposed to generate a good essential question is to reframe a standard (Smith and Wilhelm, 2006; Wilhelm, 2007). The NCTE/IRA national standards and the literature and reading standards in many states require that we highlight both the diversity and the universality of human experience.

So, let's say you are reading *Catherine Called Birdy* by Karen Cushman, which could be used in either social studies or language arts classes. You could reframe the diversity and universality standard into an essential question such as this:

- To what extent does your time and place dictate what you can do?

Or, reading *Catherine Called Birdy* could be made part of a larger inquiry about identity and context, framed by questions like these:

- How do our values reflect our time and place?
- Who are you, and how has era and place influenced your identity?

Let's say that you are studying *The Great Gatsby* as a central text, or Ann Moody's *Coming of Age in Mississippi* or M.T. Anderson's young adult novel *Feed*, or his Octavian Nothing books, or some other text where time, place, and situation are enablers or barriers to achieving one's dreams. The essential question could include a deep consideration of these factors of setting by asking:

- To what extent is the American dream accessible to all?

Once you start noodling around with including a consideration of setting into an inquiry, then you see that any inquiry can easily be given a dimension of setting. For example, here are some essential questions we have used on several occasions:

- What is a hero?

- What makes a hero?

Now, all you have to do is add a dimension to this question, or just add a sub-question to it that focuses on setting, such as "How do conceptions of heroism change over time—or place, culture, or situation?"

Jeff regularly teaches a unit on the essential question "Who will survive?" Several of the sub-questions that came up in his most recent teaching of this unit addressed literary conventions we are discussing here:

- What is necessary for survival in this setting?
- What personal characteristics and perspectives are necessary to survival?

Kindergarten teacher Angela Housley, a participant in Jeff's Boise State Writing Project, is currently pursuing an inquiry into "What is meant by 'a sense of place'?" with these sub-questions:

- What makes a neighborhood?
- What makes a good neighborhood?

Other possibilities could be: *What makes a home? What makes a school/good school? What makes a town/region/country one's own? Why do we divide settings/create borders where we do? What are the limits of an ecosystem?*

In Malcolm Gladwell's book *Outliers* (2008), he takes several looks at how context and culture shape human behavior and achievement. In fact, his essential question could be framed this way: *What is it in culture and context that explains human behavior and achievement?* Along the way he pursues many sub-questions: *Why do planes with pilots from particular cultures suffer more accidents? What explains excellence in hockey? What explains the family feuds in Appalachia? Why do some cultures achieve more highly in subjects like science and math?*

Gladwell makes a powerful case that any pattern of human behavior and achievement can be explained, and in fact can only be explained, by looking at contextual factors—many of which are amenable to revision, which leads to sub-questions such as these: *How can we improve airline safety by attending to contextual and cultural features? How can we produce more great hockey players by attending to how we identify and train those with potential? How can we fight patterns of feuding by attending to changes in context—or can we? How can we change educational settings to foster improvement in math and science?*

Such questions could work in a variety of subjects from language arts to social studies, to civics, math, and science. If you are teaching or including art in your classes, you could ask:

- How does place play out in art/impressionist art/realistic art?
- How are artists (in general or from a particular tradition like Impressionism) inspired by "a sense of place"?

- How do artists represent a sense of place in different styles of art? And in different eras? And what does this reflect about their vision of the world, of man's proper relationship to nature and other settings?

Using Graphic Organizers

Another way to focus students' attention on setting is to use a graphic organizer like the one below, which helps students focus on the various levels and dimensions of setting that they learned about in the prereading activities.

Dimensions of Setting	Description of Aspect	Impact on Character/Conflict	Level of Setting That's Most Important
Physical			
Temporal			
Social/ Psychological			

If students fill out this kind of graphic organizer as they are reading, they'll be prepared to discuss such questions as the following:

- Which dimensions were most prominently used and explored in the setting?
- How did these dimensions affect the characters and their actions?
- How did these dimensions affect the suspense and tension, the conflict and consequences?
- In what ways do you think that the dimensions of setting were effectively used? Not so effectively used?
- If you wanted to do a different version of the same story, what aspect of the setting might you change? If you changed that aspect, what other changes would have to occur?

Putting on Critical Lenses

Although we spent a good deal of time in Chapter Five talking about the importance of different levels of setting, we have a confession to make: We both tend to focus on the micro-level. As we've done this work on setting, we've become increasingly aware that we often miss much of great importance and that we need to help ourselves and our students attend more to the meso- and macro-levels of setting.

For instance, we typically think about teaching in terms of our own classrooms. We tend to home in on the micro. But sometimes in our work we find ourselves in meetings with policy people or literary theorists. It is often jarring to us how they think almost entirely at the macro-level. So, at a recent meeting Jeff attended about testing policy and how to reform it, a policy professor held forth about the political climate in the country and state, about the political beliefs in the legislature and how these are reflected on school boards, about the economy and financial situation—everything he talked about was part of larger systems. And it became clear to Jeff that if he wants to work for reforms in how his students are tested, he is going to have to attend to issues at this macro-level of his state's and the country's politics.

Likewise, Michael has noted that when he talks with a literary theorist, such as a feminist or Marxist critic, they also think about the big systems at the macro-level. They talk about the hegemony of patriarchy and its history and how this is implicitly endorsed by institutions, or about the power structure of bureaucracies and how difficult these are to define and overcome. This has reinforced to Michael that if he wants to help students see how settings affect characters and their beliefs and actions, he'll have to do more to focus their attention on issues in the macrosystem.

These exchanges have brought us to an awareness, sometimes quite surprising in how it reorients perspective, that our readings—of our classrooms, our lives, and of literature—are limited if one aspect of setting is attended to at the expense of others.

To turn to literature, if you do only a macro-level reading of setting in *Heart of Darkness*, you may miss the people and their suffering as you consider the effects of imperialism and colonialism and capitalism. But if you do focus on the characters and their suffering by doing a micro-level reading, then you may well overlook the influence of imperialism and its consequences. If so, then you are once again missing something vitally important about the text, its message, and about the world. We'd argue that for a rich reading of this text you must consider how the various levels interact.

In our experience, we aren't alone in our focus on the micro-level of setting. Perhaps the most powerful tool for correcting this tendency is to use critical theories in our teaching. Our friend and colleague Deborah Appleman has helped us to think about how to do this through her work in schools and in her wonderfully smart and practical text *Critical Encounters in High School English* (2009).

Deborah uses the metaphor of "lenses" to argue that we need to give our students new ways of seeing the world. Various critical theories (also known as literary theories) can provide just such lenses.

Here's an idea from her book that we especially like. Put on the Marxist lens (we sometimes call this the "power lens") and rank the characters in a text from most to least powerful. Then explain how you know that power is wielded according to this ranking. Now explain why the power is situated where it is. In reading *The Great Gatsby*, we would suddenly be tuned in to issues at the meso-level (New York City and the East Coast culture of the 1920s) and macro-level (how inherited versus earned wealth, status, relationship network, East Coast versus Midwest, and so on, play into power structures).

Likewise, you could put on the feminist lens and ask students to do a ranking from those who have the most "voice" to those who are most "voiceless." Who is heard and who is not? Students will be shocked to see that the women in *Gatsby* are all at the bottom. Why is this? What comment is being made? How happy are we with this situation? Any insights that have been achieved can be applied to the inquiry question "To what extent is the American dream accessible to all?"

The reader response lens, which seems to hold sway in many progressive classrooms, seems to us to focus on the micro-level of the readers' concerns vis á vis the concerns of characters. Deborah points out that different lenses can be worn simultaneously, so that the reader response lens (focusing on the micro) can be worn at the same time as one of the more political or cultural macro-lenses. However, as Deborah also points out, reader response lenses can include the macro if there are larger situational issues shaping the reader's response. But students may very well need assistance in perceiving and articulating these forces, and activities like the ranking described on pages 78–79 can help them.

We strongly recommend that anyone interested in the idea of critical lenses take a look at Deborah's book. She has a wealth of ideas and activities to make critical lenses accessible to all students.

Using Excerpts From the Studied Piece of Literature

As we've seen throughout our work on setting, the various levels and dimensions always work together in some way. So it's good to put them all together during the reading of a text so that students can consolidate and apply the understandings they have gained and use the heuristics they have developed.

To that end, you can focus on different short excerpts from what you are reading to infer all the dimensions of setting and their effects. Here is an excerpt from *Grace Flandrau* that Jeff has used in his "Who will survive?" unit:

> Calm, he must be calm, he must wait, there was still time. He must not scream or beat his
> head in blackness against the cold, stone walls of the cell. He lay with a pain across his

throat so tight he could not breathe. His hands clutching the railing of his cot could not be loosed. If only he could count the strokes when the clock struck. Last time—had it not been three or four?

Four—and then it would be five. No, no, they could not do it to him. After all, Don Fernando had promised. No matter what happens, he had said, you will be released. What you do is for the cause. We cannot do it, but you can, so we will protect you.

He had not known that he would do it, but there had been the warlike music in the square, the sudden lift and sweet, high blare of bugles when the doors above flung open and the little men appeared, sun flashing on swords, on gold crosses pinned for bravery on fine uniforms, over the hearts of traitors. At their head was the one he waited for, crushing the flowers they flung before him, tramping on lives and freedom. He put him in the crosshairs and felt taller, wider than the world.

The clock from the church struck again—Don Fernando, you must know that it is scheduled today at dawn!

To focus students' attention on setting, Jeff then had students work together on the following questions:

Physical Dimension

- Where is the main character? How do you know?
- Why is he in there?
- What is the larger setting as far as locality and country? What is the political situation? How do you know? (influence of macro- and meso-levels)

Temporal Dimension

- What is the era of the scene, and how do you know?
- What is the duration of this scene? Of the story the narrator tells? How do you know?

Human Dimension

- What was the psychological feeling when he was ready to act?
- As the clock continues to strike, what is the psychological feeling/human dimension of the excerpt?
- What accounts for the change in the character's feeling, and what does this communicate to us?
- What can we infer about Don Fernando's feelings and motivation? Why was he motivated to act in this particular way in this particular setting?

Placing Characters in New Contexts

In our work on characters, we discussed how placing characters in new contexts requires students to really know the characters. Lots of movies use the conceit of having a character travel back or forward in time. You could do something similar with the characters about whom you are reading by asking students to do in-role writing as though they were the character encountering a specific situation in the past or future or even to try a new setting in the present. Then students would share their writing, discussing both how the character would be affected by the new setting and how the character would change the nature of the setting.

Conclusion

Throughout this book we have argued that teachers must work intensively with students to deeply understand and be able to use and carry forward what is most important. We agree with researchers from every discipline, including those from cognitive science and education, that context is essential to an understanding of any human activity or achievement, both in reading and in our lives. Setting is therefore essential not only to any understanding, but also to future action and how we can choose settings or manipulate them to avoid problems and achieve success.

To do this kind of intensive work, we must go through a process of apprenticing students to deep understanding and application. This process involves modeling the work *for* them, then doing work *with* them—that is, mentoring and guiding them to develop the wide-awake meta-cognitive strategies of expert readers and thinkers; and then having them do work by themselves, in small groups and individually, so we can monitor their growth and intervene as needed to continue to assist them. This kind of deep teaching will help students to uncover understandings and develop lifelong procedures, rather than to merely cover curriculum as sets of information. We need to focus on doing more by doing less, that is, doing what we do in more depth (rather than more often) so that students gain understanding they can apply in novel situations. We believe that truly understanding setting will lead students to develop a wide repertoire of conceptual and procedural tools of immediate use to them now and in the future as readers and writers and navigators of their personal lives.

Pondering Point of View

On the day we began drafting this chapter (October 6, 2008), two stories about health insurance were on the front page of the *Philadelphia Inquirer*. One had this headline: "Rendell pushes care for the uninsured" and this second-tier header: "Looking for last-minute compromise, the governor cut back on his original plan." The other had this headline: "A caregiver is denied medical care" and this second-tier header: "The cruel irony of her life is that she cheerfully gives others what she needs—and cannot afford."

Pretty different approaches to news stories on the same issue. Let's explore for a minute just how different. What do we take from the first pair of headlines? Well, it seems that the story is going to be authoritative. Imagine that the main headline instead read, "Governor pushes care for the uninsured." Using the title seems to be a bit more deferential. The second-tier header provides an unequivocal statement of the governor's motive for scaling back his plan. The headline promises a summary of the changes in the plan, an accurate analysis of why they were made, and an analysis of the likelihood that a compromise can be reached.

The second set of headlines is much different. By repeating "care" in the main headline, the writer makes the headline almost poetic. "Is denied" has more impact than do the verbs used in the headlines in the first story. The second-tier header labels the situation as a "cruel irony." This writer seems much more emotionally involved than the writer of the first pair of headlines. The second-tier header of this story uses a dash to enhance the drama of the situation. Dashes call attention to themselves the way most other punctuation does not. We expect this second story to be more artfully constructed and less simply reported than the first one.

We could go on. And we haven't even gotten to the stories themselves yet! But we hope that we've illustrated two key points: The way a story is told—its point of view—is crucially important, and the traditional vocabulary that we have for examining how stories are told just isn't enough. Let's examine each of these two points in turn.

We manifest our understanding of the importance of point of view in myriad ways almost every day. Each of us is the father of two daughters, and over the years we figure we've said something like "I can't decide until I've heard your sister's side of the story" maybe a million times. We choose the TV news we watch because of the perspective its reporters and commentators take on the issues of the day. As we're writing this, it's campaign season, so we're assailed by political ads. We nod at some and shake our heads at others, but we're always aware that we can't simply accept what we're told. We have to understand just who's doing the telling and how they are doing it. When we read the newspaper, we know that columns, stories, features, and editorials are all different, largely because of the relationship the writer establishes with the subject and the audience.

Both in literary studies and in life, we call the way a story is told the writer's (or speaker's) point of view. And in both literature and in life, point of view is crucially important. Scholes and Kellogg go so far as to say that point of view controls "the reader's impression of everything else" (quoted in Lanser, 1981, p. 12)

Unfortunately, as a profession we have an impoverished vocabulary for talking about something so important. If you look at any literature anthology, you'll see that point of view is discussed primarily in terms of whether it's first person or third person. Third-person point of view receives another division into third-person limited and third-person omniscient. Unfortunately, those distinctions just aren't enough to do any interesting work. Let's return to our news stories for an illustration. Both are written in third person. Both are, we guess, limited, as are all tellings of true stories. Yet the stories take radically different perspective on their subjects.

Wayne Booth's *The Rhetoric of Fiction* (1983) is one of the classic critical examinations of narrative technique. In it he explains the insufficiency of the traditional labels we use: "To say that a story is told in the first or third person will tell us nothing of importance unless we become more precise and describe how the particular qualities of the narrators relate to specific effects" (p. 150). Lanser (1981) concurs. She argues that conceptions of point of view that focus on what she calls the technical "angle of vision" ignore the more significant questions of "distance, tone, and attitude" (p. 12). It appears that the traditional vocabulary we have for understanding point of view is not what we need. In this section of the book we'll explore what students need in order to understand point of view and offer some suggestions for helping them get it.

How Literary Narratives Are Told

We started this chapter by sharing the headlines of two news stories in order to provide a quick illustration of the importance of point of view. But, of course, literary narratives are different from other kinds of texts. When we read a news story, we can determine who is telling the story simply by looking at the byline. But knowing who the author of a narrative is doesn't mean we know who will be telling the story, for one of the most significant artistic decisions an author makes is the mode of narration. Lanser (1981) provides an extremely useful analysis for how to consider the nature of that decision.

The analysis is complex. We don't want to belabor the details, but we think that her scheme is worth exploring in some depth. She argues that there are three key factors to consider in evaluating any speaker's relationship to the message being sent: status, contact, and stance. By status she means "the authority, competence, and credibility which the communicator is conventionally and personally allowed" (p. 86). By contact she means the relationship a speaker or writer establishes with the audience. By stance, she means the relationship a speaker has with the message, the "ideological and psychological attitudes toward a given 'content'" (p. 93).

STATUS

Lanser points out that when we determine the authority or status of a narrator, we do so by making a variety of considerations. We believe that the four most important of these considerations are reflected in the following continua:

Equal to author	Separated from author
Uninvolved	Fully involved
Omniscient	Humanly limited
Completely reliable	Totally unreliable

Let's look a bit more carefully at each.

The first paragraph of Tim O'Brien's "Where Have You Gone, Charming Billy[1]?" gives some sense of the complexity of the first continuum. Here are the first two sentences: "One by one, like sheep in a dream, they passed through the hedgerow, crossed quietly over a meadow and came down to the rice paddy. There they stopped." At the beginning of the story the narrator appears similar to the author.[2] The simile, after all, is something an author would write. And the simple report that

---

[1] We used the version of the story found in McDougall Littell's The Language of Literature series.

[2] Booth argues that readers construct the author of a text as they read it. That is, readers imagine the kind of person who would have written the text in the way it was written. He calls that construction the *implied author*. Although we are persuaded by Booth's argument, we don't want to introduce more technical vocabulary than we need to, so we'll stick to the term our students are already familiar with.

"they stopped" indicates an angle of vision somehow above the scene, something like a camera maybe, that's simply recording the scene. The paragraph continues describing the action of the soldiers. After three sentences, this sentence appears: "Except for the sounds of their breathing, the 26 men were very quiet: some excited by the adventure, some of them afraid, some of them exhausted from the long night march, some of them looking forward to reaching the sea, where they would be safe." Is this sentence from the same perspective as the first two? It seems that the direct characterization of the narrator is something an author might do. But that last judgment—who's saying they will be safe when they reach the sea? That idea is repeated five more times through the course of the story:

> "In the morning, when they reached the sea, it would be better."
>
> "Once they reached the sea, things would be better.'"
>
> "And when they reached the sea, he would dig a deep hole in the sand and he would sleep like the high clouds and he would not be afraid anymore."
>
> "In the morning when they reached the sea, he would begin to make friends with some of the soldiers."
>
> "He would do better once he reached the sea, he thought, still smiling a little."

It seems to us that the author progressively distances himself from the judgment about what will happen when the soldiers reach the sea. And so, as a consequence, we're not surprised when the story closes: "But even when he smelled salt and heard the sea, he could not stop being afraid."

We're not trying to offer an in-depth interpretation of the story, but rather to illustrate a key point: Determining the distance of the author from the narrator is important and complex, and that distance may vary from one point in the story to the next.

Even relatively simple texts can manifest the complexity of determining the distance between author and narrator. Here are the first two paragraphs of Gordon Korman's *Why Did the Underwear Cross the Road*:

> Oh, no!
>
> Justin Zeckendorf slumped so low in his seat that his head banged on the desk. Mr. Carter was picking groups of three again. And Justin knew what that meant. He was going to get stuck with Margaret Zachary and Jessica Zander. It always worked out that way. They were the only three Z's in the fourth grade. (p. 1)

The "Oh, no!" clearly comes from Justin's perspective. It seems that a narrator who's very closely aligned with the author is telling us that Mr. Carter is picking groups again. That narrator tells us that Justin knew what that meant, tagging the next sentence as coming from Justin's perspective, so we see the phrase "get stuck with" as Justin's judgment. But who's saying that things "always worked out that way"? The perspective of that sentence is much less clear. The traditional vocabulary we have doesn't help us make that important determination; all of the sentences, despite their differences, would have to be described as third-person omniscient.

A similar complexity exists for *dramatized narrators*—that is, those narrators who are named as characters distinct from the author. On the surface it might seem that an author may be deliberately distancing himself or herself whenever he or she creates a distinct character to be the narrator. We know from the start of *The Adventures of Huckleberry Finn*, for example, that Twain doesn't want to be equated with Huck: "You don't know about me without you have read a book by the name of *The Adventures of Tom Sawyer*, but that ain't no matter." But what about Fitzgerald and Nick Carraway? Here's how *The Great Gatsby* starts: "In my younger and more vulnerable years my father gave me some advice that I've been turning over in my mind ever since. 'Whenever you feel like criticizing anyone,' he told me, 'just remember that all people in this world haven't had the advantages that you have.'" How does Fitzgerald regard Nick's father's advice? Once again our traditional vocabulary fails us. *Gatsby* and *Huck Finn* are both told from the first-person point of view, but the relationship of the author to those narrators might be very different.

The language of the narrator provides some insight into the extent to which the author might want to be identified with the narrator. The more a character's speech differs from what we might expect the author's to be, the more distance an author would seem to be establishing. (For example, Nick is more aligned with Fitzgerald than Huck is with Twain.)

But there are other clues besides language. Sometimes an author establishes distance right from the title, as Truman Capote does in the story "My Side of the Matter." The title lets us know that the narrator will be offering his particular perspective on something that's contested. Another way an author can signal distance from a narrator is to have the narrator make an obvious error. Booth (1974) cites the beginning of Twain's "Baker's Bluejay Yarn" as an example: "Animals talk to each other, of course. There can be no question about that . . ." Another way to establish distance is inconsistency in a narrator's reports or judgments. If, say, a narrator describes a character in glowing terms at one point of a story and then disparages that same character for no apparent reason later in the story, the author is signaling that the narrator's judgments are not those of the author. Finally, whenever the speaker espouses a belief that the author could not possibly endorse, we perceive irony. This is the clue that most clearly informs Swift's "A Modest Proposal," for example.

The second continuum considers the extent to which the narrator is involved in the story world. Some narrators are relatively objective and uninvolved in the particular story. Consider, for example, the first sentence of Willa Cather's "The Sentimentality of William Tavener": "It takes a strong woman to make any sort of success of living in the West and Hester undoubtedly was that." The judgment made in this sentence is not marked by any clear emotional investment. Some narrators are fully involved; Huck, for example, is both the main character and the narrator. Nick isn't the main character of *Gatsby*, but he is a participant, one who, it could be argued, becomes more and more involved as the story unfolds. A story could also be told from the perspective of a minor character or an uninvolved eyewitness.

Understanding the involvement of the narrator is crucial. On the one hand, a fully involved narrator might be suspect because of his or her self-interest in how that involvement is characterized. On the other hand, an uninvolved narrator might not have access to critically important elements of the story, such as, for example, the emotional response that involved characters have to the story's events.

The third continuum is perhaps the most conventional—at least, it makes use of conventional terminology. Some narrators are omniscient, meaning they know everything about everything. Dramatized narrators, however, who are fully involved in the story, are limited in the way we all are when we think about the events of our lives. We can only see what our involvement in a situation allows us to see. We can't know for sure what others are experiencing. We might not even know for sure what we are experiencing.

Interestingly, in both cases a reader has to recognize both what is being told and what isn't. Just because a narrator is omniscient doesn't mean that the narrator shares everything he or she knows. In fact, if an omniscient narrator shared everything, stories would get so bogged down in detail that they would be unreadable. When a character tells us a story, we have to be alert for what the character can really know. We know that it's our job to put together what the narrator can't really know—for example, what other characters might be thinking or feeling. When we read a story told by an omniscient narrator, we have to recognize what that narrator chooses not to tell us. It's often our job to fill in those blanks as well.

Evaluating the extent to which a narrator is omniscient involves determining both the narrator's spatial and temporal relationship to the events of the story. As we noted in our discussion of "Charming Billy," a bird's-eye view allows one to see things that couldn't be seen from the vantage point of the soldiers. The chestnut "Hindsight is 20-20" establishes that *when* a story is told has an effect on the extent to which the telling is limited. We know that we have better access to our feelings when we report an experience immediately, but we have better understanding of the consequences of our actions *after* the fact.

The most important continuum is the last one. Booth (1983) explains:

> For practical criticism probably the most important of these kinds of distance is that between the fallible or unreliable narrator and the implied author who carries the reader with [the author] in judging the narrator. If the reason for discussing point of view is to find out how it relates to literary effects, then surely the moral and intellectual qualities of the narrator are more important to our judgment than whether [the narrator] is referred to as "I" or "he," or whether

[the narrator] is privileged or limited. If [the narrator] is discovered to be untrustworthy, then the total effect of the work [the narrator] relays to us is transformed. (p. 158)

As we've written elsewhere (Smith & Wilhelm, 2006), we tend to judge the reliability of a narrator by considering at least the following:

1. Is the narrator too self-interested to be reliable?
2. Is the narrator sufficiently experienced to be reliable?
3. Is the narrator sufficiently knowledgeable to be reliable?
4. Is the narrator sufficiently moral to be reliable?
5. Is the narrator sufficiently emotionally balanced to be reliable?

Lanser (1981) adds social identity—the narrator's gender, race, or class, for example—as another factor that might affect the narrator's reliability. Women's judgments, she argues, have historically been less highly regarded by the society at large than have men's. Of course, just because a narrator is unreliable in some regards doesn't make that narrator entirely unreliable. When we read *The Catcher in the Rye*, for example, we may question Holden Caulfield's assessment of Mr. Spencer and accept his assessment of Stradlater just pages later. Even unreliable narrators provide some information which is to be accepted as not under dispute, and this must be differentiated from that which is under dispute.

CONTACT

Have you ever been in a situation where someone tells an offensive joke expecting you to laugh? In such a case, the joke teller is implicating you in the offensiveness. He or she is implying that you share his or her values.

Narrators develop relationships with their audience just as joke tellers do. According to Lanser, that's the second critical factor in evaluating a narrator: the narrator's relationship with the audience. Lanser discusses how narrators are more or less self-conscious about their story-telling and more or less confident in what they share. What seems most important about a reader's experience of a text, however, is the narrator's attitude toward the audience. Lanser argues that that relationship could be plotted on the following continuum:

_____

Respect   Contempt

She points out that relative equality, the mid-point, is the norm. But departures from that norm are noteworthy. Michael's experience with *The Catcher in the Rye* provides a useful illustration. When he first read it as a junior in high school, he imagined a relative equality. That is, it seemed to him that Holden trusted that Michael shared his sensibilities. Rereading the book for his book club some 35 years later, Michael saw in the opening sentences a kind of contempt:

If you really want to hear about it, the first thing you'll probably want to know is where I was born, and what my lousy childhood was like, and how my parents were occupied and all before they had me, and all that David Copperfield kind of crap, but I don't feel like going into it, if you want to know the truth.

In this recent reading, it seemed to Michael that Holden is setting up an adversarial kind of relationship with his audience, at least with those who would want to know more about Holden than the four days the novel chronicles.

In contrast, the narrator of David Yoo's story "Heartbeat" shares personal information with the audience right from the start: "My nickname's 'Heartbeat' because my friends swear that you can actually see the pulse on my bare chest." The audience may not be among the narrator's friends, but in sharing such an intimate detail, the narrator is cultivating a much more respectful relationship.

STANCE

The final factor that Lanser discusses is stance, the narrator's attitude toward the content of the narrative. Much of her discussion in this regard is closely related to the status of the narrator, but two additional continua seem to us to provide important new information:

Clear attitude	Hidden attitude

Approval	Disapproval

Lanser illustrates the first continuum by drawing on the work of Roger Fowler, a linguist and literary theorist. She contrasts three sentences: "William was mugged," "William got himself mugged," and "William was stupid enough to go out alone at night in the worst part of town, and so it's his own fault that he was mugged." The first sentence is a simple report. It's impossible to know the speaker's attitude toward the mugging. The second sentence makes that attitude clearer. The speaker seems to be placing the blame on William. The third sentence is unequivocal in its blame.

Literature works in much the same way. Here's the first sentence of Amy Tan's "Two Kinds": "My mother believed you could be anything you wanted to be in America." The narrator withholds her judgment on both her mother and America. In contrast, it's obvious from the beginning of de Maupassant's "The Necklace" that the story is being filtered through the ideological prism of the narrator: "She was one of those pretty and charming girls, born, as if by an accident of fate, into a family of clerks."

The second continuum under stance assesses whether the narrator approves or disapproves of the content being narrated. As we noted above, in the third sentence about William's being mugged, the narrator clearly shows disapproval of William. We don't have as clear a sense of the narrator's attitude toward the town, except that it does have better and worse sections.

Imagine this change: "William was mugged when he went to what had been a safe residential neighborhood before the town's disastrous new zoning laws were enacted." The attitude of the narrator is just as clear, but the focus of disapproval has shifted from William to the town. But a narrator's approval or disapproval isn't always so clear. Look again at the first sentence of "The Necklace." The sentence is marked by the narrator's ideology, but we can't be sure of the narrator's attitude. Are "pretty" and "charming" straightforward or ironic? As experienced readers, we realize that it's our job to find out. And when we write or tell a story, we have to decide how obvious we want to make our judgments.

What's a Reader to Do?

We don't want to over-complicate things. (Indeed, we have reduced Lanser's [1981] 33 scales to only seven.) As Jeff (2007) has argued, the unique power of literature resides in the fact that it does not directly tell you what it means; the reader must figure it out in ways analogous to solving a puzzle. But we do want to argue that the traditional vocabulary we provide students for understanding point of view just isn't complex enough. It is insufficient for solving the puzzle of how to understand perspective and how this impacts meaning both in literature and in life.

In the first place, as Booth and Lanser point out, the question of whether a story is told in first or third person doesn't get after the most critical issues at hand. What's key, they maintain, is that we have to sort out how closely the narrator is aligned with the author and how worthy of our trust the narrator is. In fact, applying traditional labels may even distort our understanding, as it suggests that the point of view of a story remains constant. But even if students were to use the scales that we've discussed above, they would still simply be labeling. Recognizing the point of view in operation at any given time in a story is just the start of the interpretive work we have to do. Let's think through what else is involved.

If we determine that something in a story gets told to us from a point of view that's closely aligned with the author, our job isn't done. We still need to think about what didn't or couldn't get told from that point of view. If something could have been told but wasn't, we realize that it's our job as readers to try to find out. For example, as we were working on this chapter, Michael was reading a number of books from John Harvey, a British writer of police procedurals. In *Gone to Ground*, Harvey describes what Helen Walker, one of the chief investigators of a grisly murder, does when she gets home after a day of investigation. Here's part of that description:

The CD had finished and, volume lowered, she set it to play again. In the mirror, hair unkempt and still wet, face free of makeup, she could reread all too clearly the lines around her eyes. Though she hadn't dialed the number in a long time, she still knew it by heart. She got as far as the final digit before stopping. (p. 33)

The narrator clearly could have told readers whose number it was, but the narrator chooses not to. We realize we need to be on the alert to find out.

Looking at a fairy tale can provide a quick illustration of what understanding the impact of point of view requires of readers. Here's the beginning of the version of "Cinderella" published by Reilly & Britton in 1908:

This is the story of a beautiful, motherless young girl whose father married, for the second time, a haughty and proud widow who had two daughters of her own, both vain and selfish.

No sooner was the wedding over than the wicked woman began to show herself in her true colors. She could not bear the good qualities of her pretty stepdaughter, all the more because they made her own daughters appear the less attractive. She made her wash dishes, scrub floors and wait on her own daughters. She gave her a straw bed in the garret to sleep upon, while her own daughters slept in fine rooms and upon soft beds.

We equate the narrator with the author and believe that Cinderella is beautiful, that her stepmother is haughty and proud, and that she mistreats Cinderella. But our belief doesn't mean that we can't wonder where Cinderella's father is in all of this. Our belief doesn't mean that we can't critique the story for equating beauty with goodness or diminutiveness with beauty. Indeed, it doesn't mean we can't critique the tale for offering the intervention of a man as the only way to solve a woman's problems. In other words, equating the narrator's and author's perspective does not mean that we must agree with that author's perspective.

What's true for fairy tales is also true for other literature. For example, the point of view of *To Kill a Mockingbird* seems to shift between the young Scout, who shares her experiences, and the mature Jean Louise, who is in more of a position to assess them. We see the judgments of the mature Jean Louise as being very much in line with those of the author as, for example, when she reports that Maycomb was "a tired old town when I first knew it."

However, even if we see the mature Jean Louise's judgments as closely aligned with Harper Lee's, we still can recognize the limitations of her perspective or disagree with it. For example, she shares myriad insights about the White townspeople but almost none about the African American townspeople. She seems accepting of the incremental progress toward racial equality exemplified by the fact that her father's efforts made the White jury who wrongfully convicted Tom Robinson, an African American, of rape stay out longer than it typically did in cases in which African Americans and Whites were in dispute. We're not so content with progress that's so slow. In short, as Michael has previously argued (Rabinowitz & Smith, 1998), once we've understood an author's perspective, we may choose to resist it. But whether we accept, adapt, or resist an author's perspective, we must first understand it.

If the narrator's perspective seems distant from the author's, we have another kind of work to do. Imagine this retelling of the beginning of "Cinderella":

> My daughters and I—so lucky, so lucky indeed. It's impossible for a woman to make her way in this world without the help of a man. Our world was upended when my husband died. A great and generous man he was. Not a day went by that he didn't bring a smile to my lips and laughter to our daughters.
>
> This new husband, a pale imitation. But he has property, and I have none. A woman, you see, can't hold property, so when my husband died his was given over to his brother. And we, my daughters and I, were given two weeks to leave. Little time to attract another man. But I did, and thank goodness.
>
> What a fool this new husband. Did he think two weeks would be enough time to make a place in my heart for another man? Does he see the tears that well in my eyes each day? No, he sees only my beauty and his empty bed, a bed that's been empty since his wife died. He doesn't even see his own daughter. I call her Cinderella.
>
> He didn't see her judgment when I entered the house. He doesn't see her reproach when I kindly ask her to do a chore. The household has grown. There are many chores to be done. You'd think that telling someone to scrub out the fireplace was somehow a sin. And how could I expect my daughters, grieving as they are, to do such a thing? The work will do his daughter good, spoiled as she's been. It will quiet the sparkle in her eye. It will dull her. And it must, for if he chooses ever to look at the girls, I'll not have him look down on my daughters. I'll not have him begrudge them what I've earned for them.

What to make of this story? Well, the narrator is dramatized. She's limited, as all dramatized narrators are. She doesn't see into her daughters' and Cinderella's minds. She does try to see into her husband's mind; we'll have to check her assessment. She's fully involved in the story, which means we need to be alert to see whether her self-interest undercuts her reliability. And that line about dulling Cinderella is pretty disturbing. Her attitude is clear. She disapproves of her husband. She sees his daughter as a rival. She excuses her own behavior. She seems to regard her audience as sympathetic, willing to accept the judgments that she makes.

How does the author want us to feel about what she tells us? In order to decide, we have to have something to go on. We're suspicious of her reliability, but that doesn't mean that we reject everything that she says. We believe that she's a widow. We believe that she was widowed for only two weeks.

We believe she lost her husband's property. We believe that she gave Cinderella chores and didn't give them to her daughters. Even when a narrator is highly unreliable, we have some facts that aren't under dispute. Those facts allow us, in Wayne Booth's (1974) words, to reconstruct the narrative. In this case we believe that the author wants us to see that even if she's justifiably bitter about her situation and society, she's wrong to take out her bitterness on her stepdaughter.

Okay, we realize it's easy to argue what the author wants readers to see when you are the author. But as we have explained elsewhere (Smith & Wilhelm, 2006), the process we went through to analyze this little story Michael wrote is one we should go through whenever we read.

We hope we've convinced you of just how important point of view is. Before we move on, let's review the demands that it places on us as readers:

- We have to be alert for the status of the narrator—that is, the extent to which the narrator is credible.
- We have to be alert for how the narrator regards us.
- If the narrator treats us as equals, we have to consider whether that's a club we want to be part of.
- If the narrator seems to look up to or down on us, we have to ask how we feel about that.
- We have to recognize when the narrator's judgments are explicit and when we have to infer them.
- If the author seems to want us to believe the narrator, then we have to ascertain just how we feel about the narrator's judgments; that is, we have to decide if we want to embrace or resist them.
- If the narrator isn't credible, we have to reconstruct the narrative, basing our reconstruction on what's not under dispute in the work and on our knowledge of the world.

In the next two chapters we'll share some lesson ideas to help your students understand and use tools for enacting these kinds of moves when considering point of view.

CHAPTER NINE

Putting Theory Into Practice:
Preparing Students to Understand Point of View

We hope that the last chapter convinced you that making inferences about point of view and its impact on the meaning of literary texts is a complex process, at least a more complex process than conventional terms suggest. The complexity of point of view means that it will take our students some time to get it. Indeed, as Jeff is fond of saying, every complex skill, from kissing to kayaking, takes time to master. The sequence we suggest for instruction and practice begins with an examination of dramatized first-person narrators. This is not only because dramatized narrators make the issues surrounding point of view manifest, but also because we want to build as short a bridge as possible between what students do in living their lives to what they do when they read. We want to move them with sequenced instruction from understandings that are "close to home" to those that are "further from home."

Dramatized Narrators

Understanding dramatized narrators—that is, narrators that are both clearly marked as characters in the stories they are telling and as different from the author—requires the same kind of thinking that kids do all the time as a matter of course in their daily lives. Think of the times when you've introduced a book and said, "You're going to really love this," only to hear a chorus of groans. Or of the times you've heard kids say, "He (or she) is full of it" (actually they might use a different rime) when talking about another kid or a teacher or a parent. In so doing they are commenting on reliability of a source of information, exactly what we want them to do when they read. But remember, if they are to transfer what they do in their lives to their reading, they have to be mindful of just what it is they are doing. The following initial activities are designed to help students develop that mindfulness.

USING DRAMA

One way to create the kind of mindfulness that we're looking for is to have students reflect on the tacit knowledge they employ in dramatic activities. We talked about using drama in teaching both character and setting, so we won't rehash the rationale here except to say that the following drama activities are designed to acquaint students with the first four point-of-view scales we discussed in the last chapter (equal to author/separated from author, uninvolved/fully involved, omniscient/humanly limited, completely reliable/totally unreliable).

Here's a dramatic frame for a two-person drama that should establish understanding of those four scales:

Role 1:

Imagine that you're Pat, a 14-year-old first-year student in a suburban high school. Your favorite band is coming to the city to play in a club. The place is "21 and over," but everyone tells you that the club's security lets in anyone who has a ticket, and those tickets can be bought online. The club has a great reputation for bringing in the best new music and the only trouble in recent years was the time that the crowd pushed down some barricades trying to get in, and one person fell and broke a leg. You and three friends would love to go. In fact, at lunch you told everyone at the table that the four of you were going to go. People were a bit surprised because you've never been to a club. The club is six blocks from the nearest train station. Those blocks get lots of foot-traffic during the day but not so much at night, though police cars are usually on the prowl. The concert starts at 9 and is scheduled to be over by 12, which would leave you 30 minutes to get to the station to take the last train home.

Role 2:

You're Chris, a single parent. You noticed in the paper that your son's/daughter's favorite band is coming to one of the most established clubs in the area. You went to concerts there when you were in high school. Back then they had Sunday concerts for the under-21 set, and you went to several of them, but you also snuck in twice to see bands that were special favorites. It was so convenient, just four blocks from the apartment where you lived. But things are different now. The city's crime rate is way up, and you remember hearing about some trouble at the club recently. You're afraid that your son/daughter is going to ask you to go. You don't want to fight, but you wouldn't be able to drive as you have to stay home with your other kid and you worry that your son/daughter isn't familiar enough with the city to get there safely. Plus, the last marking period, your son/daughter didn't get as good grades as usual. You've mentioned that the poorer grades will result in fewer privileges.

The Scene:

Pat (the child) has been at home taking care of his/her younger sibling as he/she always does, waiting eagerly for Chris (the parent) to come home. Pat knows that Chris likes some time after work to unwind but is worried that the tickets for the show will be sold out quickly. Chris enters the room with a sigh and starts leafing through the mail. Pat decides that there's no time like the present to ask Chris for permission to go to the concert and to buy tickets for Pat and his/her friends. They've promised to reimburse Pat. The first line is Pat's.

As we have mentioned previously, we believe that dramas that are short, scriptless, and simultaneous are especially effective. Therefore, we recommend passing out the roles sheets and pairing students up (or having them count off by twos after assigning the 1s to one role and the 2s to the other). As students are role-playing, you should circulate around the room. If a certain pair isn't working well, you can enter the drama in the role of the younger sibling or an adult friend of Chris's to help generate more discussion. (This technique is known as teacher-in-role [see Wilhelm, 2002].)

Once those dramas are complete, it's a good idea to do some debriefing by asking how many students received permission to go to the concert and how many did not. Students who played Pat (the child) should share what information they stressed and what information they left out. Students who played Chris (the parent) should then do the same.

After this debriefing, we suggest moving on to a related drama. We'd begin that drama by having all of the students who played the child stand up and count off by twos. The 1s are assigned to play the same role (Pat) while the 2s should play the role of one of the other kids who planned to go to the concert but who hasn't asked permission yet. Tell the 1s that the first line is theirs: "You can't believe what happened when I asked to go to the concert." Before students begin that drama, have all the students who played the role of the parent (Chris) stand up and count off by twos. The 1s should play the same role and the 2s should play the parent's best friend. Tell the 1s that the first line is theirs: "You know how I was dreading being asked about going to the concert? Well, it just happened." Once again, circulate as the dramas are playing out and enter as the "teacher-in-role" if you encounter any dramas that need assistance or complication. Your role will either be as one of the other kids who hoped to go to the concert or as another of the parent's friends.

Once all of the dramas are complete, we recommend extending the drama even further by putting students into groups of four and assigning each student one of the four roles that have just been dramatized. Each student should write a diary entry in which they talk about what happened. If students have difficulty with the writing, you can prompt them with one of these first lines:

"I can't believe what happened when I asked to go to the concert."

"Pat just told me what happened when he/she asked to go to the concert."

"No wonder I was dreading that conversation."

"Chris just called to talk about what happened when Pat asked to go to the concert."

After five minutes or so, the group members should read their entries to their small group. Each group should then do two things: first, identify what all of the stories have in common—that is, those things they are absolutely sure are true; and second, rank the diary entries from the one that provides the most undisputedly accurate description of what happened to the one that provides the most questionable one. To discuss their answers, we suggest putting a matrix up on the board and tallying how individuals ranked each entry. We suggest beginning with an entry about which there is some dispute and then asking students to explain their ranking. As students talk, note the criteria they apply and jot them down on the board under the heading "What makes a storyteller reliable?" For example, someone who ranked the parent's friend's diary as the most accurate description might say something like, "Well, the friend isn't involved." Another might say "Grown-ups forget what it's like to be a kid." After these comments you could write "Involvement?"

The discussion should heighten students' attention to some of the key issues authors and readers face when they are thinking about point of view. The differences among the diary entries should establish that the point of view has an enormous impact on what's being told because of the reliability of the writer and the limits to what each character can know. The rankings should help students realize that a character's involvement in the story is a critical factor in that impact, and also help them see that authors can choose narrators who are more or less distant from them, and from the central issues and emotions described in the story.

USING SIMULATED TEXTS

With that preparation, students should be ready to consider the question of reliability in greater depth. As we have written, both earlier in this book and elsewhere (Smith & Wilhelm, 2006), simulated texts are a great teaching tool because they can provide repeated practice in applying particular reading strategies much more efficiently than can actual texts. They can be written to provide what is known as a "concentrated sample" of the cues you are working on. In the following activity (pages 128–133) students are asked to think about the reliability of a number of dramatized narrators and to begin to apply the interpretive procedures that experienced readers apply when they consider stories told by unreliable narrators. We recommend asking students to work in small groups to collaborate on it.

Once the groups have completed their discussion, it's a good idea to discuss their interpretations. In that discussion, the key is to highlight why the groups came to the judgments they did. It's not important that everyone agree on the reliability of the narrators, though we suspect that most groups will agree that the narrators in monologues 1, 4, 5, and 6 aren't reliable. Students will see that the jealousy of the first narrator, the oddness of the fourth, the immorality of the fifth, and the inexperience of the sixth make them suspect. The narrators in 2 and 3 are problematic. The narrator in 2 is speaking from his or her own self-interest, but that narrator's hard work and his/her hesitance to blame the math teacher make that narrator seem more reasonable. If students believe that the math teacher really "went off" on the narrator, they're likely to join the narrator in seeing Mr. Smith as the culprit. The narrator in 3 is just an observer of the situation, but the facts that he shares seem to support his view of his friend John. Some students will argue that John is suspect because of the way he spends his weekends, but others will see his dedication to others as a point in his favor.

Again, it's not important that everyone agree. In fact, if all of the monologues were too obvious, they'd lose much of their effectiveness. What is important is that students become aware of the criteria they apply in assessing reliability and how they go about determining the truth of a situation when they suspect that a narrator isn't reliable.

In the same way, it's not important that everyone agrees on how clear the narrator's attitude is. Some students may see a grudging respect for Mr. Smith in 2; others won't. Some students will see an undercurrent of worry in 6; others won't. What is important is that students come away from their work realizing that they have to determine as best they can what the narrator's attitude is and then assess both how the author feels and how they feel about that attitude.

Another way to help students recognize how they assess the reliability of narrators is to have different narrators talk about similar situations. The activity on page 134 is a version of an activity that Michael developed for Hampton-Brown Edge, an anthology series developed for striving and ELL readers. Each monologue features an adolescent narrator talking about a disagreement with one or both of his/her parents.

After students have done the rankings, we recommend putting a matrix like the one we discussed in Chapter 3 on the board to tally the votes. Once again, it doesn't matter whether students agree. What does matter is that they can explain why they made the judgments they did and how they proceeded to craft an interpretation of the situation if they judged a narrator to be unreliable.

Rating Reliability

Please read each of the following little stories carefully and then discuss the questions following each story with your group.

1. Man, that Joe is such a loser. Just because he's the star of the football team, he goes around like he's the big shot and friends with everyone. He'll talk to anyone, even first-year students and the band geeks. But I know he's just doing it so people will like him. And when he won that award but wouldn't accept it unless the whole team was also recognized, I mean c'mon, who does that? The people I hang with usually hate jocks, but they say this guy is different. Sell-outs.

What is the narrator's attitude toward Joe? Rate it on the following two scales:

_____

Clear attitude   Hidden attitude

_____

Approval   Disapproval

Is Joe a loser? Place the narrator on the reliability scale:

_____

Completely reliable   Totally unreliable

If you think the narrator is reliable, explain what makes him/her reliable. If you think the narrator is unreliable, what makes him/her unreliable?

What in the monologue are you sure is true?

If you don't accept the narrator's interpretation of the situation, what's yours?

----→

2. Mr. Smith is so unreasonable. Music's a big thing at this school. He had to know that the spring choral concert was scheduled Thursday, Friday, and Saturday of the first week of March. It's always that week, has been for years. So what does he go and do? He schedules a major exam on Friday with study sessions after school on Wednesday and Thursday. We have dress rehearsal Wednesday after school, and all the kids in the chorus will be getting ready for our performance on Thursday. And it's not like I'm the only one. Seven other kids in the class are in chorus. I thought I could go to him and ask him to put off the test. I thought maybe he'd listen to me. I have one of the best grades in the class. Not that that makes me special, but he has to know that I care about his class. I really work hard at it. I've been to every study session so far. That's the only way I can even pass because his exams are so hard. I've never liked math, but I understand why it's important and I don't resent putting in all the extra work. When I asked him to delay the test, he just went off on me. He said something like, "So now Mr. Bigshot Director thinks he can send one of his students to tell me music is more important than math. Ridiculous." I tried to tell him that the reason I was hoping he could delay the test is because I thought math was important and I wanted to spend the time on it that it deserved. He laughed in my face. I couldn't believe it.

What is the narrator's attitude toward Mr. Smith? Rate it on the following two scales:

_____

Clear attitude   Hidden attitude

_____

Approval   Disapproval

Is Mr. Smith unreasonable? Place the narrator on the reliability scale:

_____

Completely reliable   Totally unreliable

If you think the narrator is reliable, explain what makes him/her reliable. If you think the narrator is unreliable, what makes him/her unreliable?

What in the monologue are you sure is true?

If you don't accept the narrator's interpretation of the situation, what's yours?

---→

3. John sure has had tough luck with women. First his wife leaves him for one of her co-workers. My wife and I spent lots of time with them, and neither of us saw it coming. In fact, they had just come back from a long vacation. Smiles were everywhere in the vacation photographs. But I guess no one can really know what's going on in somebody else's relationship. It took two years to get him to even consider going out again. And after a few false starts, he really seemed to find someone great. Joanne is smart and funny. I thought it was weird that they never went out on the weekend, but John didn't seem to mind. He sees his Little Brother—you know, the Big Brother/Big Sister deal—on Saturdays. His Little Brother usually has soccer or baseball or something during the day, so John takes him out to dinner. On Sundays he usually spends time with his mother or goes to some kind of sporting event. So I guess Joanne's schedule suited him. So what happens? He's at the game last week and runs into Joanne, who's with her four-year-old kid. She only sees the kid on weekends because she has a high-powered job and keeps late hours. But she never even told John about the boy, and they've been out about 10 times. Of course, John didn't mind. He loves kids, which is why he's doing the Big Brother thing. So after they run into each other, she calls him up and says, "Look, I need to keep my son separate from the other parts of my life. It gets too complicated otherwise." Then she drops the bombshell and says "So now that you know about him, I can't see you anymore." Cold. John is devastated. He told me that he would have been happy to become part of the boy's life or to stay away if that's what Joanne wanted. He's crushed. I bet it'll be another two years before he goes out with someone else. It's so sad. He's such a good guy. If I had a sister, he's just the kind of person I'd want for her.

What is the narrator's attitude toward John? Rate it on the following two scales:

Clear attitude	Hidden attitude

Approval	Disapproval

Has John had tough luck with women? Place the narrator on the reliability scale:

Completely reliable	Totally unreliable

If you think the narrator is reliable, explain what makes him/her reliable. If you think the narrator is unreliable, what makes him/her unreliable?

What in the monologue are you sure is true?

If you don't accept the narrator's interpretation of the situation, what's yours?

---→

4. I have to admit, I'm baffled by Gloria's behavior. She refuses to go out on a second date with me. I'm willing to go out again and I'm the one who had to put up with all of the bad stuff on the first date. In the first place, she made me wait three minutes from the time I arrived at her house until the time she was ready to leave. I just hate being late and I had calculated exactly how long it would take us to get to the restaurant on time for our reservation. Instead we arrive 45 seconds late. I was humiliated. Good thing I built some extra time into the schedule or it would have been worse. And then when we split the check she calculated her portion by adding 15% to the cost of her food. Everyone knows that sales tax is 6% so she should have added 21%. And I didn't even complain about how long it took her to get the difference out of her purse. You'd think she would be happy to find someone so considerate.

What is the narrator's attitude toward Gloria? Rate it on the following two scales:

_____

Clear attitude   Hidden attitude

_____

Approval   Disapproval

Is the narrator considerate? Place the narrator on the reliability scale:

_____

Completely reliable   Totally unreliable

If you think the narrator is reliable, explain what makes him/her reliable. If you think the narrator is unreliable, what makes him/her unreliable?

What in the monologue are you sure is true?

If you don't accept the narrator's interpretation of the situation, what's yours?

5. In tough times like these, the only way to get ahead is to do whatever it takes. That's why I'm such a great asset to the company. My job is government relations. I take care of government officials to make sure that they don't get in the way of what the company wants to do. So I reach out to those officials whenever the company is making new plans. And when I reach out, I always have some money in my hand, if you know what I mean. My strategy always worked when the old mayor was in office, except that one time when I had to put money together with some photos that the mayor didn't want his wife to see. But things are changing. The new mayor ran on a platform of cleaning up corruption. All of the people she brought in with her have the reputation of being do-gooders. I've talked with people who have worked with the new mayor, and they say she's serious about it. All that means to me is that I'm going to have to up the ante. Everyone has a price. We have a big expansion coming up and we need the support of the mayor's office. So money is no object. But I'm going to have to do some creative bookkeeping to get the money I need. People at the company think all I do is persuade officials that our plans will benefit the city. Yeah, right. None of them know that the office equipment I put in for really went to bribes. But this is going to cost more. I may have to use the money I get under the table from the contractor I promised the construction bid to. But it'll be worth it. An investment in the future.

What is the narrator's attitude toward himself? Rate it on the following two scales:

Clear attitude   Hidden attitude

Approval   Disapproval

Is the narrator an asset to the company? Place the narrator on the reliability scale:

Completely reliable   Totally unreliable

If you think the narrator is reliable, explain what makes him/her reliable. If you think the narrator is unreliable, what makes him/her unreliable?

What in the monologue are you sure is true?

If you don't accept the narrator's interpretation of the situation, what's yours?

--->

6. My dad is the best dad ever. I mean, how many fathers quit their jobs just so they can be their kid's little league coach? My dad says he knows that selling the house and moving to an apartment will be hard on Mom and my two sisters, but he's willing to make the sacrifice because he thinks I'm going to be great some day. Even though I'm the smallest kid in our league, I'm one of the best. At least that's what Dad says. And he doesn't trust anyone else to coach me. He even got into a fight when I made the traveling team and the league asked someone else to coach that team. They said something about pressure and that he should remember we're only 11. But my dad says this is the age when the great ones start. That's another reason we moved. He doesn't want me hanging around with losers who just play the game and don't take it seriously. Me and my dad take it seriously, though. We work at least three hours a day on my hitting, even when I'm sick. Even in the off season. I used to play soccer and I like that, too, but my dad says he wants me to be dedicated. He never played soccer because after all, it's not even an American game. I miss it sometimes, mostly because I could see my friends when we played. Nobody else practices all the time like me. But I'll have a leg up on them next season, that's for sure. At least that's what Dad says.

What is the narrator's attitude toward his dad? Rate it on the following two scales:

_____

Clear attitude   Hidden attitude

_____

Approval   Disapproval

Is the narrator's dad the best dad ever? Place the narrator on the reliability scale:

_____

Completely reliable   Totally unreliable

If you think the narrator is reliable, explain what makes him/her reliable. If you think the narrator is unreliable, what makes him/her unreliable?

What in the monologue are you sure is true?

If you don't accept the narrator's interpretation of the situation, what's yours?

Evaluating Narrators

Rank the narrators of each of the following monologues from the one you think is most reliable (1) to the one you think is least reliable (4). Be prepared to explain not only your rankings but also what the truth of each situation is.

_____1. Oh my God. I can't believe that they'd ground me for that. Who do they think they are, anyway? They're SO unfair. So what if I took a little something from my mother's purse. She would have given it to me anyway. I just didn't feel like asking.

_____ 2. Man, my mom must have really been tired last night. I'll admit that my room was a little messy, but she just went ballistic when she saw my papers spread out on the floor. I don't know why she got so upset—maybe it was the jet lag. I understand that traveling's hard on her. But she should know I always get my papers picked up before school starts. I just like to spread out to do my homework.

_____ 3. I'm worried about Mom and Dad. They seem to be fighting all the time. Mom was crying when Dad came home late last night. I heard a little of the blow-up. Something about, "Can't a guy work late to try to catch up?" and then, "You're trying to catch something all right." Dad has been working a lot lately, but he told me not to worry, that things would be all right in the end. I wasn't sure what he meant but I didn't ask. He looked so sad. Something must be bothering him at work. I tried to talk to Mom this morning about what happened last night, but she told me to keep my ears to myself. And then she hugged me and started crying. I'm sure things will be back to normal once Dad catches up at work.

_____ 4. I'm so stressed and things at home aren't making it any easier for me. Chores, chores, chores, that's all I have. All I hear is, "Take your dishes to the sink. Take out the garbage. Bring down your laundry so I can do it." All that for a measly $20 a week allowance. And then every night they ask me whether I've done my homework. My parents are so unreasonable—it's a miracle I haven't had a breakdown.

USING STUDENTS' WRITING

As we argued in Chapter 1, we believe that casting students as writers is an enormously powerful way to help them understand what they need to do as readers. A great follow-up to the work with the simulated texts we just presented is to have students write a monologue themselves. They can choose whether to create a reliable or unreliable narrator. We recommend having students read their monologues to each other, either in a whole-class read-around or after dividing the class into two or three big groups. After each reading, the students should assess the narrator's reliability and discuss the clues that led them to their assessment.

Fred Hamel (Hamel & Smith, 1998, pp. 364–366) shares the wonderful range of writing his lower-track eleventh grade students did after working with a similar set of simulated texts. One student wrote: "It was a dark and stormy night when I was unjustly accused of hitting someone with my car. I vaguely remember that night. . . ." The narrator goes on to provide what Hamel calls an "exacting" alibi. The contradiction clearly marks the narrator as unreliable. Another student begins her monologue this way: "I am sitting here chatting on the phone with one of my close friends. He is only a friend, and nothing else. In fact, he's like a brother to me. I know for a fact that I don't like him any more than that!" Students found it easy to see that the narrator's protestations belied her true feelings.

Another way to have students use their writing to help them better understand their reading is to have them retell familiar stories from a different perspective. Most students will be familiar with Jon Scieszka's *The True Story of the 3 Little Pigs*, so you can use that as a model after reading it to the class first to refresh their memories. Having students rewrite fairy tales and fables from the perspective of one of the characters (as we did to "Cinderella" on page 121) will help students see how the teller affects the tale.

It's especially effective to have groups of students write multiple versions of the same tale. Let's take "Cinderella" as an example. Students could rewrite "Cinderella" from the perspective of the stepmother, either of the stepsisters, Cinderella, Cinderella's father, the prince, or the fairy godmother. Creating multiple versions of the same story provides a clear demonstration of the impact that different dramatized narrators have on a story.

Creating multiple versions of the same story can also help students recognize two other dimensions to point of view: the relative distance of the narrator from the author and the relationship of the narrator to the audience. Before the groups compose their monologues, we recommend having them place the narrators on these two continua:

Equal to author	Separated from author

Respect for audience	Contempt for audience

What matters is that they come to understand how those dimensions affect the way a story is told and received and that they are mindful about what they do as readers so that they can transfer that understanding to new reading situations.

After receiving prereading instruction similar to what we've described so far, Hakeem Oliver, a Philadelphia seventh grader, wrote the suggestion at right to be included in the *Good Readers Handbook* his class was writing for the fourth graders at their school.

USING POPULAR CULTURAL MATERIAL

Popular cultural material also provides fertile ground to help students understand the impact of point of view.

Films and Television Shows

A number of films present stories told from multiple perspectives. Cinemagora (http://www.cinemagora.co.uk/tag-7347-multiple-perspectives.html) provides the following list of the best multiple-perspective movies as voted on by

Figure 9.1: How to Be a Point of View Detective

visitors to the site: 1. *Rashomon* 2. *Elephant* 3. *I'm Not There* 4. *Eve's Bayou* 5. *Hoodwinked* 6. *Basic* 7. *One Night at McCool's* 8. *Vantage Point*. We're not suggesting showing these films in class, as showing a complete film takes so much class time (and some of these movies are quite disturbing), but you could ask students to view them outside class, depending on the age of the students. (*Rashoman* is unrated. *Hoodwinked* is PG, and *Vantage Point* is PG 13. The rest are R-rated.) We suggest having students track the perspectives that the movie presents, analyze how those perspectives compare to one another, identify what they're sure of and what they feel is open for interpretation, and then think about what they see as the truth of the situation. They could discuss their findings in "movie clubs" (Wilhelm, 2004), especially if they're used to working in literature circles.

An even more effective way to move from the known to the new is to tap students' knowledge of television shows. This is easy to do by showing an episode of a sitcom and having students tell the story from the perspectives of different characters, once again asking them to place the characters on

tive is closest to that of Matt Groening, the show's creator, and does that change within or across episodes? Asking students to assess how Groening and the show's writers feel about the judgments the characters make is crucial to understanding the targets of the satire. Students could discuss when Bart and Homer are the targets of satire and when their criticisms of the established order are shared by the show's creator and writers. Some students will see Lisa's and Marge's perspectives as being less distant; others will take the opposite view. As always, it doesn't matter what position students take on the question. What is important is that they see they have to determine the distance and reliability of narrators, that they recognize how they make similar determinations as a matter of course in their out-of-school lives, and that they begin to develop conscious control over just how they make those determinations.

Music

Yet another way to help students develop an understanding of the importance of determining the reliability of a narrator is to turn to music. In our study of the literate lives of young men both in and out of school, we found that music, albeit different kinds of music, was without question the most universally held passion. And many songs feature dramatized narrators. You might remember the furor in the 1970's surrounding Randy Newman's "Short People," which was taken at face value by a surprising number of people instead of as an ironic monologue.

Other speakers are more problematic. Our classes used to debate whether Sting's "Every Breath You Take" was a sympathetic look at a jilted lover or a warning from a dangerous stalker. Bruce Springsteen has written many monologues (we used to use an early one, "Meeting Across the River," which could be compared to "Born in the USA" or the more recent "Working on a Dream," both of which have dramatized narrators). If you take a careful listen to some of your favorite songs, you'll be sure to find a number that may have dramatized narrators, both reliable and unreliable. Most of our students didn't share our musical tastes, so it's important to bring in music that they may enjoy more and be more familiar with. To that end, asking the class whether the misogyny of "'97 Bonnie and Clyde" is Eminem's or his dramatized speaker's should foster some interesting conversation.

But you don't have to be an expert on contemporary music (we're not, much to the dismay of our daughters) in order to include music as part of the study of point of view. Because it's hard to keep up with the current musical scene, we recommend tapping your students' expertise. You could simply ask students to bring in the lyrics of two songs, one that they're pretty sure is from the perspective of the singer/band and one that they're pretty sure isn't. Students could share their lyrics in groups of four or five, and then each group could share one example of each type with the class. You'll need to set up some guidelines for appropriateness, but it will be well worth the effort to show how the work you're doing in the study of literature matters in students' lives outside school.

doing in the study of literature matters in students' lives outside school.

Before we move on to talk about teaching narrators who aren't dramatized, we'd like to take a minute to look back over the activities we've shared thus far. If you had a class of 24 students and did all of the activities we presented above, it might take six or seven 45-minute periods. During that time students would be very actively reading, writing, and reflecting on both content and strategies. They would be getting repeated practice on a focused set of strategies that make up a heuristic for understanding point of view. They would grapple with at least 30 dramatized narrators, which would provide more focused and repeated practice than they would otherwise be likely to get during their entire middle school or high school career. (Remember Jeff's mantra: Complex skills take time and repetition to learn.) And as Haskell (2000) emphasizes, students need lots of practice if they're to transfer what they've learned to new situations. But the research base shows that students rarely get enough practice to allow them to learn a strategy deeply enough that they can transfer and use it. The instruction that we've just sketched out provides the kind of practice that students need, as Michael's research (Smith, 1989, 1992) has borne out.

Narrators Who Are Not Dramatized

Understanding the impact of narrators who aren't dramatized is often more difficult than understanding the impact of dramatized narrators, for the narrative perspective can shift more quickly and with less notice.

USING SIMULATED TEXTS

Once again, simulated texts are a very efficient way to help students recognize the variety of effects that third-person point of view can achieve. Here's a version of another activity Michael developed for Hampton-Brown's anthology series, Edge (Moore, Short, Smith, & Tatum, 2007).

Retelling a Familiar Tale

Authors can tell stories in many ways. One way to think about how the way a story is told affects the story and its meaning is to look at three different versions of a familiar story.

Version 1

Humpty Dumpty sat on a wall.
Humpty Dumpty had a great fall
All the king's horses
And all the king's men,
Couldn't put Humpty together again.

Version 2

Humpty Dumpty sat on a wall, his thoughts racing. "You old fool. What's an egg like you doing on a wall in the first place? You always have to be the one to take a risk. You always have to be the one who defies the rules. You always have to be the one who pretends that being fragile as an egg is no big deal."

Humpty surveyed the landscape. He saw the king's men, sitting on their horses, waiting. Waiting for what? "For you to take a risk that will really get you scrambled, that's what," Humpty thought. He sighed. He asked himself whether the view was worth it, and as he looked at the fields below him, he told himself "Yes." Then the wind started to blow. He wondered what the king's men would think if he just climbed down. "I'll never give them the satisfaction," he muttered.

But soon climbing down wasn't an option. Humpty felt himself tipping, then falling. As he fell, he thought that it hadn't been a bad life at all. At least not for an egg.

Version 3

Humpty Dumpty sat on a wall, his thoughts racing. "You old fool. What's an egg like you doing on a wall in the first place? You always have to be the one to take a risk. You always have to be the one who defies the rules. You always have to be the one who pretends that being fragile as an egg is no big deal."

Humpty wasn't the only one whose mind was racing. For many of the king's men, the Humpty Dumpty detail was no big deal. They had seen splattered eggs before. They made jokes about past efforts to reassemble cracked eggs. But for Joshua Jones, this was the first time. He was nervous. And queasy. He thought about all of the training he had received, all of the wonderfully modern techniques that his teachers had taught for fixing cracked eggs. They convinced him that it was possible, at least in theory. But he knew that the classroom and the kingdom were very different places. He might be called upon to put what he learned into practice. He might be the one to finally succeed in putting an egg back together. And if he did, well, then his name would be celebrated throughout the world. He'd be as famous as the Dumpty family themselves.

---→

Joshua looked up. He saw Humpty teeter and then fall. His heart went out to the great egg. "He must be so frightened. He must be so disappointed to have it end this way."

The splatter echoed throughout the kingdom. People rushed out of their houses to see what had made such a great noise. They saw the broken egg and were filled with concern. They heard the clattering of hooves as the king's men raced to repair Humpty. Joshua was among them. His queasiness was over. As he raced to the egg, he was certain. He would be the one. He would be the one.

But alas, the king's men couldn't repair the great egg. The damage was too great. Joshua saw the determination on the other men's faces. He saw the care they gave to their efforts. He himself rushed to the front to try some of the techniques he had learned. But nothing worked. The king's horses and king's men stood defeated. They couldn't put Humpty back together.

Thinking about all three stories, rank the following statements from the one you're surest is true (1) to the one that you're least sure is true (8).

_____ Humpty Dumpty sat on a wall.

_____ The view was worth the risks.

_____ The king's men exercised great care as they tried to put Humpty back together.

_____ Humpty was frightened as he sat on the wall.

_____ Joshua had learned wonderfully modern techniques for putting eggs back together.

_____ People who rushed out were full of concern.

_____ The Dumpty family was famous.

_____ Humpty's life hadn't been a bad one.

In order for students to do this ranking, they have to determine from whose perspective they received the information. After the class discusses their rankings, it would be a great time to introduce the terms _third-person omniscient_ and _third-person limited_. Contrasting the different versions of the nursery rhyme should help students recognize that having an omniscient narrator doesn't mean that readers are directly told everything that is important to know. It should also help them understand that they have to assess the information they receive from the third-person limited perspective just as they do when they assess first-person narrations.

Another set of simulated texts can heighten students' awareness of how the point of view might shift from one part of a story to the next. We suggest having students work on this activity independently before sharing their responses.

Checking Out Changing Perspectives

Imagine that each item is the first paragraph of a story. Your job as a reader is to figure out from whose perspective you're getting information. Rate each sentence as to whether it represents the author's perspective or is distant from it.

1. (a) Jake had always been among the youngest kids in his grade. (b) That had never been much of a problem. (c) He remembered back to first grade when he was the shortest kid in the class. (d) But he was also one of the fastest, so he still got picked for playground games of soccer. (e) But being fast didn't matter now. (f) Now all that mattered was who was sixteen. (g) For at sixteen, you see, you could get a driver's license. (h) And getting a license was clearly the most important thing in the world.

a. _____

    Equal to author   Separated from author

b. _____

    Equal to author   Separated from author

c. _____

    Equal to author   Separated from author

d. _____

    Equal to author   Separated from author

e. _____

    Equal to author   Separated from author

f. _____

    Equal to author   Separated from author

g. _____

    Equal to author   Separated from author

h. _____

    Equal to author   Separated from author

2. (a) Jeffrey Whitmire had been teaching now for 30 years. (b) And for 30 years he'd been one of the best. (c) When he didn't win Teacher of the Year, he always finished close to the top. (d) He earned those awards, for he was more devoted than most, spending hours upon hours outside school planning lessons, responding to papers, writing letters of recommendation. (e) And more than that, he also attended soccer, football, and baseball games, choral concerts, and the like. (f) His dedication to school was rewarded by the affection of his stu

---→

dents. (g) Every year they came back to thank him. (h) It made all the sacrifices worth it, he thought. (i) One couldn't expect to have a marriage last—let alone prosper—when one was so dedicated to such important work.

a. _____

   Equal to author   Separated from author

b. _____

   Equal to author   Separated from author

c. _____

   Equal to author   Separated from author

d. _____

   Equal to author   Separated from author

e. _____

   Equal to author   Separated from author

f. _____

   Equal to author   Separated from author

g. _____

   Equal to author   Separated from author

h. _____

   Equal to author   Separated from author

i. _____

   Equal to author   Separated from author

3. (a) Has any party ever been so BORING? (b) Janice glanced around the room. (c) People scattered in groups of two or three around the edges of the room talking quietly—some weird techno music in the background. (d) No one would ever dance to that. (e) But suddenly things got more interesting. (f) Who's this? (g) Janice had never seen him before. (h) She would have remembered if she had. (i) He looked like a movie star. (j) He gave a quick glance around the room, and then his eyes settled on Janice. (k) She smiled and turned away to get a drink, but she felt his eyes still on her. (l) He started to walk over to her. (m) "Have we met? (n) You look so familiar." (o) And so beautiful, he thought. (p) But probably out of my league. (q) Just like all the people here.

a. _____

   Equal to author   Separated from author

⋯→

b. _____

   Equal to author   Separated from author

c. _____

   Equal to author   Separated from author

d. _____

   Equal to author   Separated from author

e. _____

   Equal to author   Separated from author

f. _____

   Equal to author   Separated from author

g. _____

   Equal to author   Separated from author

h. _____

   Equal to author   Separated from author

i. _____

   Equal to author   Separated from author

j. _____

   Equal to author   Separated from author

k. _____

   Equal to author   Separated from author

l. _____

   Equal to author   Separated from author

m. _____

   Equal to author   Separated from author

n. _____

   Equal to author   Separated from author

o. _____

   Equal to author   Separated from author

p. _____

   Equal to author   Separated from author

q. _____

   Equal to author   Separated from author

Many of these items are reasonably clear cut. Nevertheless, in the discussion it is important to encourage students to say how they knew which items were clear cut. Each little story does, however, have at least one sentence that could be problematic. Sentence (d) in story 1 seems to come from a perspective very close to the author's. But some students might see a change in tone in sentences (e) and (f) and consequently see those as being more from Jake's perspective. And who's making the judgment of sentence (i) in set 2 or of sentences (h) and (i) in set 3?

We recommend that students work in groups of four or five to discuss their ratings. If you give each group another copy of the activity, they'll be able to display the range of opinions about each of the sentences. It's important for groups to discuss both where they agree and disagree. The key is to establish that students have to pay careful attention to the narrative perspective and its shifts, and to have students see how they and their classmates do that.

USING STUDENTS' WRITING

You can also raise students' awareness of how authors manipulate point of view by having students recast stories told from a first-person point of view. One way to do so would be to have students rewrite one of the items from the Rating Reliability activity (pages 128–133). Here's a model you can share with them:

At precisely 7:30 Gloria's doorbell rang. "Who's that punctual?" she thought as she rushed to finish putting on her makeup. But she put her annoyance aside. Starting a date out annoyed doesn't do anyone any good. When she opened the door, she found Glenn, staring intently at his watch. He smiled quickly and said, "We'd better be going. It takes exactly 12 minutes to get to the restaurant and we don't want to be late."

They made it on time, at least what most people would think of as on time. But not Glenn. He couldn't stop apologizing for being late, no matter how many times the people at the restaurant assured him it was okay. "It's better to be safe than sorry," he said with a smile. "This is one of the most popular restaurants in the city."

Their meal went better. For all of his obsession with being on time, Glenn was, surprisingly, a great conversationalist. He seemed to know something about any topic Gloria introduced. By the time the check arrived, Gloria was feeling much better. When it did, she reached right for her purse. "How much is it?" she asked. After a just a quick glance, he told her it would be $43.75 plus tax and tip. Gloria reviewed her order in her head and found that he was right. She handed him a fifty. "Umm, you're $2.93 short," he said. He smiled but made no effort to leave. Gloria fumbled through her purse, getting madder by the minute. "Here," she said, handing him the three stray bills she found. "And here," he said handing her back a nickel and two pennies. "It's best to keep everything precise, don't you think?"

They rode back to Gloria's apartment in silence. The car had barely stopped when she ran out.

After students have done their writing, we recommend that they share their work in groups, first with the other students who rewrote the same item and then with students who rewrote different items. After the sharing is complete, the class can discuss the extent to which different versions of the same basic story resembled and differed from each other. Students can discuss how different perspectives can create different kinds of reading experiences. They can share how and why they changed the stories in the ways that they did.

With this preparation students will be well equipped to think critically about the point of view of the stories, poems, and novels you want them to read. In the next chapter we'll share some ideas for addressing the issue of point of view in your work with particular units and texts and, we hope, illustrate how those ideas will enrich students' reading.

CHAPTER TEN

Putting Theory Into Practice:
Teaching Point of View With Particular Units and Texts

A s we've argued throughout this book, we believe that designing inquiry units around essential questions is one of the most powerful tools we have available to us. Inquiry units make learning matter in the here and now because they allow students to use their reading to grapple with important questions. Embedding skill and strategy instruction in inquiry units allows us to prepare our students for their future reading, writing, and living, even as we're motivating them to engage in their current work. Doing so shows students why learning strategies is important—because applying the strategies allows readers to think about issues of real importance.

Devising Inquiry Units That Foster Attention to Point of View

A variety of essential questions provide easy opportunities for a focus on understanding point of view. One we're especially interested in is "To what extent can people really understand the experience of someone who differs from them in some fundamental way?" If the fundamental difference you wanted to consider was, say, physical disability, addressing this question would likely involve comparing and contrasting texts written from the perspective of a person with a physical disability both when the author himself or herself is also physically disabled and when he or she is not. It could also involve comparing and contrasting those texts both with texts about a physically disabled person from the perspective of an able-bodied observer and with texts that have third-person narrators of various sorts. You could take up this question in a similar way in terms of a whole range of fundamental differences: gender, generation, geography, linguistic background, race, social class, and on and on. This can lead to a consideration of a sub-issue such as "Who has the 'right to write' about disability (in this case)—or (in other cases) about race, gender, injustice, history—or any other topic you might be inquiring into?"

These inquiry units not only provide an opportunity to embed literacy instruction into a meaningful context but they also provide an opportunity to make significant interdisciplinary connections. Health classes might also take up the issue of disability. Social studies takes up the extent to which race, class, generation, and geography impact people's experience. Foreign language classes could consider the effect of ethnicity and linguistic background.

If we can help to incorporate literature into other content area classes as a unique and powerful way of knowing, or better yet, integrate instruction and content across curricular areas, we will have done a huge favor for ourselves and for our students. As David Perkins, the famous cognitive scientist from Harvard often argues, knowledge is a network, not a line; it is an interconnected web, not a set of disconnected ideas. By working to relate the study of literature to other curricular areas, we foster students' capacities to see how knowledge is patterned and how issues work across disciplines and curricular areas. In so doing, we give them a compelling reason to learn what we want to teach them.

Another essential question that would work well to motivate a careful consideration of point of view is "To what extent is the American Dream equally accessible to all people?" Determining why a character did or did not achieve his or her dream would require sorting through a wide range of perspectives. It could also provide an excellent opportunity to teach students to transfer this important literary strategy to nonfiction by comparing and contrasting the perspectives of a variety of literary texts with the perspectives of writers who take a historical or sociological perspective on the same issue. Doing so allows students to transfer what they have learned into new reading contexts and to consider the different kinds of work that different texts can do.

Other essential questions could also work to foster a careful attention to point of view. Any question that is controversial—controversy is a key element of essential questions—requires students to compare the perspectives of different authors and characters. Understanding point of view and engaging seriously in essential questions require students to do more than decide what they think. Students must also consider why they think what they think in relation to the other perspectives that they could take.

In fact, current conceptions of understanding (Nickerson, 1985) require that various perspectives on any issue be examined. A person who "understands," it is now argued, must know the various positions and ways of thinking about particular issues, and must know why she currently embraces a particular position and certain methods in contrast to the other possibilities. To know only one point of view or one method of solving a problem does not constitute understanding. This is true even in math. Inquiry approaches such as CGI (Cognitively Guided Instruction) engage students in the various ways of solving a particular problem, comparing and contrasting the efficiencies and inefficiencies of each, and of articulating why various methods work more effectively than others in different situations. Such an approach meets the "correspondence concept," since no mathematician thinks there is only one way to solve a particular problem. It also meets the standard of understanding, since various perspectives and methods are played out before an informed decision about how to proceed and what to think in a specific instance is made.

Our point about point of view is simply this: If students are to understand anything, they must understand the various perspectives in play around that issue or idea. The general takeaway: If we want our students to value the skills and strategies we teach them, we have to demonstrate that those skills and strategies help them do important and engaging work.

Drawing on Previous Work With Character

It's likely that you and your students will already have done some work analyzing narrators, especially dramatized narrators, through your work on character. Any of the stock-taking activities we shared in Chapter Four will help students assess the reliability of dramatized narrators. You can also use those activities to consider the relationship between authors and dramatized narrators by asking students to do the same work they did on characters to help them think about authors. Take, for example, the values-ranking activity. After students rank a narrator's most and least important values, they can do the same for the author, with discussion focused on how they made their determinations. When students determine a difference between what they perceive as a character's values and what they perceive as an author's values, they're establishing the necessity of reconstructing the narrator's understanding of the events of the narrative.

Point of View Tracking Sheets

Another issue that we've addressed throughout this book is the importance and difficulty of transfer. If we're mindful of teaching for transfer, then we have to do more than ask story-specific questions about how particular literary elements are working in particular stories. At the very least, we need to supplement these questions with heuristics that work across stories. One very easy way to do this with point of view is to segment the reading that students are doing and have them assess the point of view using the scales that we presented in Chapter 8:

Equal to author	Separated from author
Uninvolved	Fully involved
Omniscient	Humanly limited
Completely reliable	Totally unreliable
Respect for audience	Contempt for audience
Clear attitude	Hidden attitude
Approval	Disapproval

The work we discussed in the last chapter will have prepared students to employ the scales. Their repeated use will cement their importance, especially if students' responses on the same set of the scales change significantly as they are reading. As students repeatedly apply the same scales, they will internalize a heuristic for understanding point of view that they can use throughout their lives whenever they read literature or the news, view political advertisements, or even engage in discussion.

Transforming Texts

Another way to help students grapple with the point of view of particular texts is to have students transform them into new genres. More and more our profession is focusing on the importance of new literacies. Indeed the theme of NCTE's 2008 conference was "Shift Happens," the shift being an expanded understanding about what counts as literate activity. We've argued elsewhere (Smith & Wilhelm, 2002, 2006) about the importance of new literacies as subjects of instruction in their own right. Miller (2007) is among the many others who illustrate why they are important. She documents the transformative power of digital video composing.

Such composing could also be a bridge to the development of conventional literacies. We recommend asking students to recast stories told by dramatized narrators into videos that do not have voice-over narrations. When they do, they are, in essence, transforming a first-person narration into a limited third-person narration. In order to do so, they have to sort out the facts that are not under dispute from those that are. They have to decide how to cue their audience into what perspectives are closest to their own. The techniques they employ will give them insight into how other filmmakers and other authors accomplish the same goals. Creating a new text that tells the same story from a different point of view provides a powerful contrast that will allow the class to see the different challenges and effects of different aesthetic choices.

But digital video isn't the only way to achieve these powerful instructional outcomes. Comic books or storyboards would achieve much the same result. *Visual Tools for Differentiating Reading & Writing Instruction* (Essley, with Rief and Rocci, 2008) is an excellent resource for using storyboards with students in grades 3–8.

Using Drama

We've also talked at some length at various points about using drama as an instructional tool, so we won't belabor the point here. However, we do want to note that there are different kinds of drama strategies that are especially useful in focusing students' attention on point of view.

Asking students to do in-role writing from the perspective of characters who are not narrators and comparing and contrasting those versions of stories (or some set of incidents within a story) with the actual story illustrates the impact of point of view in much the same way creating multiple versions of fairy tales did. (See the prereading activities we discussed in Chapter Nine.)

These in-role writings, whether in the form of letters, diaries, op-ed pieces, or the like, can be shared with other students and responded to (e.g., with a return letter, a letter to the editor about the op-ed, etc.) with a different perspective from inside or outside the story. (It's often useful to have a character or author of a previous text in the inquiry unit respond, which gets at text-to-text connections.) The most powerful words, phrases, or lines for exhibiting perspective from this in-role writing can be circled. These can then be strung together to create choral montages (Wilhelm, 2002).

A choral montage can include competing voices and perspectives (e.g., those of the king's men and Humpty Dumpty, or Gatsby and Daisy and Tom from *The Great Gatsby*) or a poem can be created from a single perspective and then contrasted with another poem written from a competing point of view (e.g., a poem from Gatsby's perspective contrasted with one from Daisy's). We find that our students enjoy this kind of collaborative writing. They've already chosen the most powerful words and phrases for expressing perspective, and then they consider how to sequence and revise these to create a coherent short text expressing that perspective. It makes both perspective and the process of revision visible to them. We sometimes videotape the resulting performances. This activity often gets at expressions of theme, which we will explore in the next chapter.

Alter-ego or inner voice dramas (dramas in which a character tells a public version of a story and then the inner voice says what the character really thinks) provide a stark illustration of the fact that what narrators say is often not what they mean, nor what the authors mean.

Another way to illustrate that crucially important point is to have students dramatize authors. Have students cast the author of a story as the character's alter ego or play the author in a conversation with a character about an event or idea. Authors and characters can be "hotseated" and interviewed, separately with the same questions, or together in a kind of press conference or "Crossfire." Dramatizing the author as separate from the characters, especially when characters are narrators, forces students to consider carefully the issues of distance and reliability.

Conclusion

We believe that Scholes and Kellogg are right when they assert that point of view is critically important because it controls "the reader's impression of everything else" (quoted in Lanser, 1981, p. 12). As a result, we also believe that it's essential to teach point of view deeply. That means we have to teach students to evaluate the reliability of the narrator as they are reading and to provide alternative interpretations when narrators are unreliable. Those abilities can't be developed by learning definitions or by answering story-specific questions. But they can be developed by providing plenty of practice and plenty of opportunity to transfer what is learned to new reading situations. We hope these chapters give you what you need to provide that practice and those opportunities to your students.

CHAPTER ELEVEN

Thinking About Themes

Theme is the last topic of this book. Theme is where all the other literary elements come together to give a story's ultimate reward and fulfill its consummate purpose. When we see characters play out various values and perspectives in particular circumstances, when we see situations, perspectives, and values change, we see themes come to life. Remember back in Chapter Two, where we shared some of the literature that has been most meaningful to our lives? What Michael learned about teaching from Parson Adams in *Joseph Andrews* and what Jeff learned about parenting from the father in *Too Late the Phalarope* were thematic generalizations from those texts that they applied to their lives. Thematic generalizations provide the discovery, the understanding, the pleasure in recognizing, "Yes, that's the way it is" or "That's a powerful idea to consider" or "That's something I can use to navigate that kind of challenge in my life" or even "I profoundly disagree with that idea." Theme is the element that addresses the question "What does it all mean?"

As we'll explore in this chapter, one can read solely for information or simply to experience and enjoy story. However, the most powerful reading—the kind that can help us communicate with other perspectives and ideas we have never before encountered, the kind that can transform us and help us outgrow our current selves, the kind of reading that literature requires of us and most deeply rewards—is the kind of reading we want our students to do. That kind of reading, what we'll call point-driven reading or reading for thematic understandings, is what we will now pursue.

The Importance of Thematic Understandings

A few years ago, Jeff was listening to NPR and heard an interview with a cowboy poet and storyteller. The interview amused him and its message has stuck with him. The topic was what we should want out of life. The cowboy argued that Americans have it all wrong. We get faced with these important choices in our lives, and we apply the value of materialism to it. We think: What choice would bring me the most material gain, or the most power and prestige? He said that this attitude reminded him of the cheesy bumper sticker "Whoever dies with the most toys wins!" Well, this was all a bunch of cockamamie hooey to our cowboy poet. The bumper sticker should announce, he maintained, this thematic statement: "Whoever dies with the most stories wins!"

His contention was that whenever faced with a choice, we should consider the choice by applying this rule: What choice will give me the most interesting stories? If we did so, he maintained, we would choose adventure and challenge. Our choices would lead to a rich life of constantly outgrowing ourselves. We would have lives full of more excitement, but even more important, we would gain a rich reservoir of understandings we could use to navigate and subsequently enrich the rest of our lives. "Always go for the best stories; go for the life choices that will give you stories to tell and think with!" was the way he ended the interview.

This urge—to experience and then tell stories to make sense of that experience and of ourselves—seems to be at the essence of the human condition. Some anthropologists have proclaimed man to be the storytelling animal; there are brain researchers who find narrative to be the primary mode of mind. We know that we use stories to think through, think with, and reflect upon what speaks to us.

Jeff is a passionate Nordic ski racer, and he does cross-country marathons around the world. He has the goal of skiing all the races sponsored by Worldloppet, an international sports federation of cross-country skiing marathons. But really his motivation is tied up with storytelling. Whenever he goes to an event, he meets new people in a new place. He faces circumstances from the culture, the race course, and the conditions that are new and challenging to him. He doesn't have his usual support network. All this, and the act of marathoning itself, serves to put "my butt over the yawning gulf" as he likes to say—in other words, to challenge him in an exciting and sometimes unnerving way. The result of these extraordinary circumstances is going to be some kind of change, some development of values and thinking, and maybe even a story. The stories Jeff likes to tell about his skiing fall into success stories (when things went really well), disaster stories (the folly of using the wrong wax, broken ski poles, pile-ups, a leap into a ravine), and ironic or tragic-comic stories (with ambiguous results and combinations of success and failure).

Of course, not all stories need be so dramatic. When Michael works with teachers, he is constantly telling stories about the kids that he taught. They, too, may be tragic or comedic or ironic and may feature a yawning gulf (though it may be metaphoric). Michael's work in schools is marked by his telling stories and sharing what he learned from them. His work in schools is rewarded by his getting more stories to tell and to think with as he navigates subsequent challenges.

If stories didn't have this kind of pay-off, there would be much less reason to tell them. We want to learn how to repeat our successes, to avoid future disasters, and to prepare for and deal with new situations. Lukens (1995) puts it this way:

> [T]he Storyteller we especially value is someone whose stories awaken us to awareness of new meaning—of the inconsistency of people, or the mixed joys of family living, or the pain of social exclusion, for example. The storyteller is aware of meaning and has reached for idea, for theme. (p. 93)

Theme as Conversation

You'll notice that our discussion of theme has thus far focused on conversation and oral storytelling. We made that choice for a reason. Our understanding of theme is informed by what we do when we engage in conversation. But we're not talking about the kind of conversation we engage in with our wives when we're talking about our days or puzzling out our families' schedules. Rather we have a larger cultural conversation in mind, the kind of conversations Kenneth Burke (1941) describes in his famous parlor metaphor:

> Imagine you enter a parlor. You come late. When you arrive, others have long preceded you, and they are engaged in a heated discussion, a discussion too heated for them to pause and tell you exactly what it is about. In fact, the discussion had already begun long before any of them got there, so that no one present is qualified to retrace for you all the steps that had gone before. You listen for a while, until you decide that you have caught the tenor of the argument; then you put in your oar. Someone answers; you answer him; another comes to your defense; another aligns himself against you, to either the embarrassment or gratification of your opponent, depending upon the quality of your ally's assistance. However, the discussion is interminable. The hour grows late, and you must depart. And you do depart, with the discussion still vigorously in progress. (Word Works, 2009)

The notion of theme has a lot of near-synonyms: *aphorism, main idea, moral, central focus, gist*. But theme, we think, is richer and more complex than these other ideas (some of which we will use in our instructional sequence in the next chapter as steps toward getting at theme). Here's the point: What makes a theme more than an aphorism, a main idea, or a moral is that theme is a rich understanding, expressed through a crafted work of art but applicable to life beyond the work, and situated in an ongoing cultural conversation that tests and complicates it.

One of the reasons we gravitate to Burke's parlor metaphor is how well it jibes with the argument we've been making about structuring units around essential questions. Any essential question is about an ongoing disciplinary debate or cultural conversation. If it is not, it's not an essential question. And if it is not, then it cannot do the work of engaging students and of furthering more expert understandings from the disciplines and the world. What is learned cannot be applied and used. Recognizing how texts and data and knowledge are parts of a conversation helps us to avoid being too reductive in how we express themes.

Burke is not alone in recognizing how ongoing cultural conversations are generative. Polanyi (1979) has shown that the issues authors and narrators address are going to be culturally shared and culturally contested values and beliefs. These are the topics and themes that are available for debate and that are recognizable and accessible to readers. This is a point that Gee (1999) also makes about "discourse communities" and disciplines—which are kinds of micro-cultures. According to Gee, different themes are a focus of different cultures and subcultures.

If you see theme as an author's putting his or her oar into an ongoing cultural conversation, you'll recognize that even themes that can be elegantly expressed in a single sentence are going to require elaboration and evidentiary justification. If a story were not part of a larger conversation, as in Burke's parlor metaphor, it would not be compelling enough to write or to read; we write and read and think about topics of important debate at play in our cultural surroundings. Because themes are a part of an ongoing conversation, they don't provide the last word. Readers can choose to embrace them *in toto*, embrace them in part, or interrogate, adapt, or even resist them.

Moreover, any cocktail party that we've been to features more than one conversation. This means that the more rich and complex the work of art, the harder it will be to reduce that work to a single theme. Quite often a rich work of art will express multiple themes, some major and others minor. Typically those themes will relate but in some cases they may be more separate (as is true in some picaresque texts).

Let's take the case of *Romeo and Juliet*. When Jeff taught the play as part of his "What makes and breaks relationships?" unit (Wilhelm, 2007) a year ago, he did a debate activity in which different groups chose to justify very different themes as the central one for the play. One group said, "Love bites." Another group posited, "Love is always changing." Another group maintained, "We are controlled by fate." A fourth group argued, "Deceit causes all human problems and tragedies." Any of the themes expressed by the groups in the first round of the debate can be justified by the play. But all of them ring a little hollow and sound a little flat.

Ah, but if stating and justifying the theme is your entry into an ongoing conversation, suddenly the dynamic is changed. Stating the theme isn't the end of conversation—it is the start of one. Even if you can justify that *Romeo and Juliet* expresses the theme that destiny is absolute, you will need to contend with the other authors, characters, classmates, popular culture figures, even President Obama—who clearly do not believe that fate controls all but believe, instead, that we can create our own destinies, at least to some degree. All of these perspectives can be brought into the unit itself, by the teacher or even by the students.

If the conversation is ongoing, then no one can be silenced, no one perspective holds the trump card or the answer. Exploring theme opens up discussion instead of closing it down. Even a compelling argument is taken as categorically tentative: Is this always true? Or is it true only under certain conditions? Responding to those questions makes a theme more than an aphorism or a bumper sticker.

And that's crucially important. Michael and Peter Rabinowitz (Rabinowitz & Smith, 1998) have written extensively about how treating narratives as though they are only about big ideas instead of about people who are worthy of our attention and concern is ethically problematic. But if we see texts as part of an ongoing cultural conversation, then we can't simply make some kind of intellectual pronouncement. We may do so when we first dip our oars into the water. But then our conversational partners will ask, "What makes you say so?" Our answer will depend on the details of the narrative, the lived experience of the characters in the text, our lived experience reading it, and how our lived experience outside the text connects and comments upon all this.

Mikhail Bakhtin (1981), the Russian literary theorist who has had so much influence on English studies, makes an even stronger statement when he contrasts authoritative discourse with internally persuasive discourse. Authoritative discourse "demands that we acknowledge it" (p. 342). That is, it puts itself beyond question and conversation. (We'd use the example of telling our daughters to do something, but sadly, our discourse seldom gets the acknowledgment of authority we're hoping for!) According to Bakhtin, "Authoritative discourse can not be represented—it is only transmitted" (p. 344). It becomes "an object, a *relic*, a *thing*" (p. 344, italics in original). If authoritative discourse cannot be represented, it is not the stuff of stories.

In a recent television interview on TMC, Ron Howard was reflecting on his 50 years in show business and made much the same point. He argued that what ruins art is when the author, or artist or director, can't keep from preaching a little bit—from trying to indicate directly the message of the work. Howard explains that this kind of move demonstrates a profound mistrust of your own artwork and of your audience, and undermines the experience, turning art into a didactic essay, reducing it to a statement.

Internally persuasive discourse, on the other hand, according to Bakhtin, "is affirmed through assimilation" (p. 345). When we live through characters, we do that kind of assimilation. In Booth's (1988) words, we "stretch our own capacities for thinking about how life should be lived" (p. 187). Internally persuasive discourse doesn't become a relic. Rather,

> it is . . . applied to new material, new conditions; it enters into interanimating relationships
> with new contexts. More than that, it enters into an intense interaction, a struggle with other

internally persuasive discourses. Our ideological development is just such an intense struggle within us. (Bakhtin, 1981, pp. 343–344)

Even as we imagine an ongoing cultural conversation, we can also imagine an ongoing internal conversation that guides us to become who we become.

This reminds us of Vygotsky's contention that the self is only the self in relationship. It follows that we can only become a new self through relationship—relationships with texts, characters and authors, the world, each other—by taking on, however tentatively, a different point of view through dialogue. This kind of powerful and potentially transformative experience is exactly what literature is uniquely poised to provide.

What Theme Is Not

When we posit a literary text as a turn in an ongoing cultural conversation, we see not only what theme is, but also what it is not. Remember the scene in *Dead Poet's Society* in which Mr. Keating (the Robin Williams character) has his students read aloud poems that they have written? One young man writes about the girl who is the object of his affection. His classmates laugh, and as he returns to his desk, the young man says, "I'm sorry. It's stupid." Mr. Keating intercedes with the following: "No, it's not stupid. It's a good effort. It touched on one of the major themes. Love."

We may admire how Mr. Keating sticks up for one of his charges, but we don't admire what appears to be his definition of theme. "Love" is certainly the topic of an ongoing cultural conversation, but it's not a conversational turn. As Johnston and Afflerbach (1985) put it, identifying the topic of a text is only the "halfway" point (p. 214). Experienced readers recognize that understanding a theme requires more. It requires them to qualify the topic, or general subject, with some kind of comment, what Johnston and Afflerbach call the "topic-comment" strategy.

What Readers Must Do to Understand Theme

Any teacher knows that students have difficulty in applying this topic-comment strategy. This makes sense, for as we argued earlier, making thematic generalizations depends on identifying key literal information as well as on making myriad simple and complex inferences.

Hillocks and Ludlow's (1984) hierarchy of literary skills gives some sense of what is involved in interpreting themes. Their research demonstrates that making an authorial generalization depends on a reader's ability to do each of the following:

- Understand basic stated information
- Identify key details
- Recognize stated relationships
- Make simple inferences that tie together details that are in close proximity
- Make complex inferences that require applying information gleaned from across the text

Research from Graesser, Singer, and Trabasso (1994) is consistent with that of Hillocks and Ludlow (1984). Their work shows that experienced readers are engaged in a "search for meaning," and as they do so, they create a "situation model" or representation of what the text is about. Experienced readers attend directly to clues about character, setting, perspective, and events, and infer—using their own personal and world knowledge—to fill in gaps, and see and interpret implied relationships. Throughout their reading, experienced readers attempt to construct a meaning that fulfills their own goals and is coherent at both local and global levels of the text. That is, they work to develop an understanding that is consistent with the details of the text and that can be applied to other situations in our lived experience out in the world.

Vipond and Hunt (1984) add specificity to the discussion of what readers must do to understand theme. They begin their consideration of point-driven reading by examining what listeners do in conversation. They argue that listeners are motivated to figure out what the speaker is "getting at." They consider this a form of what they call "point-driven understanding." They consider how people try to understand points in the context of conversations and daily interactions, and then apply this process to literary reading.

Before Vipond and Hunt detail the strategies that point-driven readers apply, they contrast a point-driven orientation with two other orientations: information-driven and story-driven. These researchers posit that sometimes readers engage in "information-driven" reading in which they only wish to take away snippets of content, such as when reading a bus schedule or a grocery list. This orientation is akin to Rosenblatt's (1938, 1978) efferent stance. It is most likely to occur when the task is to remember something, when the text is fragmented, or when the text is read solely inside a local context (taking the bus downtown or buying milk at the grocery store) and outside of a meaningful global context.

A second kind of reading is called "story-driven," in which readers "live through" the text but only on the story level and not on what could be called the discourse level (Chatman, 1978). Story-driven readings attend to character, plot, and event but ignore the discourse through which these are presented. That is, readers using such a stance do not attend to how texts are constructed to help readers come to the understanding of a point. They are engaged solely in looking for a "good read."

AUTHORS MATTER

Point-driven readings not only offer a powerful lived-through experience, but they also attend to experiencing and reflecting on the discourse level, on the construction of text by an implied author who is trying to communicate something of import to the reader. (Both point-driven and story-driven readings would be aesthetic readings in Rosenblatt's terms.)

This is key: People who read for a point think about the texts they read as being the result of choices made by another human being in order to communicate to their readers. Since this is what expert readers do, it is crucial for students to understand that authors matter and must be specifically considered as part of the reading transaction.

More specifically, Vipond and Hunt (1984) cite three types of strategies that expert readers use to attend to the points made by the implied author of a text. The first is what they call *coherence strategies*—reading with the purpose of putting things together. Expert readers try to understand the text as a whole and think about how the parts contribute to that whole. They assume that new topics, new details, shifts in perspective, ruptures in plot and tone, and so forth, are all going to be meaningful in contributing to the communication of an overall point.

> # Three Key Strategies Used by Expert Readers
>
> Coherence Strategies
>
> Narrative Surface Strategies
>
> Transactional Strategies

The second set of strategies is what Vipond and Hunt call *narrative surface strategies*—attending to story elements like character, setting, and plot, focusing especially on how characters and situations and values change. Peter Rabinowitz's (1987) first meta-rule for plot is simply this: Something happens. You can't write a story about stasis—or if you do, it's surprising, as in *Waiting for Godot*—and the stasis is going to be essential to the theme.

Attending to change, to what happens and evolves, means we must attend to the other literary elements we've written about in this book. And indeed expert readers, according to Vipond and Hunt, also attend to discourse aspects of narrative such as point of view, tone, diction, and style. This means they go beyond experiencing the story to think both about how the text was constructed to create that experience and about what the experience is constructed to mean or communicate. Experienced readers notice any unusual structural features and think about how they contribute to the point the author is trying to make.

The final set of strategies is what Vipond and Hunt call *transactional strategies*. That is, point-driven readers realize that texts are artifacts created by another human being. They see that what happens in a text is not inevitable but is rather the result of a rhetorical choice on the part of an author. In recognizing the constructedness of a text, they consider the impact of the choices an author makes and contrast these choices with the potential impact of the choices an author chose not to make.

But, as Vipond and Hunt explain, readers (and listeners) do not apply these three strategies in a vacuum. They note that the readers' generic expectations affect their understanding of a point. Here, their work resonates with that of Northrop Frye, the famous literary critic.

GENRE MATTERS

Frye (1957) posits that there are four basic narrative patterns: romance, tragedy, satire/irony, and comedy. Although texts that have similar patterns may have different themes, those themes resemble one another. According to Frye, the patterns form a circle of stories, with one type blending into the next at its edges. He sees the patterns as representing the seasons of the year, and the larger human journey, both individual and collective.

The first pattern is romance. Romances tell of beginnings, of innocence, satisfaction, splendor, and possibility. It is the pattern of childhood and success, and happily concluded quests. It is about adventure, conflict overcome, and triumph. There may be an element of magic, of powers working unseen, which love and sustain us. Romances are stories of enjoyment and have uplifting and positive themes. They are associated with summer.

The second pattern is tragedy. Tragedies tell of challenge and failure and profound disappointment. It is the pattern of adolescence, of disappointment, of misguided and failed quests. This pattern can be seen as a reaching toward maturity, of the struggle and failure that is necessary to growth. Seasonally, it is autumnal. The themes of tragedies focus on the loss of innocence or of life, and on the inevitability of decline.

The third story pattern is irony/satire, which identifies and faces and even rails against weakness and folly in the world of experience. This story is intended to bring the world to its senses, to shake us out of our accepted ways of thinking and doing, to the development of a new consciousness and conscience. This is not a world of heroes, but of people brought low striving to become something new. It is winter. This is a time of recuperation and preparation for the spring, of looking forward. The themes of irony and satire speak to what needs to be critiqued, challenged, and reformed.

The fourth and final story is that of comedy. It tells of rebirth, of nature reasserting its power, of seeing the possibilities of renewal and of love. Here there is a vision of humanity as humane, of being successful in undertaking and progressing in the quest. This is the story of integration, of becoming complete, of looking upward. It is the tale of both a metaphorical and a very real spring. The themes of comedy center on how we can achieve what is possible.

When we understand the genre of a text, then we will know what kind of conversational turn is being taken on the issues, and we will know what kinds of themes can be expressed.

What Readers Should Do in Addition to Understanding

If a story is a turn in an ongoing cultural conversation, a reader's obligation doesn't end with interpreting a theme. Rather, a reader must respond to that theme in some way. To be sure, we hope that some of the texts our students read will be internally persuasive. We hope that they will make them part of their thinking and living the way we have made use of *Joseph Andrews* and *Too Late the Phalarope*. But we also want students to be able to resist the texts that they do not find internally persuasive.

Let's take the example of *To Kill a Mockingbird*, a very commonly taught novel. We've mentioned previously that one theme of that novel is that change must be gradual. We think that Harper Lee sees Atticus's efforts to raise kids who aren't prejudiced and his causing the jury to stay out longer than it typically would to convict an African American defendant as signs of real progress. We disagree.

Michael is the father of two children of color. Jeff has two close family members who are gay. We are simply not willing to accept the idea that change must be incremental. We don't want to wait for the world to change in small increments. In Dr. King's words, we don't want to accept "the tranquilizing drug of graduation (i.e., gradual change)." We can't wait for generations of progressive parents to do their work. We don't want to tolerate unjust convictions no matter how hotly contested. We think that the message of *To Kill a Mockingbird* is too passive. We want ourselves and others to work with more agency and more urgency toward the goal of a less prejudiced society. Harper Lee dips her oar into the water to talk about what kind of change is possible. We can respectfully listen, identify her message, and then respectfully disagree.

What Teachers Must Do

So looking back on our discussion of theme, what can we say a teacher must do?

- Help students recognize the existence of ongoing cultural conversations and place their reading in those conversations (for example, by using essential questions).
- Help students see the importance of coherence and develop and name useful coherence strategies (for example, by recognizing and making inferences and understanding genre patterns).
- Help students recognize the narrative surface strategies they have available, especially recognizing what changes in a story.
- Help students apply transactional strategies; that is, help students understand that the stories

they are reading are the product of an author's choices and that, as a consequence, they need to think about the impact of what the author has chosen to do, compared to what the author could have done.

- Create an environment in which students feel free to discuss and ultimately to accept, adapt, or resist an author's theme or themes.

All of these goals can only be achieved in what Nystrand and his colleagues (Gamoran, Kachur, & Prendergast, 1997) call a "dialogic classroom"—a classroom that is itself built on conversation and not on authoritative pronouncements or leading questions. Unfortunately, that kind of classroom is all too rare. In a series of studies, Nystrand and his colleagues found that actual classroom dialogue and inquiry for the purpose of understanding (as opposed to recitation/information coverage) occurs infrequently. Most of what teachers identified as discussion in their own classrooms, Nystrand found to be recitation (thinly veiled lectures in which questions were used to fill in the blanks of a prepared interpretation). Disturbingly, this seems to be particularly true in lower-track classes. In fact, a recent study by Applebee and his colleagues (2002) indicated that they could not find enough authentic discussion in lower-track classes to study it! Despite arguments by Delpit (1995) and Lee (2001) that authentic discussion and "dialogic" instruction need to become standard for all classes of all students of all cultural backgrounds in all schools, particularly for students who have struggled as learners or been marginalized by society, these classrooms remain stringently monologic (i.e., the only substantive contributions are determined by the teacher and the curriculum). Likewise, reviews of textbook questions have found that upwards of 80 percent of such questions are factual and have only one legitimate response.

When Nystrand and his colleagues encountered authentic classroom discussion, they found that it was extremely beneficial in terms of engagement and comprehension. Indeed, discussion-based approaches were strongly related to achievement across a wide range of contexts with students of various levels of classroom proficiency.

Conclusion

We have dedicated our professional lives largely to the teaching of literature. We have done so because we understand the power of literature to inform, transform, and give meaning to the deepest aspects and most profound needs of human beings. Today, with schools ever more focused on preparation for test scores or jobs, we know that literature fulfills a unique niche. But this richness can only be actualized if students are not told what to think, but are instead shown how to experience and think for themselves about works of art in order to help them think about the world.

One of the great tragedies of education, one that is brought home to us by our daughters' experiences through much of their schooling, is that so much of school—and so much of literature teaching—is bland, impersonal, boring, and without meaning to the students. What is particularly tragic is how easily a different view of teaching and of reading could lead to empowering and exciting and transformative experiences for our students. Figuring out theme is a challenge. But it is one we can help our students meet. And if we do, we have done them a lifelong favor as readers, conversants, and democratic citizens.

CHAPTER TWELVE

Putting Theory Into Practice:
Preparing Students to Understand Theme

We hope that the conversation metaphor that we spun out in the last chapter has enriched your understanding of what it means to understand theme. If students see texts as products of real human beings who have something to communicate, then they're far more likely to employ their well-developed skill of understanding the point of the conversation to their literary reading.

Connecting Theme to Students' Lives: Using Simulated Texts

One way to help students see the importance of theme is to build a bridge between what they do as a matter of course in their day-to-day lives and their literary reading. Simulated texts are a great way to do just that.

You may recall that our houses are full of teenage daughters with all of the attendant *sturm und drang.* Our daughters are often deep in conversation (actual and virtual), in which they are sharing the latest that's happened. They offer advice to their friends and receive advice in return. Giving that advice, we've come to understand, very much resembles what one needs to do to develop thematic understandings. Think for a minute about someone's explaining a problem in a relationship and seeking your advice. Before you offer it, you have to pay careful attention to the particular details of the situation. But when you offer advice, you typically comment on more than that immediate situation. "Don't expect him (or her) to change just because of the relationship." "It's important for people to maintain their separate interests." "Don't make too big a deal about the little things." And on and on. The following activity is designed to help students apply their advice-giving skills to their literary reading. It begins by reading aloud to students the following little story that Michael composed.

Out to Lunch

Lunch time was always the worst, thought Gabrielle. All eyes were on her, she was sure of it. All those perfectly put together girls laughing at her clothes that weren't quite right. All those too cool boys making fun of her ungainly walk.

But on the ice—on the ice it was different. On the ice, thought Gabrielle, I'm not an ugly duckling anymore. I'm a swan. She thought back to practice that morning and how she had hit that triple-triple combination, a jump only a few people can make, most of them way older than she was. There was no one there to see it. Her mom was asleep in the car. Who could blame her. Practice started at 5 a.m., and the rink was a 30-minute drive from her house. Just Gabrielle and her coach. The coach was always pushing Gabrielle, but even he had to smile. Not many 13-year-olds can pull off such a feat.

But no one at school knows. No one else skates. Football, basketball, softball are the sports that rule at school. If they only knew, thought Gabrielle. But no one did. No one knew that Nationals were coming up. No one knew that Gabrielle's coach felt she might have a chance to medal.

Gabrielle trudged through the lunch line like she always did, head down. As she picked up her plate of sloppy joes—at least that's what she thought it was—she heard a burst of laughter and flushed. And then she heard a voice.

"It's not you they're laughing at. It's me." Gabrielle turned her head to the voice. It was Jessica, the girl from her science class who seemed to know everything. But, thought Gabrielle, not in a show-offy way. Jessica was just so enthusiastic about science that she couldn't contain herself. Gabrielle had heard something about her being interested in rockets or something.

"We were talking about values today in English class, and I made the mistake of saying that being smart was more important than being popular or pretty. You should have seen the eyes roll. You'd think I'd be used to it. But I'm not."

They were through the lunch line now. Gabrielle usually sat alone at a table near the back. But Jessica followed her. She set down her tray and asked, "Okay?" Gabrielle nodded.

That's how it started. Gabrielle and Jessica started eating together every day. At first the conversations were slow in coming. Lots of pauses. Lots of quick mentions of things neither of them really cared about, like the latest TV shows or movies. But slowly they started

⋯→

FRESH TAKES ON TEACHING LITERARY ELEMENTS

to bring up the things that really mattered. Gabrielle shared her joy in skating, and Jessica astonished her by explaining some of the science behind what Gabrielle was doing. Jessica talked about her rocketry and how she felt about being dismissed as a science geek. They both talked about their parents, both the joys and the trials.

Jessica even decorated Gabrielle's locker the day before she was leaving for Nationals. And when Gabrielle won the silver medal, the first person she called was Jessica. "Can you believe it?" Gabrielle said. "And get this, a local TV show wants to follow me around for a day at school. Something about wanting to see the daily life of a 'champion.' Can you believe it?"

Nobody at school knew about Gabrielle's skating before Nationals. But her winning a medal and the prospect of a TV crew following her around was a hot topic. And all of a sudden, the kids who had been laughing were calling out her name and making space for her at their lunch tables.

Jessica laughed nervously. "I guess you won't have time for me anymore now that you're a star," she said quietly. Gabrielle flashed her a quick smile. "Are you kidding? The TV crew wants to know what a day in my life's really like. I want to show them how important good friends are. And how hard it is for kids like us who are different. Let's get to our table."

After reading the story ask students to pretend that they were the author of the story and that they also worked as an advice columnist. Explain that you want them to respond to the letter at right.

Then ask students to offer advice to the same letter writer as though they were the author of a story that ended this way instead:

Jessica laughed nervously. "I guess you won't have time for me anymore now that you're a star," she said quietly. Gabrielle flashed her a quick smile. "There's room for two at this table, right?" she said to the girls at the table as she sat down.

I have a dilemma. Each spring our school competes in a field day with another local school. It's really a big deal. And it's my one chance to shine. You see I don't have too many friends at school. I'm too quiet, I guess. But I can really run. Over the past two years, I've helped our school win field day. Everybody congratulates me, and for a few days at least, I'm one of the in-crowd. Things get back to normal pretty quick, but for those days it's like I'm one of the popular kids, too. But this year field day is the same day as the try-out for the community theater spring musical. I can run, but what I really love to do is sing and act. And I'm good at it, too. But being good at singing and acting doesn't get you much at my school. Try-outs can't be rescheduled, so I have to choose. What should I do?
~ Perplexed in Peoria

We suggest having students share both letters in pairs, discuss how the letters were different and why, and then to share their findings with the whole group. The discussions are sure to focus on the differences between the stories and what those differences mean for the themes.

A great follow-up activity is to read Frank Stockton's "The Lady or the Tiger?" As you may recall, that story, which was published in 1882, is set in a kingdom in which justice is meted out by having those accused of crimes choose one of two doors. Behind one is a lovely maiden whom the accused will marry. Behind the other is a savage tiger. The story centers around the king's discovering that his daughter has taken a lover far below her station in life. The king imprisons the lover. The princess is able to discover behind which doors stand the lady and the tiger. She makes a small signal to her lover. Stockton doesn't reveal the choice and instead ask readers to "engage in a study of the human heart" and determine for themselves which choice the princess made.

Rather than asking students to discuss what choice the princess made, we suggest asking them to pretend that the princess's choice was the lady and that they were the author of the story that ended that way. Then ask them to identify which of the following quotes they would most agree with and which they would most disagree with:

1. Anne Morrow Lindbergh:

Him that I love, I wish to be free—even from me.

2. C. S. Lewis:

Why love if losing hurts so much? We love to know that we are not alone.

3. Euripides:

He is not a lover who does not love forever.

4. Margaret Anderson:

In real love you want the other person's good. In romantic love you want the other person.

5. Rose Walker (a character in Neil Gaiman's *The Sandman 9, The Kindly Ones*):

Have you ever been in love? Horrible, isn't it? It makes you so vulnerable. It opens your chest and it opens your heart and it means someone can get inside you and mess you up. You build up all these defenses. You build up this whole armor, for years, so nothing can hurt you, then one stupid person, no different from any other stupid person, wanders into your stupid life . . .

6. St. Augustine:

Better to have loved and lost, than to have never loved at all.

After a whole-group discussion of students' choices, we suggest repeating the process, asking them to pretend that they are the author of a story that ended with the princess telling her lover to choose the tiger. How would the author of this text respond to the various statements?

These activities should help students recognize that the choices authors make have consequences for what they are communicating and help them develop the powerful strategy of asking themselves, "What would it mean if an author had chosen Y instead of X?" Their work choosing quotes will also help them see both the kinds of generalizations about key topics that tend to be developed as themes and the fact that people take different positions on those topics.

Helping Students Recognize and Articulate Themes: Using Fables

Another way to help students recognize the kinds of generalizations that stories tend to be about is to have them work with fables, for fables are relatively simple stories whose structure focuses readers on the theme.

We suggest reading a number of fables that relate to the particular essential question that you will be pursuing. Here are three of Aesop's fables that work well with the question "What does it take to be happy?"

Three Fables

The Flies and the Honey-Pot
A number of flies were attracted to a jar of honey that had been overturned in a house-keeper's room and, placing their feet in it, ate greedily. Their feet, however, became so smeared with the honey that their wings could not lift them, nor could they release themselves, and they slowly sank and were slowly suffocated in the honey itself.
Moral: Greed for pleasure can lead to pain.
Question: What comment on how to achieve happiness does the fable make?

The Lioness
A controversy prevailed among the beasts of the field as to which of the animals deserved the most credit for producing the greatest number of whelps at a birth. They rushed clamorously into the presence of the Lioness and demanded of her the settlement of the dispute. "And you," they said, "how many sons have you at a birth?' The Lioness laughed at them, and said: "Why! I have only one; but that one is altogether a thoroughbred Lion, king and master of the savannah, and my protector!"
Moral: The value is in the worth, not in the number.
Question: What comment on achievement and happiness does the fable make?

----→

> **The Miser**
>
> A miser sold all that he had and bought a lump of gold, which he buried in a hole in the ground by the side of an old wall and went to look at daily. One of his workmen observed his frequent visits to the spot and decided to watch his movements. He soon discovered the secret of the hidden treasure, and digging down, came to the lump of gold, and stole it. The Miser, on his next visit, found the hole empty and began to tear at his hair and to make loud lamentations. A neighbor, seeing him overcome with grief and learning the cause, said, "Just put a stone in the hole and cover it again, for it will fulfill the same purpose and do you just as much good as the gold."
>
> *Question: What do you think is the moral?*
>
> *Question: What comment on achievement and happiness does the fable make?*

Our suggestion is to read a couple of fables with your class and once they are familiar with the form, present them fables with the moral lines omitted. Students could then work in pairs or small groups to write the missing morals. They can then debate who has written the best one by tying their particular moral to data in the fable and explaining how their moral matches the story, and finally how their moral connects to life in general.

With this preparation, students are ready to write their own fables. We suggest starting with *procedural knowledge of substance* by having the class brainstorm qualities or kinds of people that really get on their nerves, since most fables have as their target some kind of human foible. Then you could choose one foible for the whole class to address, and have students brainstorm the following: "What kinds of problems are caused by that foible? What are the consequences of the foible?"

Once students have ideas for the substance of their fable, move on to *procedural knowledge of form*. You could first lead a discussion on an animal or animals that would best symbolize the foible. Then consider how the foible will change an initial situation, complicating it and leading to particular consequences. Finally, students can be helped to see how a moral must reflect the trajectory of the story, in this case, how the moral reflects the changes wrought or problems caused by this particular foible.

Students can then work in groups of three to compose their own version of the fable. Once the groups have completed their fables, we recommend jigsawing the groups—that is, dividing the class into three large groups with one representative from each group in each of the larger groups. After a read-around of each fable, students discuss the choices they made and why they made them.

You could also return to the idea of having students write advice from the perspective of the author, in this case Aesop. The RAFT technique can be a useful organizing and brainstorming device.

- R = Role = Aesop
- A = Audience = a person who needs advice about happiness—for example, someone who cares too much about money (The Miser) or who wants more than what they need (The Flies and the Honey Pot).
- F = Form = Advice Letter
- T = Topic = Advice about happiness based on a particular fable

Here's an example from a student at Jeff's school, advising a modern miser in ways that reflect the theme of Aesop's fable:

Dear Modern Miser:

What were you thinking, putting all your investment into one stock! So you invested all your money in the stock market and then wasted your time tracking it every day and then getting all depressed when the arrows were pointing to red. How much better would it be to take your money and put it into something you and other people could use and enjoy over time. If this thing is something that can be used and keeps value over time, like a house—so much the better! Think of the pleasure you and others will get from buying something enjoyable to use—like a bicycle. That's a freedom machine! You can get around for cheap and see your friends! That's what you should put your money into! When you earn some more coin, do yourself a favor and don't stick it somewhere to be watched—use it for something that benefits you and other people!

Sincerely, Dr. "Phil" Aesop

Students can then be asked to justify their advice—does it reflect the same theme as expressed in the original fable? Does it work outside the text in its application to another person and to his or her situation in the world outside the text? If so, you have captured theme.

Then students can be asked to change the ending of the fable and write a second letter reflecting the change. This helps students to see how the details of the stories, when changed, add up to something different—a different conversational turn and perspective in the ongoing cultural discussion about the inquiry topic, in this case, of happiness.

For example, one group of students rewrote "The Miser" as "The Saver" so that the main character put the gold into a hole and then forgot about it. Then a great recession came and his bank failed. He couldn't get any money out and his family was hungry. Then he remembered the gold, and some silver he had also buried somewhere else. When he dug it up and took it to the goldsmith, he found that the price of gold had doubled.

This revised story expresses an entirely different moral about saving, and maybe about not trusting institutions with your money. The resulting letters expressed variations on these ideas.

Helping Students Perceive Patterns and Their Import: Collages and More

Remember in the last chapter when we made a distinction between topic and theme? We think that distinction is important enough to reiterate here because many of our students, even sometimes our college students, confuse the two. The topic of a text is its general subject—love or fate or friendship. In the final fable we presented above, the topic is wishes or desires. As Johnston and Afflerbach (1985) point out, though, identifying the general subject only gets one halfway to theme. A theme is more specific as it contains both a topic and a comment. The comment on the topic of wishes or happiness that Aesop makes in the first fable is that if people had all that they wished for, they would often be ruined. The activities we've presented already will help students see that theme means more than topic, but because it's such a common confusion, we think that a little more work to clinch the idea might be in order.

COLLAGES

Asking students to interpret and create collages is one way to cement the topic-theme distinction in their minds. Over the years we've seen many collages, and often students simply cut out any pictures that relate at all to the topic and paste them on a poster board. What we're calling for instead is to have them create and interpret thematic collages.

One idea Jeff often uses is called "floorstorming" (Wilhelm, 2004). In floorstorming, the teacher brings in photos, pictures, or sometimes even headlines or phrases associated with the upcoming inquiry. Once students are familiar with the technique, we like to farm out the work to them and ask students to bring in several images they think are typical of an era, an issue, an edgy topic of some kind related to the inquiry.

The pictures, objects, and phrases can be strewn across the floor. Then small or large groups are asked to classify the images and to ask the following questions:

> *What is the general topic? Subtopics?*
> *What seem to be the crucial details or ideas about the topic that are expressed?*
> *What point might we take away from the pattern of all details related to the topic?*

Students can then be asked to create a collage with the images—or challenged to use the images with others they can find to create a collage.

Teacher Melissa LaPrath's students created the collage on page 173 after a floorstorming activity prior to reading *The Great Gatsby*:

Collages on various topics are also readily available online. Likewise, students can create collages from photos and other representations. They should be asked to create a collage with a clear topic and to include only those details that indicate their comment on that topic—that is, the theme they are trying to communicate.

In a unit on the essential question "Do Americans overemphasize sports?" some of Jeff's students created the collage below. The class identified the most specific topic that captured all the photos as "Competitive ball sports." There was some discussion of whether a frisbee is a "ball," before ultimately noting the

Gatsby collage

Sport inquiry collage

skier and track runner engaged in sports that involve no ball, so they retreated to "Competitive sports." They were thinking productively about how to pitch a topic at the most specific level possible that accommodates all the key details. The students noted that the key details all involved focus, concentration, or emotion. Students subsequently identified themes like "Competitive sports require concentration and focus." Or "Competitive sports involve emotion." And "Sports involve emotion before, during, and after the competition." Students could then be asked to *create* collages that make similar or different points about the topic, or that express the same theme as a reading. Collages allow students, both as composers and readers, to practice identifying and communicating themes about a topic before doing so in their reading.

TIMELINES

Students can likewise collect images to be put on timelines about various aspects of a topic (general historical events, history of civil rights in America—for sports, for immigrants, in business, in the arts; see our chapter on teaching setting). If the scales for the timelines are the same, they can then easily compare events on each timeline and posit patterns within each topic and across topics.

Students can create their own museums, gallery walks, timelines, and Webquests for other students to work on as they identify the topic, details, and implied points that are expressed by these. Exhibits and Web sites can be rearranged, or items deleted and added, so that students can see how such choices make a difference to the implied point of the complete exhibit or Webquest.

PAINTINGS/PHOTOS

Any painting or photograph that has an implied story can also be used. We've used such paintings as Wood's *American Gothic* (Wilhelm, 2004), Renoir's *La Loge*, Munch's *The Scream*, and the paintings of Hopper, Benton, and many others. We first ask students to identify the topic of the painting or photograph. Then we ask them to focus on the details, to notice patterns that connect those details, and finally to articulate the comment the artist is making by including this pattern of those details. We've found that it's especially effective to show a painting alongside a parody of it. (Jeff found over 200 parodies of *American Gothic* online.) The contrast makes it clear to students that new or different details might change the topic or the theme of the work.

PRECIOUS OBJECT

As a front-loading activity before a unit, Jeff often asks his students to bring in a "precious object" (O'Neill & Lambert, 1982; Wilhelm, 2002) or a photo or picture of such an object. This object should be related to the inquiry. For example, in the unit on the question "What does it take to be happy?" Jeff asked students to bring in an object that represented their response to the question.

Students then work in small groups to look for similarities and differences and any other patterns they see across the objects. (When Jeff last did this, students found that most of the objects reminded them of important relationships.) Likewise, before a unit built around the question "What does it take for a person (or culture or species) to survive?" you could ask students to bring one thing that they think would aid their survival on a trip into space, across a desert, in case of a natural disaster, a recession, and so forth. For a unit on heroes, they could be asked to represent the gift a hero might want before a quest. This activity is quick, but it helps students notice key details and how they relate and form patterns. It also helps them notice how significant objects in the text can aid in understanding the theme (Wilhelm, 2002).

FACEBOOK PAGES

We talked about using Facebook pages in our work on character. Returning to those pages will be useful in your work on theme. We ask students to study a celebrity's Facebook or MySpace page and consider the details that are included. Then we ask, "What point is the celebrity trying to make about his or her identity or career, from the pattern of details that are included? How could the celebrity design (or redesign) a Facebook page to make a different point? How could he or she do it explicitly? How could this be accomplished more subtly and implicitly? Which approach would work more powerfully? Students could then plan to design or redesign their own Facebook page or home page.

Likewise, students could look at college promotional materials or resumes and examine the details that are offered, and in what order, then deduce the point the people or institutions are trying to make about themselves and how they make it. More and less successful efforts can be ranked. The same thing can be done with regular Web sites, advertisements, and other media.

Helping Students to Monitor Genre Patterns for Understanding Theme

In the last chapter we drew on the work of Northrop Frye (1957) to explain how the genre of a text orients us as experienced readers to that text's potential theme. The direction of the ending of a story is crucial in identifying which of Frye's four genres it belongs to. Romances end with complete satisfaction and are forward-looking to more of the same. Tragedies end with some kind of disaster and the endings are downward-looking in their view of humanity. Satires and ironic stories may end on a down note, but they are upward looking when it comes to the future—if people will only attend to the offered critique, that is. Comedies deal with troubles (boy loses girl, etc.) but all is sorted out, so comedies end in an upward-looking trajectory.

INTRODUCING AND IDENTIFYING GENRE

To introduce Frye's notion of genre, we have sometimes simply asked students, "Why do people laugh?" Students offer a range of responses: "satisfaction," "pride," "joy," surprise," "incongruity," and so on. Satisfaction and pride relate to romance. Joy relates to romance but is more typically associated with comedy. Surprise can be comedy but is more likely irony/satire. Incongruity is definitely irony/satire. When asked why people cry, students typically respond with "sadness," "a bad shock," "being overwhelmed," "feeling abandoned or betrayed"; all this is the stuff of tragedy. When asked why people poke fun, students respond with a variety of ideas, but they generally revolve around being angry or disappointed that things aren't different and better and more just—and this is the stuff of irony and satire. What is important here is not only that students recognize the general shapes of the literary genres, but also that they understand how the ending of a text is crucially important to understanding the theme.

CLASSIFYING COMICS

Another way to give kids lots of practice with short versions of genre is to have them read the comics page and to think about what happens and what direction things are heading. Now, some comics merely offer gags or a joke, but most are some kind of narrative. If there is a narrative, you can discern the direction of the ending. As always, it doesn't matter what exactly kids say if there is disagreement. (It should be noted that most cartoons are somewhat comedic, or funny, but they can still offer a trajectory that fits another genre). What matters here is if students get the concept of change and directionality.

In the past week (the one after President Obama's inauguration), while we are writing this chapter, here's what's going on in the comics world. Sally, the main character in *Sally Forth*, has a new job as marketing director, but she finds out that everyone in the marketing department is a frustrated, off-beat, back-biting, self-absorbed person. Though the strips are funny, the movement is toward tragedy: it looks like Sally is in for more trouble at work. *Doonesbury* offers Roland Smedley's critique of the George W. Bush legacy. The critique offers implicit hope that Obama's presidency will transcend these shortcomings. The trajectory is ironic/satiric, since the ending is forward-looking after the downer. *For Better or Worse* currently strikes us as moving in the direction of comedy. Michael is overcoming a cold and his friend Deanna's move to another town. But he feels better, he's excited to get back to school, his family loves him, and he still has friends. It's upward-moving, and one has the sense that all will be well despite the inevitable trouble. *The Family Circus* strikes us as being constantly in the mode of romance. Life is good. The kids are amusing. There's no foreseeable trouble on the horizon, except for PJ's coloring the wall and Dolly's commenting on it—nothing to greatly disturb the idyll of family life—in fact, the few problems help us to appreciate the idyll all the more.

This kind of work is a problem-solving exercise that helps kids understand the basics of literary genres, and teaches them to pay attention to how the movement at the end will shape the theme. Since *Sally Forth* is in a tragic movement downward at work, the topic will be work, and the current theme will be something along these lines: The workplace is a battleground, full of intractable problems. *The Family Circus*, looking forward in an upward trend, is commenting on family life with this theme: Family life is good if you can laugh at the little stuff. And so on. Again, the exact topics and theme statements aren't the issue, since there are many justifiable topics or themes even for something as short as a comic strip. What is important is that the students discern the movement of the comic and how to write a theme that reflects that movement. This tunes in students to how genre shapes and constrains themes.

As students are doing this classification work, they'll notice that distinctions among genre blur at the edges. That is, tragedy can be more romantic or tend more toward irony, depending on the narrative's specific details. This recognition will help students understand the range of potential themes available in any genre.

Of course, your students needn't work on comics. They could do the same thing with favorite movies, television shows, YouTube videos, and other popular culture texts. Any classification work of this kind will fit nicely into an understanding of how genres work.

GENRE COLLECTIONS AND COLLAGES

Another way to develop the understanding of genre's influence on theme is to show students sets of photos, paintings, cartoons, advertisements, and so on, that express a genre and therefore a particular kind of theme. For example, you could show depictions of an attractive rebel and the forces that seek unsuccessfully to constrain him or her, a pattern of many comedies. We know who will win and that the theme will be about ways of affirming life and achieving growth, progress, and integration. We've already suggested working with Apple's Mac versus PC campaign. You could return to this campaign in your work on theme. Students will see that the ads suggest that the young, hip Mac is superior in every way to the old, entrenched PC, so that Mac will eventually overcome PC because of his hip energy. Volkswagen likewise overcomes older and bigger rivals because of the comedic, upward outlook and energy of its advertising campaign.

After this discussion you could ask students to collect other ads (e.g., Volkswagen's campaign in which the VW Beetle interviews celebrities) or other images that show the life force triumphing over images of constraint and death (e.g., a bud opening, a chicken coming out of an egg, transformations like the chrysalis, something else entering a new state of becoming, and so on). These could be put into a portfolio, mural, or collage that could hang in the classroom.

Similar work with romance could include idealized images of wish fulfillment, family, community, and society. Students could brainstorm their deepest personal dreams and wishes, and what their ideal community would look like, and then collect images of these. (Ads often use images of such idylls and wishful fantasies.) Students could likewise do searches for paintings of earthly paradises and see what images are there. They could be asked to journal and record their thoughts about what things they feel are absolutely necessary to their well being, along with what they feel they could do without and still be happy and fulfilled. They might consider what they are missing and how they could achieve this for themselves. Again, this could be turned into an individually or collectively composed poem, choral collage, visual collage, drama tableau, or mural. Best/worst tableaux could be created visually or dramatically (Wilhelm, 2002, 2004) to show the idyllic romantic world and the tragic fallen version of it. They could be asked to explain how the romantic world was achieved and lost to get at the causes of romance and tragedy. A visual display of a completed quest is another possibility. The teacher should make it clear that this kind of wish fulfillment and attainment is the province of the romance genre.

Tragedy is about death and/or the loss of a greater destiny and possibilities. Romantic tragedies tend to have a cause in the setting; more ironic ones have the cause in the self. Tragedy often explores what humans can bear and overcome. Tragedy always makes us say "This should not be!" which is another way of affirming a higher order that we must strive for. A collage about tragedy would include damaged life—people, animals, vegetation that is hurt or destroyed or mangled in some way. Traps and containers and images of control are also appropriate. Students could choose images, label these images with graffiti or thought balloons, talk about why they chose the images they did, and compare these to what others chose. Students could likewise look for fatally wrong choices from people, historical figures, or literary characters. They can be asked what wrong choice was made and how this led to a "fall." This cause will be part of the tragic theme for that story.

Satire is a little trickier, but students could collect satiric political slogans, cartoons, bumper stickers, and even popular expressions. Students can be asked to identify the target and the moral norm the target does not yet meet. A collage of such statements could be made, with or without images that relate to them. Fables are typically satiric, especially those of Thurber, and students could be invited to illustrate these.

Students can also be asked to create a collage that reconstructs the seasons of the genres and the ways in which they flow into one another. Students should induce, express, or explain the various elements of each genre and their relationships to each other—for example, romance is integration and satisfaction with the order of things (summer); tragedy is fall and chaos (autumn); satire/irony is disintegration and critique/revolt (winter); and comedy is the effort at reintegration and wholeness— for rebirth and the reestablishment of order (spring).

Why It's Worth It: Themes Matter

The activities described here focus our students' attention on how experiences and texts come to mean something. This in turn helps them read more powerfully. Whenever we want to go beyond a casual experience with a text, we need to consider what the text is about (its topic) and what the text is saying about the topic (its theme) as well as how it says that (the way the text forms patterns and relates events and details).

This approach will benefit students not only as readers and writers, but also as democratic citizens and integrated human beings pursuing their most vital possible lives. After all, what is life if not a search for meaning, and knowing how to achieve or at least approach the meaning one seeks, whether this is to love and be loved, achieve a measure of the heroic, or survive in tough economic times. Likewise, what is reading if not a search for meaning, whether we are reading expository or narrative texts, classic literature or comics? In our living and our reading, understanding the point is crucially important.

CHAPTER THIRTEEN

Putting Theory Into Practice:
Teaching Theme With Particular Units and Texts

A s we maintained in Chapter Eleven, we believe that experienced readers see the theme of a work of art as a conversational turn in ongoing cultural conversations. Teaching students to understand theme, then, requires helping them recognize those conversations.

Creating a Context That Fosters Attention to Theme

Inquiry units take the idea of a cultural conversation from the realm of the metaphoric to the realm of the actual and experienced. That is, when students read texts that take different positions on the same topic, they come to see this author agreeing with that one or disagreeing with another. They have to move from topic to theme because all of the texts center on the same topic.

GETTING STARTED

We've talked throughout the book about the power of inquiry units, so we thought it would be worthwhile to spend some time developing some ideas on how you might construct one. We've written elsewhere (Smith & Wilhelm, 2006; Wilhelm, 2007) about how to choose a focal question. In short, though, we recommend 1) paying special attention to what draws you to the literature you read or teach or to the new stories that attract your attention, 2) listening to your students to find out the issues that engage their attention, identifying issues that have a special local import, and 3) examining the assumptions that undergird your state standards or cumulative progress indicators.

Once you've identified a question, it is essential to start the unit with front-loading activities that foreground purpose, elicit student interest, and connect the inquiry to what students already know and care about. For example, in a unit organized around the question that we used as an example earlier, "What does it take to be happy?" Boise State Writing Project fellow Erika Boas began her unit by having students work in pairs to create lists of things that make people happy. Students reflected on what makes them happy and what would be absolutely necessary for them to be happy, then wrote a short autobiographical piece on what makes them happy or what they believe they need to be happy.

Next, students completed the following opinionnaire. They had to answer each question with a "yes" or "no."

Opinionnaire:
What does it take to be happy?

Respond to each statement by agreeing or disagreeing. Be prepared to justify your answers.

Dreams and goals are essential to happiness.	Yes/No
The happiest people are satisfied with what they already have.	Yes/No
Happiness doesn't happen overnight; it is a long journey.	Yes/No
We are most happy when we are helping others find happiness.	Yes/No
Increased intelligence brings greater happiness.	Yes/No
Money is essential to a person's happiness.	Yes/No
Relationships are essential to one's happiness.	Yes/No
Having a job that one loves is a key element of happiness.	Yes/No
Not everyone needs the same things to be happy.	Yes/No
You cannot be lonely and happy.	Yes/No

After students filled out the opinionnaire individually, they discussed their responses in groups of four or five, focusing especially on the items about which there was disagreement. After the groups reported on what items resulted in the most disputes, students reflected on their original thoughts about happiness and whether they'd changed as a result of the opinionnaire and discussion.

Then Erika presented her students with the following quote from Ayn Rand: "Happiness is that state of consciousness which proceeds from the achievement of one's values." (1963). Students wrote a response to the quote that provided an example or event from their experience that endorsed or disputed the quote. Erika then invited students to find quotes about happiness to bring in for class discussion and response.

WORKING TOWARD A CULMINATING PROJECT

Throughout the unit, Erika returned to these front-loading activities. For example, students did in-role writing as characters or authors of the texts they read, making lists of things that make them happy and exploring what it is they want that would make them happier. Students worked in groups or individually to take the opinionnaire in role as an author or character, using examples from the text to illustrate how they knew a character or author would respond in a particular way. They regularly wrote short journal entries about new ideas they were considering or rejecting regarding happiness. They talked about which of the quotes they found would particularly appeal to or be rejected by different authors or characters.

In returning to the front-loads as templates, Erika provided curricular coherence by focusing on a range of themes on the topic of happiness. Because of this coherence, students were always thinking about and collecting data for the unit's culminating project in which they wrote an argument about what is necessary for happiness, using examples and non-examples from their own life and from various readings in the unit.

Teaching Students the Questioning Hierarchy

In Chapter Eleven, we discussed Hillocks and Ludlow's (1984) hierarchy of literary skills, noting that their research establishes that students must have command of the basic skills in order to be successful with higher-level skills such as understanding an author's generalization. One way to help students develop and apply those skills is to give them conscious control by applying the hierarchy to the particular texts that they are reading. In Jeff's national demonstration site, several elementary school teachers adapted Hillocks's scheme to make it more accessible to their students, even at the lower elementary level. Following is a version from elementary school teacher Kelli Olson, which we applied to *Roll of Thunder, Hear My Cry* by Mildred Taylor.

Just the Facts! Questions to Help Us Establish the Facts

STEP 1: Obvious Information

Create a question that asks about a detail that is repeated and can be found "right there" and that is important throughout the book.

Example: *What is the social situation of African Americans in the South at this time in history?*

STEP 2: Key Detail

Create a question that asks about a detail that is very important to the story's plot and helps move this plot forward.

Example: *What does the Logan family own that is so important to them?*

STEP 3: Explain Relationships/How come?

Create a question that focuses attention on a direct statement about how two events or details are related. This question might explain why or "how come" something happened between two people or events.

Example: *How come Cassie is nice to Lillian Jean after Lillian Jean humiliates her?*

But What Does It Mean? Questions to Help Us Figure Things Out

STEP 4: Connect Some Dots/Playing Detective

Create a question about how two or three clues that are close together are connected and work together. The question should ask the reader to "connect the dots" to determine a solution or meaning that is not stated in the text.

Example: *Why do Little Man and Mama respond as they do to the textbooks used in their school, and what various events follow from their responses?*

STEP 5: Connecting Lots of Dots/Playing Super Detective

Create a question where a person has to use many details from throughout the whole text to arrive at a solution that isn't specifically stated in the book.

Example: *In what different ways do the members of the Logan family fight for their rights, and which ways seem to be less and more effective?*

STEP 6: Walking in the Author's Shoes

Create a question that asks about one of the author's BIG IDEAS expressed by the story.

This should be an idea we can apply to our lives and the world beyond the story.

Example: *What is the author saying about the best way to protect and promote civil rights?*

DRAMA TECHNIQUES THAT FOSTER ATTENTION TO AUTHORS AND THEIR EXPRESSION OF THEME

We've argued that authors must explicitly be part of the discussion about their work and about the inquiry topics their work explores. Authors matter and must be considered as part of the reading transaction. After all, who created the text, constructed its meaning, and did all the patterning?

Drama activities are especially excellent for conversing with authors. In all drama work, as Jeff explores in his research on drama (Wilhelm & Edmiston, 1998; Wilhelm, 2002), success depends on adequate *framing*. At a minimum, successful framing assumes the following:

1. Students understand the purpose of the activity and how it relates to the inquiry.
2. Students understand their roles and have some assistance and time to prepare for their roles. (This can be just a minute or two.)
3. Students understand how the task/drama work is structured (what they are being asked to do and in what order).
4. Students understand how they are going to be accountable for what they will need to produce or report out within or after the drama work.

When these conditions are met, drama work is likely to be highly engaging and successful. In fact, these principles apply to successful small-group work and other classroom situations where students are actively engaged.

CORRESPONDENCE DRAMAS

Students could also undertake conversations with authors through correspondence dramas such as writing letters, notes, questions, or advice requests to the author. These texts can be exchanged, and students then respond to each other in role as the author, taking care to note how they know or why they think the author would respond in this way. (The advice letters on page 167 are a variation of this dramatic technique.)

HOTSEATING THE AUTHOR

Hotseating is a more active drama technique in which a student (or the teacher) sits in the "hotseat" in role as an author (of course, this can be done with characters, as well). Students in the classroom take on roles of those who would have an interest in questioning or learning from the author. They question the author, and the hotseated student playing the author responds in ways justified by the text. Variations include letting the hotseated author have a "lifeline group" to confer with before answering, or an "alter ego" or "shadow self" who stands behind the author to reveal what the author is really thinking but not saying after each comment. There are many other variations (see Wilhelm, 2002 for examples).

TO TELL THE TRUTH

In this hotseat variation, three or four people play the role of author and are asked questions by the audience. At the end, the students in the forum vote for the student who did the best job playing the author, but must justify their vote with evidence from the responses and from the text.

RADIO CALL-IN SHOWS

In this technique, the teacher or a student acts as emcee for a call-in radio show to the author (played by the teacher or a student). Students "calling in" must be in the role of someone from the unit or popular culture who is interested in the topic of the author's text. When calling in, the caller identifies his or her role and then asks an appropriate question or makes a comment for the author to respond to: ("Hello, this is Dr. Martin Luther King, Jr. I'm wondering why the author sent Uncle Hammer back to Chicago after the near fistfight, an action I disagree with due to my belief in nonviolence. I also want to know how the story might have turned out if Uncle Hammer had stayed.") The author answers the callers. We have also done a variation of this through online discussions where students IM an author (played by the teacher or a group of students), who responds to the submitted questions. The technique is excellent not only for understanding and conversing with authors and their thematic statements, but also for putting authors in conversation with each other so multiple perspectives on the inquiry can be highlighted.

PRESS CONFERENCE

Students can take the role of author (and major characters) after the reading of a climactic scene or after completing the reading of the text. The rest of the students are the press corps and must bring five questions to ask the author and characters, who respond as if at a press conference. Oftentimes, we get interesting interactions and differences expressed among author and characters. For example, after reading Jodi Picoult's *My Sister's Keeper*, a student role-playing the protagonist told the author that "you treated me disrespectfully by killing me." A long, emotional exchange ensued between different characters and the author about whether the death was essential to the theme of the story. As with all the techniques, students could participate in a large-group enactment of this technique so they understand it, and then pursue it in smaller groups.

As always, small-group work and pair work goes particularly well if students have seen a model of the technique. Students will also benefit and be motivated when they know why they're doing the activity (the purpose it serves), how to pursue it, and how they will be accountable—for example, by writing a news release based on the interview, or turning in a question along with the author's response and an evaluation of the response. We've also found that drama work is best done quickly, with episodes lasting one to three minutes, followed by reporting out and reflecting.

MEETING OF THE MINDS

At the end of an inquiry unit, small groups of students can be cast as different authors of three or four important texts from the unit (articles, stories, poems, novels). Initial questions to the authors regarding their takes on the inquiry question can be posed by the teacher and then submitted by students. Students, in role as the different authors, then discuss their views on the questions. Students might also be asked to fill out a Venn diagram or another kind of chart reflecting the authors' varied responses. A variation is to jigsaw students so they meet in expert groups with other students who are taking on the same role prior to the exchange with other authors. They can rehearse responses to the questions and how they know these responses are justified before going to meet the other "minds." This technique also works quite well to review themes and authorial perspectives on hotseat questions related to the inquiry. Another variation is to have small-group discussions in which everyone is playing the role of a different author.

Keeping Track of Patterns in a Story

In Chapter Eleven we talked about how change and changes in values, and what accounts for these changes, are essential considerations in understanding theme. At the beginning and end of a reading, we like to have students fill out a chart that focuses their attention on such changes and the reasons for them. This can then be used as a tool to help them reflect on theme. On page 188 you'll find an example from a student's work on *Number the Stars* by Lois Lowry, which makes note of patterns of change in the novel. The chart is then used to identify and justify the themes expressed by these patterns.

This chart, like the Character Response Sheet, the graphic organizer for setting, and the Point of View Tracking Sheet, explicitly reinforces the preparatory work students have been doing. Because the same chart could be used for any story or novel students are reading, it fosters transfer. Because it highlights only one kind of detail students should be alert for and leaves them to notice for themselves the most significant particular details, it fosters independence from teacher questions.

Figure 13.1 PATTERNS OF CHANGE IN A NOVEL				
Number the Stars by Lois Lowry	**Situation**	**Actions, Qualities, and/or Values of Major Character/s**	**Actions, Qualities, and/or Values of Opposing Characters and/or Forces**	**Actions, Qualities, and/or Values of Allied Characters and/or Forces**
Beginning	Nazis are running Denmark. The Jewish people are being threatened. Everyone is being harassed and has no freedom whatsoever. It looks like things are only going to get worse.	Annemarie loves her family and friends, especially Ellen. She is kind of unaware of the political struggles and problems faced by those around her as she is being protected by her family.	Nazis are the worst in going after and controlling and hurting the population. They are forceful and threatening. They are controlling. They are the worst.	King is courageous and provides a model for the people by riding through the streets without guards and flying the flag. Family is protective and brave and working hard to help each other. Ellen is a strong friend. Resistance is courageous and fights the Nazis in any way they can.
Ending	Lise and Peter are dead, killed by the Nazis for their work in the resistance. Denmark is free and the people once again wave the Danish flag, sing their national anthem, and express their pride in ways that would have had them shot during the Nazi time. The Johansens await the safe return of the Rosens, their Jewish friends who are safe in Sweden. They've taken care of their home and business for them.	Annemarie loves and appreciates her family and friendships even more. She is aware of the struggles and what it took to end the war and regain freedom. Annemarie is grateful to Lise and Peter but sad about their deaths. She now knows that people must actively work together to protect and promote each other's freedoms.	The Nazis are totally defeated and kicked out of Denmark. They are powerless to hurt anyone anymore.	The King is still king and loved by his people for his leadership in times of trouble. The family shares their struggles and some of what they protected Annemarie from. They remain strong despite their losses and suffering and being sad. Ellen is safe in Sweden but should return home soon. The Resistance is victorious and is recognized and given its proper due.
Causes of Change/s	The courage and work and sticking together of the Danish people, the freedom fighters, and of the family Families and friends protected and helped each other over time.	The ordeal of living through an occupation has given her awareness. The talking of her uncle and mother have added to that awareness	The resistance and persistence of the Danish people, and their creativity in resisting, and the work of the Allied forces (not really in the story, but I know about it).	Courage, persistence, creativity, knowing what could be done and not trying to do less or more. Hitting it "just right."

Picture Mapping

A technique known as picture mapping (Wilhelm, 2004) is another excellent tool for helping students identify and understand two kinds of patterns:

- Local textual patterns are used for organizing details that are embedded into a particular place in the text. Such structural patterns include simple listing, time order (chronology), cause and effect, comparison and contrast, classification, and definition.

- Global/genre and text-structure patterns, those patterns that organize a whole text, give it coherence and provide an overall roadmap for reading. Some of the same patterns that work locally can also organize a whole text—for example, comparison and contrast, classification, extended definition, narrative chronology (which is sometimes rearranged for effect). Other generic superstructure patterns include argument, ironic monologue, fable, and dramatic script.

The patterns demonstrated by the relationships among details can be made part of a picture map where idea development and the relationships of various details are visually portrayed. This helps students to understand deeply how text structures work to develop and express particular meanings. The picture map then provides a powerful visual summary of the topic (what all the key details have in common) and the key details themselves. It also shows the structured relationships of ideas—how ideas are organized to create patterns with other ideas and how this expresses meaning (e.g., how the text signals what is of importance through placement, relationship to other ideas, markers, etc.) and the thematic meaning.

We typically have students work in groups of three or four. These groups are small enough so that everyone will be involved but large enough that there will be plenty of discussion. We give the following directions:

1. Read through a text excerpt, underlining what seem to be key details. Pay attention to the key detail clues we have studied:
    - First and last sentences of the text; introductions and conclusions. (Remember, paragraphs often signal a new key idea.)
    - Highlights, bolds, italics, bullets, boxes, font changes
    - Quoted material
    - Surprises, shifts, and changes in focus, direction, or emphasis
2. Identify the topic of the reading (the general subject that all the major ideas or events share in common).
3. Consider how to represent or symbolize each key idea with a picture—an icon that directly

represents it, an "index" that suggests it, or a symbol that reverberates with meanings about it. Do this as simply and clearly as you can. NO WORDS MAY BE USED!

4. Identify how the key details work together to create a deep meaning and statement about the world outside the text. This is the point or central focus statement (also known as a thematic generalization). Consider how to represent this point in a single picture.

Once students have done several picture maps, we suggest adding one or more of the following additional challenges:

- Add to each key detail picture how you knew that each key detail was essential, instead of just providing texture to the reading.

- Demonstrate several key ideas with one picture or symbol.

- Show the patterns and connections between ideas or progressions of ideas if the organization and structure of the text is important to the point it makes. For example, organize the picture map into a timeline if there is historical cause and effect, into a family tree if it involves relationships or classes of information, into Venn diagrams if it involves definition or comparison-contrast.

- Add a response corner (or area on the back of the picture map) depicting your response to the text and your feelings about the information presented and issues raised. Here, you could indicate what surprised you or what you want to do as a result of this reading. You might also show to what degree you accept, would adapt, or resist the message and implications for thinking and living provided by the text. If several of you worked on the picture map together, you could each take a corner for your different responses.

- Use a picture map to summarize our whole unit. Be sure to show the key details across various texts and experiences, the ways they relate to each other, and the conclusion (big understandings/central foci) you gleaned from the unit as a whole.

- Show your picture map to another group. Let them guess what each symbol/picture and the various placements/relationships mean.

- Use your picture map to show students in other groups what was important about your text. If individuals or groups are reading different texts for the same inquiry unit, make sure your picture map is strong enough that they will know the most important things you learned about the inquiry topic so they can think with these ideas, too.

- Use your picture map to study for a test, write a paper, or just to jog your memory. How well does it work in meeting these purposes?

- Hang the picture maps in the classroom and use them as references for writing assignments, tests, and discussions.

Picture map of Tim Flannery's *The Weather Makers*, depicting the topic of global warming and the theme of human responsibility for climate change

Written Think-Alouds

Another technique that helps students notice and track patterns within a text is the written think-aloud (Wilhelm, 2001). There are many variations of the technique. Students can use sticky notes to jot down every key detail they see and post them in the text where they encounter them. As with other activities, they could be asked to explain how they know these are key details. If students are allowed to write in a text, they could annotate the text by underlining or highlighting key words and phrases. Comments could be made in the margins.

While reading, and afterwards, students can go back to look at the highlights and comments and search for patterns: repetitions, development of an idea or event, similarities, differences, contradictions, interruptions, and ruptures. You could also cue students to look for something specific, such as key details, symbols, or clues to unreliable narrators. For a cued think-aloud, you can model looking for such cues and how to think aloud about them. Then you might underline cues later in the text for students to respond to as they work together. (See Wilhelm, 2001, for more details on using think-alouds.)

Keeping Track of the Conversation Across Stories

If we understand themes as turns in an ongoing conversation, you will aid students in identifying the themes of what they are reading by helping them track the conversation. Charts and graphic organizers are excellent ways to keep track of patterns across texts. Here is a semantic feature analysis for a survival unit looking at the features of survivability of the animal characters from Sheila Burnford's *The Incredible Journey*, and of characters and animals from other readings in the unit.

The students brainstormed the features, made sure they were all phrased positively, then ranked each character as having the feature (or not) to a particular degree. (To differentiate the degree to which characters possessed a feature the students used + and – marks.) This chart was kept throughout the unit and updated after readings. At the end of the unit, students added individuals and cultural groups they knew about so they could assess the individual's or group's "survivability" and test their emerging theory about what determines the capacity to survive.

SFA Who will survive?	Persistence	Physical strength	Psychic strength	Capacity for team work	Adaptability	Vitality/Energy	Available food sources	Available habitat	Independence	Creativity	Quick thinking
Tao		X	X		X+	X+	X	X	X+	X	X
Luath	X	X	X	X		X X-			X	X	X
Bodger	X+	X-	X+	X		X-				X	
Cockroaches	X+	X	?	X+	X+	X+	X++	X+	X		
Shackleton	X+++	X+	X+++	X+++	X+	X+			X	X	X
Horseshoe crabs	X++	X		X		X					

Semantic Features Analysis Chart: Who will survive?

Keeping Track of Strategies to Understand Theme

After the kind of instruction we've described here, students should have an articulated understanding of what they need to do to understand theme. As we've argued throughout the book, having such an understanding is crucial if students are to be able to transfer what they've learned to novel situations. We'll close this chapter with how one group of seventh graders (adapted from Wilhelm, 2001) explained how they worked to understand theme.

IDENTIFY THE TOPIC (OR GENERAL SUBJECT) OF THE PIECE

To find CLUES to topic:

- Look at the title.
- Look at the first and last paragraph: the topic is often named and always implied. (For narrative, you might have to look a little further.)
- Ask yourself: What is discussed through the whole selection? What general subject spreads across the whole text?
- Look at captions, pictures, words in boldface, headings, and so forth for clues to topic. What do all of these have in common? What do they all have to do with?
- Remind yourself: the topic must connect to all the major details and events from the selection. Caution: not every detail has something to do with the topic. The topic is the common element or connection among the major details.
- What do all the major details and events have in common as far as what they are about or are concerned with?

CHECK YOURSELF: It's not a true topic if . . .

- it's too general or too big. (The topic statement suggests or could include many ideas not stated in the text.)
- it's off the mark, totally missing the point.
- it captures only one detail rather than all of the key details.
- it captures only some of the details (for example, maybe you didn't think about the ending, or the climax, or a shift or major change of some kind).

QUESTIONS to ask yourself:

- Does the topic I've identified give an accurate picture of what the whole selection is about?
- Was I as specific as possible in accommodating all of the key details?

- After naming the topic, can I now fairly specifically picture in my mind what happened or was communicated in the text? Or might I picture something radically different that also fits my topic statement? If so, how can I revise my topic statement to correct this problem?

IDENTIFY THE KEY DETAILS/EVENTS AND THE PATTERN AND TRAJECTORY THESE CREATE BY WORKING TOGETHER

Authors often plant important ideas in rules of notice. For example:

- Details that reflect or refer to the title
- Details at the beginning of the text/or front and center of an image
- Details at the end
- Surprises, revelations, whenever your expectations are not met
- Evolving changes/sudden ruptures in character, situation, tone, mood, setting, plot twists
- All changes/development (particularly in narrative): in values, attitude, relationships, situation
- Reasons for changes/development (particularly in narrative): actions, decisions, helpful and opposing influences or forces, situational conditions in the setting
- Escalations in intensity/emotional charges
- Repetition, or repetition with slight variations—of words, events, ideas, etc.
- Lots of attention given to a detail, for instance, long explanation or description
- Subheads, bold, italics, chapter titles
- Single-sentence paragraphs
- A question near the beginning or the end

CHECK YOURSELF: It's not a key detail or event if . . .

- it's interesting, but it doesn't develop the topic or lead to the controlling idea/theme.
- it can be removed from the piece without causing the work to lose any significant meaning or impact. (This can be true even of things that seem important.)

QUESTIONS to ask yourself:

- Are all the details related to the topic?
- How do the key details relate to each other? Caution: This will quite often have to be inferred—particularly in narrative—as the connection will not be directly stated!
- What pattern do the details make when they are added together? In narrative you will have to infer. In expository texts the controlling idea may be directly stated.

- What point does this pattern add up to and imply? In narrative, you will have to infer.
- What can we extrapolate or interpolate from the pattern? You will have to infer.

IDENTIFY THE MAIN IDEA/CONTROLLING IDEA (the theme or point the author makes about the topic)

- The statement of main idea you name must make a point about the topic and cover the whole selection.
- It must apply to the world beyond the text and be useful in thinking and acting in real life.
- Ask, "Is the main idea directly stated?" If not, it must be inferred from the pattern and relationship of the key details.
- Which details help determine the main idea? Why are these details important?
- The controlling idea considers how the details relate to one another or lead to one another (what caused or correlated or led to what?).
- The main ideas must consider the ending and how the details, characters, setting, perspectives, interactions of these and the events led to this conclusion.

CHECK YOURSELF: It's not the main idea if . . .

- It is so literal and specific it doesn't allow the reader to apply the main idea to his or her own life.
- It is too general—more like a topic statement than a main idea or point.
- It is true but misses the point of this text. It wasn't what the author was saying through this combination of these details.
- It misses the point.
- It only fits one detail, event, or part of the story, not the coherent whole.
- It does not incorporate all the details, but only a few.
- It doesn't fit the ending or final situation.

QUESTIONS to Ask Yourself:

- What point do the key details repeat and add up to when taken all together?
- Is the main idea or point a statement about the topic?
- Is the main point something useful that can help you think or act in the world?
- Also consider, Do you agree with the statement as it applies to life? Will you use this idea to undertake action in the world or to think about the world? Why or why not?

Conclusion

Northrop Frye (1957) argued that the inner possession of literature (i.e., an understanding of the circle of stories) could be the mightiest imaginative force, a power that the reader can internalize to deal with fears, nourish hopes, inspire journeys, sustain successes, guard against weaknesses and the shadow self, and to reveal the rich potential in ourselves, and in society, both in the moment and in the trajectory of all life.

To own this power we must cultivate our imagination to see beyond, to transcend our current moment. William Blake likewise posited that there is nothing real beyond the imaginative patterns people apply to their lives. All meaning, all action and belief, emanate and take shape from the social vision constructed by our imagination. The purpose of reading literature, according to Frye, is to make what we read part of our own developing vision, and to understand something of its function in shaping this vision.

Such a project can be undertaken only if our students learn to read for theme, develop the capacity to justify themes, and appreciate how these understandings play out in their lives and in the world.

CHAPTER FOURTEEN

Looking Back, Looking Forward

I f you know Jeff, then you know that he is a "full court press" kind of guy. He is always trying to pack the absolute maximum into every day, and into every class he teaches. If you know Michael, then you know that he is more thoughtful and thorough. (At this point Michael has to add that his family would be astonished at that characterization. He's famous for getting distracted in the middle of one thing and moving on to the next, what his family has come to call the 82 percent approach.)

One of the most important things that Jeff has learned from Michael (among many others) is to slow down, and to achieve more by doing less. When Michael saw Jeff's first undergraduate methods syllabus, he told Jeff, "You can't do all of this." But Jeff was concerned with what his students needed to know to be successful teachers, and he wanted to prepare them completely. Michael argued that you can't completely prepare a person to teach in a semester course, and so you have to think about what is most important, what is prerequisite, what—if put in place—will help the students to develop as teachers in the future. "You can only get so much done," Michael told Jeff. "So only do what you can actually get done. *And then make sure that this actually gets done!*"

Because Jeff is a slow learner, he has only gradually taken Michael's advice. But over the years, he has prioritized his teaching, doing less and less each semester. It turns out that his students are happier and more successful at consolidating central stances, strategies, and reflective attitudes of mind.

Jeff's had an analogous experience with his Nordic skiing. For years every workout was a two- to three-hour endurance ski. Jeff has limited opportunities to ski and he races marathons, so this seemed most expedient. When he moved to Idaho and joined the Idaho Nordic Club, his coaches, Joe and Eric Jensen, put the kibosh on this training regimen. They pointed out that he used only a couple of techniques and he wasn't very good at those—even after 20 years of racing. They pointed out that although he was in great shape by the end of each ski season, he had not achieved or learned a single thing that he could bring forward to the next season—things like poling strategies, waxing techniques, and improved skating techniques. Now Jeff spends one third of his workouts on endurance, one third on general technique work, and one third on a new goal. This year it is step turning on steep downhill turns. Guess what? Jeff is happier, and even at the age of 50, he is improving every year and doing better in his races. He has found that it is fun to learn and fun to see demonstrable improvement. When he starts a new ski season, he uses what he learned the previous year that can be carried forward—and these are always procedural knowledge and techniques. Although he may be starting from scratch in training his muscles and achieving fitness, he has a repertoire of techniques to bring forward.

We want to stress that this is exactly what we have argued for in this book. Choose the strategies that are most important and transferable right now for your students, and spend the time on really developing and consolidating those procedures so they can be transferred for use in their future reading and their lives. We've argued that character, setting, point of view, and theme are four literary elements that we would put at the top of our list of things to teach about literature—if they are taught as more than terms. If taught as procedural understandings, these elements are at the top of our lists because of the pay-off they give to students in engaging and improving their capacity to do reading in more expert ways. And they're also important because if they are taught deeply, students might be able to apply these procedural understandings to other disciplines and life settings.

Now, we think an individual teacher could thoroughly cover all of these elements in a single school year to great effect. But one of the things we've proposed elsewhere (see especially Smith & Wilhelm, 2007) is that teachers can divide up the work. Think of a middle school where the sixth-grade teachers agreed to focus on character throughout the year, and maybe even across the curriculum. The seventh-grade teachers could focus on setting and the power of context in some way in all major units and assignments throughout the year. The eighth-grade teachers could focus on point of view and theme. The same principle could work in a high school. Different grades could focus on different critical understandings with various genres and through various units.

In our experience, it's often the case that every teacher—like Jeff throughout most of his career—is trying to do everything. As a result, nothing at all really gets adequately done. In the classroom Jeff is working in this year, not a single student can use apostrophes or quotation marks correctly, although it is part of the grades 4–6 curriculum. This is the result of every teacher every year trying to do too much and therefore not helping students to consolidate and master central strategies.

When we wrote this book, we too thought about trying to do more. But we resisted the impulse. Before we look back and review more specifically what we hope we've accomplished in this book, we thought we'd take a little bit of time to explain what we chose not to do: devote sections of the book to plot and conflict.

Plot

Our decision not to include a section on plot was informed in part by the fact that we take up a variety of issues related to plot in our section on setting. Our discussion about how the setting constrains what's possible is a discussion of plot. But that decision was also informed by our belief that of all the traditional elements, plot is the most complex and, as a consequence, the most difficult element to teach in a way that transfers. We know that this flies in the face of conventional wisdom, so let us explain.

Our trouble with plot is the use of the singular. It seems to us that plots vary enormously from genre to genre. Hero quests have different structures than do detective stories, than do comedies of mistaken identity, than do Russian fairy tales, than do classic westerns, and on and on and on.

Peter Rabinowitz (1987), whose work on the conventions of literary understanding is, we believe, nothing short of brilliant, writes that our understanding of how stories are structured, what he calls "rules of configuration," seems "almost trivial when made explicit" (p. 116). Indeed, take a look at his first two principles: "Something happens," and "What happens happens according to some pattern." He talks about two more specific rules upon which most texts are structured. "Rules of undermining" allow readers to expect that narratives will focus in some way on changing situations. "Rules of balance" allow readers to expect that those changes will be patterned in some way. But the precise way that these rules play out, is, according to Rabinowitz, "radically genre-bound" (p. 139).

Let's take a quick look at the traditional diagram of the action of a story: rising action, climax, dénouement. To be sure, lots of stories adhere to this pattern. But lots don't. Think of the most recent Bourne or Bond movie. No rising action there. The movies start with intense action that continues unabated through the whole movie. Think of any story that ends with a twist. Those stories don't have a dénouement. If they did, their effect would be dissipated.

If we can't identify strategies that work across stories, then we're left with asking questions about particular stories. And as we've argued throughout this book, literal-level, story-specific questions by themselves aren't an effective teaching technology, as they are nearly impossible to transfer into new understandings and strategic facilities.

To be frank, we're stumped in figuring out how to teach the immense variety of plot types, except to recommend that you give students repeated opportunities to engage with the genres that matter most to you. Moreover, some essential questions lend themselves to explorations of a particular genre. For example, "What does it mean to grow up?" requires reading coming-of-age stories, most of which have a similar structure. "What makes a hero?" obviously lends itself to reading hero quests.

And to be frank again, our ideas about plot have been met by more skepticism when we're working with preservice and in-service teachers than have our ideas about the others elements that we've shared with you. We see genres as much narrower than do many others. You'll notice we haven't talked about short stories or novels but rather about particular kinds of stories and novels. We strongly believe that many teachers conceive of genres too widely to be helpful to students. In our minds, poetry is not a genre because it is too widely conceived. Lyric poetry is a genre. Ironic monologues are a genre. Why? Because these narrower conceptions of genre share features across all examples of that type that can be taught and applied to all examples. So for us poetry is not a genre (neither are novels or short stories). But we're afraid that we're fighting a losing battle on that front.

But to be frank yet again, before we move on, we do want to offer a caution when you are teaching plot: make sure what you ask students to do is something that you really did as a reader the first time you read the story. For example, our preservice teachers regularly want to ask their students what a particular passage foreshadows. Our concern is that foreshadowing only becomes obvious once you've completed a text. We worry that sometimes our questions distort what readers actually do when they read. One great way to make sure that you're asking students to do what you yourself did is to teach texts that you're reading for the first time along with your students (Rabinowitz & Smith, 1998; Smith & Connolly, 2005; Wilhelm, 2001).

Conflict

Our reason for not including a section on conflict is also informed by the fact that we discuss conflict in some detail in our work on setting. But there's more to it than that. Of all the conventional terminology, what we find least useful is the four varieties of conflict: person versus person, person versus nature, person versus society, person versus him- or herself. In the first place, the terms presume that stories have one kind of conflict to the exclusion of the others. We don't think that's true. If it is true, however, one can typically label the conflict simply by looking at the cover or the book or title of the story or at the very least, the first couple of paragraphs. If a reader can do that labeling so easily, we're convinced that the construct isn't generative. It just doesn't help one understand.

What We Hope We Have Accomplished

What we do think helps our students become better readers and achieve deep understandings is the deep teaching of powerful strategies. We hope we've convinced you of the power of an approach that begins by thinking hard about how experienced readers understand texts and then sequences instruction so that students get repeated practice in doing what experienced readers do, in reflecting on what they have done, and in doing it some more. We hope that we have convinced you of the importance of creating a context that engages students in experiencing the benefits of what we are teaching them (the importance of the *how*), that focuses on procedural knowledge (the application of the *how*), that teaches for transfer, that builds careful sequences, that provides opportunities for choice and for authentic discussion, and that taps the power of writing to help students become more powerful readers.

We hope you are convinced that teachers must connect what is learned to new situations inside and outside the classroom.

But we worry that in providing all of the instructional suggestions that we may be raising a red flag. When we work with teachers in the field, we're often asked, "How can we do all of this and still teach all the novels that we have in our curriculum?"

The truthful answer is you can't. As we've recently argued (Wilhelm & Smith, in press), the currency that we have to spend as teachers is time. When we do one thing, we have to give up doing another. The prereading work that we've suggested in this book takes some time. Doing it might mean that you'll have to replace a novel with several stories or have groups of students choose one of the novels you want to teach to read and work on it together rather than having every student read them all.

Even when we've persuaded people of the benefits of achieving more by doing less, we still encounter some resistance. "What about the curriculum?" we're asked. "We have to cover everything." Our response: State standard documents demonstrate that that's just not true. We admit that we haven't studied all of the standards in all of the states, but we've spent a great deal of time looking at many of them. And we can't recall ever seeing one that specified a particular text that had to be read. Instead they focus on the development of skills and strategies. Rather than seeing standards as the enemy, then, we think that we can use them as levers for progressive practice.

The Pennsylvania (Michael's home state) eighth-grade standards don't specify any particular readings, but they do call for students to "analyze drama to determine the reasons for a character's actions, taking into account the situation and basic motivation of the character." We think that the instruction on characterization that we're calling for clearly works toward achieving that standard. The Idaho (Jeff's home state) eighth-grade standard doesn't specify reading any particular text, but it does call for students to be able to "explain the author's point of view and interpret how it influences the story." We think that our instruction in the areas of point of view and theme clearly work to achieve that standard as well.

Our point is simply this: The standards movement has dramatically changed teachers' lives, and in many cases those changes have not been for the better. We shouldn't lose the opportunity to use standards as allies to achieve more engaging and powerful instruction whenever we can. Rather than worrying about coverage, we need to keep in mind the "correspondence concept" we discussed in Chapter One. Our job isn't to hurry through lots and lots of texts. Our job isn't to struggle through a few difficult canonical texts. Our job isn't to have kids memorize lists of literary terms or label stories for how they use those terms. Our job is rather to help our students be more engaged and passionate readers and to read more like experts. We hope this book helps you achieve exactly that.

A Final Note

Nobel-winning psychologist Herbert Simon (1996) distinguished the sciences as being about describing the world as it is, and the arts and professions as being concerned about the world as it could and ought to be. In this book, we have described how we think literature could and ought to be taught for the purposes of helping students to explore what their lives could and ought to be like.

Many recent studies, reviews, and meta-analyses of achievement find that instruction is the central factor that leads to learning (Fullan, Hill, & Crevola, 2006). As the National Writing Project (2003) puts it in their review on instruction in *Writing Matters*, improvement in learning is about instruction, and only about instruction. If we do not transform how we teach, we cannot transform how students engage and learn.

There are quite literally thousands of studies on effective instruction that reach the same conclusions about the overriding importance of three factors in explaining student achievement: 1) motivating contexts and high expectations, 2) opportunity to learn and extended time on task, and 3) focused instruction (Fullan, Hill, & Crevola, 2006).

In this book we have made the case that student motivation can be achieved through a clear purpose that connects to students' interests and needs through the use of essential questions and the contextualizing of literary study in an environment of inquiry. We have likewise asserted that we need to identify the heart of the matter about understanding literature *and* understanding our lived experience—and then to provide in-depth practice over time on these concepts and procedures in a context in which they can be learned, used, and applied to situations beyond the classroom.

Throughout our lives, as children, adolescents, and adults, the two of us have found the reading of literature to be a unique and powerful way of exploring, reflecting, and knowing. We have found the reading of literature such a profoundly worthwhile pursuit that we have chosen the teaching of literature—or perhaps it has called and chosen us—as our life's central pursuit.

Through our 60 years of combined classroom experience (yikes!), we have come to know that when we teach literature most powerfully, we are helping our students come into conversation with important perspectives that will help them navigate their own lives. We have learned that once we emphasize procedural knowledge, it changes the way we think about teaching—focusing on the heart of the matter, on action, on understanding, and on application—and taking us away from information transmission. In this book, we have shared some of what we have learned. We hope that it will help you to teach deeply, and that it will help your students to read deeply in ways that will inform their future living.

References

Anderson, R. C., Reynolds, R. E., Schallert, D. L., & Goetz, E. T. (1977). Frameworks for comprehending discourse. *American Educational Research Journal, 14*, 367–381.

Applebee, A., Bermúdez, A., Blau, S., Caplan, R., Elbow, P., Hynds, S., Langer, J., Marshall, J. (2002). *The language of literature.* Evanston, IL: McDougal Littell.

Applebee, A. N., Burroughs, R., & Stevens, A. S. (2000). Shaping conversations: A study of continuity and coherence in high school literature curricula. *Research in the Teaching of English, 34*, 396–429.

Appleman, D. (2009). *Critical encounters in high school English* (2nd ed.). New York: Teachers College Press.

Asch, S. E. (1946). Forming impressions of personality. *Journal of Abnormal and Social Psychology, 41*, 258–290.

Bakhtin, M. (1981). *The dialogic imagination: Four essays.* Austin, TX and London: University of Texas Press.

Bandura, A. (1977). *Social learning theory.* Englewood Cliffs, NJ: Prentice-Hall.

Benton, M. (1983). Secondary worlds. *Journal of Research and Development in Education, 16*(3), 68–75.

Bereiter, C. (2004). Reflections on depth. In K. Leithwood, P. McAdie, N. Bascia, & A. Rodrigue (Eds.), *Teaching for deep understanding.* (pp. 8–12). Toronto: OISE/UT and EFTO.

Biancarosa, C., & Snow, C. (2006). *Reading next—A vision for action and research in middle and high school literacy: A report to the Carnegie Corporation of New York* (2nd ed.). Washington, DC: Alliance for Excellent Education.

Bleich, D. (1975). *Readings and feelings.* Urbana, IL: National Council of Teachers of English.

Booth, W. C. (1974). *A rhetoric of irony.* Chicago: University of Chicago Press.

Booth, W. C. (1983a). *The rhetoric of fiction* (2nd ed.). Chicago: University of Chicago Press.

Booth, W. C. (1983b). A new strategy for establishing a truly democratic criticism. *Daedalus, 112*, 193–214.

Booth, W. C. (1988). *The company we keep.* Berkeley, CA: University of California Press.

Bransford, J., & Johnson, M. (1972). Contextual prerequisites for understanding: Some investigations of comprehension and recall. *Journal of Verbal Learning and Verbal Behavior, 11*, 717–726.

Bridge, R., Judd, C., & Moock, P. (1979). *The determinants of educational outcomes: The impact of families, peers, teachers, and schools.* Cambridge, MA: Ballinger Publishing Co.

Bronfenbrenner, U. (1977). Toward an experimental ecology of human development. *American Psychologist, 32*, 513–530.

Bronfenbrenner, U. (1979). *The ecology of human development.* Cambridge, MA: Harvard University Press.

Bronfenbrenner, U. (1989). Ecological systems theory. In R. Vasta (Ed.). *Annals of child development, 6* (pp. 187–251). Greenwich, CT: JAI.

Brown, J., Collins, A., & DuGuid, P. (1989). Situated cognition and the culture of learning. *Educational Researcher, 18,* 32–42.

Burke, K. The parlor metaphor. Retrieved from Word Works on January 15, 2009. http://www.boisestate.edu/wcenter/ww82.htm.

Chatman, S. (1978). *Story and discourse.* Ithaca, NY: Cornell University Press.

Coles, R. (1989). *The call of stories: Teaching and the moral imagination.* Boston: Houghton Mifflin.

Delpit, L. (1995). *Other people's children: Cultural conflict in the classroom.* New York: New York Press.

Downie, R. S., & Tefler, E. (1970). *Respect for persons.* New York: Schocken.

Durkin, D. (1979). What classroom observations reveal about reading comprehension instruction. *Reading Research Quarterly, 14,* 481–533.

Dysktra, D. (2006). Testimony to Education at the Idaho State Legislature, Education Committee of the House of Representatives, April 3, 2006— see URL of cited resources: http://www.ipn.uni-kiel.de/aktuell/stcse/stcse.html.

Engeström, Y. (1993). Developmental studies of work as a testbench of activity theory: The case of primary care medical practice. In S. Chaiklin & J. Lave (Eds.), *Understanding practice: Perspectives on activity and context* (pp. 64–103). Cambridge, UK: Cambridge University Press.

Erikson, E. (1963). *Childhood and society* (2nd ed.). New York: Norton.

Essley, R. with Rief, L. and Rocci, A. (2008). *Visual tools for differentiating reading & writing instruction: Strategies to help students make abstract ideas concrete & accessible.* New York: Scholastic.

Fishman, A. (1995). Finding ways in: Redefining multicultural literature. *English Journal, 84*(8), 73–79.

Frye, H. N. (1957). *Anatomy of criticism: Four essays.* Princeton, NJ: Princeton University Press.

Fullan, M., Hill, P., & Crevola, C. (2006). *Breakthrough.* Thousand Oaks, CA: Corwin Press.

Gee, J. P. (1999). *An introduction to discourse analysis: Theory and method.* London: Routledge.

Gee, J. (2003). *What video games have to teach us about learning and literacy.* New York: Palgrave-Macmillan.

Gerson, M. (1996). *The embedded self.* Hillsdale, NJ: The Analytic Press.

Gladwell, M. (2008). *Outliers.* New York: Little, Brown.

Gordon, I. (1975). *Human development: A transactional perspective.* New York: Harper & Row.

Grabes, H. (2004). Turning words on the page into "real" people. *Style, 38,* 221–235.

Graesser, A., Singer, M. & Trabasso, T. (1994). Constructing inferencing during narrative text comprehension. *Psychological Review, 101,* 371–395.

Hamel, F., & Smith, M. W. (1998). You can't play if you don't know the rules: Interpretive conventions and the teaching of literature to students in lower-track classes. *Reading & Writing Quarterly, 14,* 355–378.

FRESH TAKES ON TEACHING LITERARY ELEMENTS

Haskell, R. (2000). *Transfer of learning: Cognition, instruction, and reasoning.* San Diego: Academic Press.

Heathcote, D., & Bolton, G. (1995). *Drama for learning: Dorothy Heathcote's mantle of the expert approach for teaching drama.* Portsmouth, NH: Heinemann.

Hillocks, G., Jr. (1980). Towards a hierarchy of skills in the comprehension of literature. *English Journal, 69,* 54–59.

Hillocks, G., Jr. (1986). The writer's knowledge: Theory, research and implications for practice. In D. Barthalomae and A. Petrosky, Eds., *The Teaching of Writing, 85th Yearbook of the National Society of the Study of Education* (pp. 71–94.) Chicago: University of Chicago Press.

Hillocks, G., Jr. (1995). *Teaching writing as reflective practice.* New York: Teachers College Press.

Hillocks, G., Jr. (1999). *Ways of thinking, ways of teaching.* New York: Teachers College Press.

Hillocks, G., Jr. (2002). *The testing trap: How state writing assessments control learning.* New York: Teachers College Press.

Hillocks, G., Jr. (2007). *Narrative writing: Learning a new model for teaching.* Portsmouth, NH: Heinemann.

Hillocks, G., Jr., & Ludlow. L. (1984). A taxonomy of skills in reading and interpreting fiction. *American Educational Research Journal, 21,* 7–24.

Hubbard, R., & Power, B. (1993). *The art of classroom inquiry.* Portsmouth, NH: Heinemann.

Huitt, W. (2003). A systems model of human behavior. *Educational Psychology Interactive.* Valdosta, GA: Valdosta State University. Retrieved January 9, 2009 from http://chiron.valdosta.edu/whuitt/materials/sysmdlo.html.

Hynds, S., & Appleman, D. (1997). Walking our talk: Between response and responsibility in the literature classroom. *English Education, 29,* 272–294.

Johnston, P., & Afflerbach, P. (1985). The process of constructing main ideas from text. *Cognition and Instruction, 2,* 207–232.

Kahn, E., Walter, C. C., & Johannessen, L. (2009). *Writing about literature* (2nd ed.). Urbana, IL: National Council of Teachers of English.

Kunda, Z., & Thagard, P. (1996). Forming impressions from stereotypes, traits, and behaviors: A parallel constraint-satisfaction theory. *Psychological Review, 103,* 284–308.

Langer, J. A. (2001) Beating the odds: Teaching middle and high school students to read and write well. *American Educational Research Journal, 38,* 837–880.

Lanser, S. (1981). *The narrative act: Point of view in prose fiction.* Princeton, NJ: Princeton University Press.

Lee, C. (2001). Is October Brown Chinese? A cultural modeling activity system for underachieving students. *American Educational Research Journal, 38,* 97–141.

Lukens, R. (1995). *A critical handbook of children's literature.* New York: Harper Collins.

Marshall, J. D., Smagorinsky, P., & Smith, M. W. (1995). *The language of interpretation: Patterns of discourse in discussions of literature.* Urbana, IL: National Council of Teachers of English.

McCloud, S. (1994). *Understanding comics: The invisible art*. New York: HarperCollins.

McKee, R. (1997). *STORY*. New York: Harper-Collins.

McQuade, D., & McQuade, C. (2006). *Seeing and Writing 3*. Boston: Bedford/St. Martin's.

Miller, S. (2007). English teacher learning for new times: Digital video composing as multimodal literacy practice. *English Education, 40,* 61–83.

Moore, D. W., Short, D. J., Smith, M. W., & Tatum, A. W. (2007). *Hampton-Brown Edge* (Levels A, B, C). Carmel, CA: National Geographic School Publishing/Hampton Brown.

National Writing Project, & Nagin, C. (2003). *Because writing matters*. San Francisco: Jossey-Bass.

Nickerson, R. S. (1985). Understanding understanding. *American Journal of Education, 93,* 201–239.

Norton, W., & Gretton, W. (1972). *Writing incredibly short stories, poems and plays*. New York: Norton.

Nystrand, M., & Gamoran, A. (1991). Student engagement: When recitation becomes conversation. In H. C. Waxman & H. J. Walberg (Eds.), *Effective teaching: Current research* (pp. 257–276). Berkeley, CA: McCutchin Publishing.

Nystrand, M., with Gamoran, A., Kachur, R., & Prendergast, C. (1997). *Opening dialogue: Understanding the dynamics of language and learning in the English classroom*. New York: Teachers College Press.

O'Donnell-Allen, C., & Smagorinsky, P. (1999). Revising Ophelia: Rethinking questions of gender and power in school. *English Journal, 88*(3), 35–42.

O'Neill, C., & Lambert, A. (1982). *Drama structures: A practical handbook for teachers*. Portsmouth, NH: Heinemann.

Omi, M., & Winant, H. (1994). *Racial formation in the United States: From the 1960s to the 1990s* (2nd ed.). New York: Routledge.

Perkins, D. N. (1986). *Knowledge as design*. Hillsdale, NJ: Erlbaum.

Perkins, D., & Salomon, G. (1988). Teaching for transfer. *Educational Leadership, 46*(1), 22–32.

Phillips, K. (2006). *It's all about me: Personality quizzes for you and your friends*. Palo Alto, CA: Klutz.

Polanyi, L. (1979). So what's the point? *Semiotica, 25,* 207–241.

Postman, N. (1996). *The ends of education… and how to get there*. CEE keynote at NCTE Spring meeting, Boston, MA. March 21, 2006.

Probst, R. (1992). Five kinds of literary knowing. In J. Langer (Ed.), *Literature instruction: A focus on student response* (pp. 54–77). Urbana, IL: National Council of Teachers of English.

Rabinowitz, P. (1987). *Before reading: Narrative, conventions and the politics of interpretation*. Ithaca, NY: Cornell University Press.

Rabinowitz, P., & Smith, M. W. (1998). *Authorizing readers: Resistance and respect in the reading of literature*. New York: Teachers College Press.

Rand, A. (1963). *For the new intellectual: The philosophy of Ayn Rand*. New York: Signet.

Riesman, R. (1994). Leaving out to pull in: Using reader response to teach multicultural literature. *English Journal, 83*(2), 20–23.

Rosenblatt, L. R. (1938). *Literature as exploration*. New York: Appleton-Century.

Rosenblatt, L. R. (1978). *The reader, the text, the poem*. Carbondale: Southern Illinois University Press.

Rosenblatt, L. R. (1993). The transitional theory: Against dualism. *College English, 55*, 380.

Roth, W., & Lee, Y. (2007). Vygotsky's neglected legacy: Cultural-historical activity theory. *Review of Educational Research, 77*. DOI: 10.3102/0034654306298273. Retrieved on January 10, 2009 at http://rer.sagepub.com/cgi/content/abstract/77/2/186

Schiamberg, L., & Smith, K. (1982). *Human development*. New York: Macmillan.

Scruggs, M., & McKnight, K. (2008). *Improv in the classroom: Using improvisation exercises to teach the content areas, grades K–12*. San Francisco: Jossey-Bass.

Scholes, R. (2001). *The crafty reader*. New Haven, CT: Yale University Press.

Science Media Group. (1989). *A private universe*. Cambridge, MA: Harvard University, Smithsonian Institution.

Simon, H. (1996). *The sciences of the artificial*. Cambridge, MA: MIT Press.

Smagorinsky, P. (2000). Reflecting on character through literary themes. *English Journal, 89*(5), 64–69.

Smagorinsky, P., & O'Donnell-Allen, C. (1998a). The depth and dynamics of context: Tracing the sources and channels of engagement and disengagement in students' response to literature. *Journal of Literacy Research, 30*, 515–559.

Smagorinsky, P., & O'Donnell-Allen, C. (1998b). Reading as mediated and mediating action: Composing meaning for literature through multimedia interpretive texts. *Reading Research Quarterly, 33*, 198–226.

Smith, M. W. (1989). Teaching the interpretation of irony in poetry. *Research in the Teaching of English, 23*, 254–272.

Smith, M. W. (1992). The effects of direct instruction in understanding unreliable narrators. *Journal of Educational Research, 85*, 339–347.

Smith, M. W., & Connolly, B. (2005). The effects of interpretive authority on classroom discussions of poetry: Lessons from one teacher. *Communication Education, 54*, 271–288.

Smith, M. W., & Strickland, D. (2001). Complements or conflicts: Conceptions of discussion and multicultural literature in a teachers-as-readers discussion group. *Journal of Literacy Research, 33*,137–168.

Smith, M. W., & Wilhelm. J. (2002). *"Reading don't fix no Chevys": Literacy in the lives of young men*. Portsmouth, NH: Heinemann.

Smith, M. W., & Wilhelm, J. (2006). *Going with the flow: How to engage boys (and girls) in their literacy learning*. Portsmouth, NH: Heinemann.

Smith, M. W., & Wilhelm, J. (2007). *Getting it right*. New York: Scholastic.

Steichen, E. (1955). *The family of man*. New York: The Museum of Modern Art.

Thompson, R. (1971). *A systems approach to instruction*. Hamden, CT: Linnet Books.

Vipond, R., & Hunt, R. (1984). Point-driven understanding: Pragmatic and cognitive dimensions of literary reading. *Poetics, 13*, 261–277.

Vygotsky, L. (1978). Mind in society. (M. Cole, V. John-Steiner, S. Scribner, & E. Souberman, Eds.). Cambridge, MA: Harvard University Press.

West, C., & Zimmerman, D. (1991). Doing gender. In J. Lorber & S. Farrell (Eds.), *The social construction of gender* (pp. 13–37). Newbury Park, CA: Sage.

White, B. (1995). Effects of autobiographical writing before reading on students' responses to short stories. *Journal of Educational Research, 88*, 173–184.

Wieman, C. (2005). *Learning physics through inquiry.* Keynote for Southern Colorado Literacy Conference, Pueblo, CO, July 21, 2005.

Wilhelm, J. (2001). *Improving comprehension with think alouds.* New York: Scholastic.

Wilhelm, J. (2002). *Action strategies for deepening comprehension.* New York: Scholastic.

Wilhelm, J. (2004). *Reading IS seeing.* New York: Scholastic.

Wilhelm, J. (2007). *Engaging readers and writers with inquiry.* New York: Scholastic.

Wilhelm, J. (2008). *You gotta BE the book: Teaching engaged and reflective reading with adolescents* (2nd ed.). New York: Teachers College Press.

Wilhelm, J., Baker, T., & Dube-Hackett, J. (2001). *Strategic reading.* Portsmouth, NH: Heinemann.

Wilhelm, J., & Edmiston, B. (1998). *Imagining to learn: Inquiry, ethics and integration through drama.* Portsmouth, NH: Heinemann.

Wilhelm, J., & Smith, M. W. (in press). A call for action: Building bridges between literacy in school and out. In J. Manuel & S. Brindley (Eds.), Teenagers and reading: Literacy heritages, cultural contexts and contemporary reading practices. Norwood, South Australia: Wakefield Press/Australian Association of Teachers of English.